M000002390

THE AGILE ARCHITECTURE REVOLUTION

WILEY CIO SERIES

Founded in 1807, John Wiley & Sons is the oldest independent publishing company in the United States. With offices in North America, Europe, Asia, and Australia, Wiley is globally committed to developing and marketing print and electronic products and services for our customers' professional and personal knowledge and understanding.

The Wiley CIO series provides information, tools, and insights to IT executives and managers. The products in this series cover a wide range of topics that supply strategic and implementation guidance on the latest technology trends, leadership, and emerging best practices.

Titles in the Wiley CIO series include:

The Agile Architecture Revolution: How Cloud Computing, REST-Based SOA, and Mobile Computing Are Changing Enterprise IT by Jason Bloomberg

Big Data, Big Analytics: Emerging Business Intelligence and Analytic Trends for Today's Businesses by Michele Chambers, Ambiga Dhiraj, and Michael Minelli

The Chief Information Officer's Body of Knowledge: People, Process, and Technology by Dean Lane

CIO Best Practices: Enabling Strategic Value with Information Technology by Joe Stenzel, Randy Betancourt, Gary Cokins, Alyssa Farrell, Bill Flemming, Michael H. Hugos, Jonathan Hujsak, and Karl D. Schubert

The CIO Playbook: Strategies and Best Practices for IT Leaders to Deliver Value by Nicholas R. Colisto

Enterprise IT Strategy, + Website: An Executive Guide for Generating Optimal ROI from Critical IT Investments by Gregory J. Fell

Executive's Guide to Virtual Worlds: How Avatars Are Transforming Your Business and Your Brand by Lonnie Benson

Innovating for Growth and Value: How CIOs Lead Continuous Transformation in the Modern Enterprise by Hunter Muller

IT Leadership Manual: Roadmap to Becoming a Trusted Business Partner by Alan R. Guibord

Managing Electronic Records: Methods, Best Practices, and Technologies by Robert F. Smallwood

On Top of the Cloud: How CIOs Leverage New Technologies to Drive Change and Build Value Across the Enterprise by Hunter Muller

Straight to the Top: CIO Leadership in a Mobile, Social, and Cloud-based (Second Edition) by Gregory S. Smith

Strategic IT: Best Practices for IT Managers and Executives by Arthur M. Langer

Strategic IT Management: Transforming Business in Turbulent Times by Robert J. Benson

Transforming IT Culture: How to Use Social Intelligence, Human Factors and Collaboration to Create an IT Department That Outperforms by Frank Wander

Unleashing the Power of IT: Bringing People, Business, and Technology Together by Dan Roberts

The U.S. Technology Skills Gap: What Every Technology Executive Must Know to Save America's Future by Gary Beach

THE AGILE ARCHITECTURE REVOLUTION

HOW CLOUD COMPUTING, REST-BASED SOA, AND MOBILE COMPUTING ARE CHANGING ENTERPRISE IT

Jason Bloomberg

with contributions from Ronald Schmelzer

WILEY

John Wiley & Sons, Inc.

Cover image: © 4X-image/iStockphoto
Cover design: John Wiley & Sons, Inc.

Copyright © 2013 by Jason Bloomberg. All rights reserved.

Published by John Wiley & Sons, Inc., Hoboken, New Jersey.

Published simultaneously in Canada.

No part of this publication may be reproduced, stored in a retrieval system, or transmitted in any form or by any means, electronic, mechanical, photocopying, recording, scanning, or otherwise, except as permitted under Section 107 or 108 of the 1976 United States Copyright Act, without either the prior written permission of the Publisher, or authorization through payment of the appropriate per-copy fee to the Copyright Clearance Center, Inc., 222 Rosewood Drive, Danvers, MA 01923, (978) 750-8400, fax (978) 646-8600, or on the Web at www.copyright.com. Requests to the Publisher for permission should be addressed to the Permissions Department, John Wiley & Sons, Inc., 111 River Street, Hoboken, NJ 07030, (201) 748-6011, fax (201) 748-6008, or online at http://www.wiley.com/go/permissions.

Limit of Liability/Disclaimer of Warranty: While the publisher and author have used their best efforts in preparing this book, they make no representations or warranties with respect to the accuracy or completeness of the contents of this book and specifically disclaim any implied warranties of merchantability or fitness for a particular purpose. No warranty may be created or extended by sales representatives or written sales materials. The advice and strategies contained herein may not be suitable for your situation. You should consult with a professional where appropriate. Neither the publisher nor author shall be liable for any loss of profit or any other commercial damages, including but not limited to special, incidental, consequential, or other damages.

For general information on our other products and services or for technical support, please contact our Customer Care Department within the United States at (800) 762-2974, outside the United States at (317) 572-3993 or fax (317) 572-4002.

Wiley publishes in a variety of print and electronic formats and by print-on-demand. Some material included with standard print versions of this book may not be included in e-books or in print-on-demand. If this book refers to media such as a CD or DVD that is not included in the version you purchased, you may download this material at http://booksupport.wiley.com. For more information about Wiley products, visit www.wiley.com.

Library of Congress Cataloging-in-Publication Data:

Bloomberg, Jason, 1961-
    The agile architecture revolution : how cloud computing, REST-based SOA, and mobile computing are changing enterprise IT / Jason Bloomberg ; with contributions from Ronald Schmelzer.
        pages cm
    Includes index.
    ISBN 978-1-118-40977-0 (hbk.); ISBN 978-1-118-42199-4 (ebk); ISBN 978-1-118-55405-0 (ebk); ISBN 978-1-118-41787-4 (ebk); 1.   Business enterprises—Technological innovations.
2.   Management information systems. 3.   Service-oriented architecture (Computer science)
I.   Title.
    HD45.B5466 2013
    658.4'038—dc23   2012038783

Printed in the United States of America

10 9 8 7 6 5 4 3 2 1

To Ronald Schmelzer—business partner, mentor, colleague, parallel entrepreneur, curmudgeon, and friend.

CONTENTS

PART THREE—Implementing Agile Architecture 147

FOREWORD: THE AGILE ARCHITECTURE REVOLUTION

The core thrust of architecture has been to define core business requirements, and then construct the IT solution to meet those requirements, typically as instances of software. While this seems like a simple concept, many in enterprise IT went way off course in the last 10 to 15 years.

IT does not provide the value it once did, meaning IT does not meet the objectives and expectations of the business. Indeed, IT has become a cost center where the resource burn increased significantly over the last 20 years, while the value to the business decreased relative to costs. This can't continue.

We've tried all of the tricks. With "waterfall" types of approaches to application architecture, the time it takes to move from understanding the requirements to the final deployed system could be years. Thus, by the time the system is completed and deployed, the business requirements likely have changed, you're back to the drawing board, and the delivered system has significantly diminished in value.

To address the latency issues around the waterfall, those who design and build systems turned to the concept of interaction. This means moving through cycles of understand-design-develop-deploy, over and over again, until there is something that resembles the desired business solution. Iteration approaches to software development often lead to poorly designed and lower-quality systems because you get it wrong over and over again, seemingly to get it right once. Moreover, as requirements change, it's back to the iterations again, sometimes in a never-ending loop.

The core benefit IT should provide is that of achieving business agility, or the ability to allow the business to change rapidly around changing business requirements and business opportunities. Thus, businesses can move quickly into newer and more profitable product lines, acquire companies to expand their position in the market, or quickly align with regulatory changes that could stop their business in its tracks.

So, if business agility is good, how can IT achieve it? The current thinking is that we need to change our approach to design and development, again, and move to newer methods and approaches around software architecture. The right answer is that we need to change *what* we build, not *how* we build it.

This book describes a true revolution, a different way of thinking about how we build and leverage software. The idea is to address business requirements in a different way. Instead of thinking about what the business needs the software to do, the business should define the software to support agility. Thus, the software is not designed to provide specific static functionality, but instead it is designed to change as the needs of the business change.

In this book, Jason calls this requirement "the meta-requirement of agility," which defines how you approach the other requirements around the software system. The idea is to build a system that can change its behavior and data semantics on demand, in support of a changing business.

The concept of SOA has always promoted the notion of agility, and many of the architectural patterns of SOA have a place within Agile Architecture, the revolution defined in this book. SOA has taken a beating the last several years, mostly because vendors hijacked the term and took it for a wild ride, to the point of it being declared dead.

SOA once meant an approach to architecture where the end state was defined sets of services, and the ability to configure and reconfigure those services into business solutions. These days, most consider it just another category of technology. However, SOA is a fundamental approach to achieving business agility, and is deeply seeded in the concepts defined in this book. It's time that we understand the true value of SOA as an architecture pattern, and make proper use of it.

The rise of cloud computing provides us with another opportunity. We now have the ability to access massive compute and storage services on demand over the open Internet. These services are at a price point more affordable to the smallest and most frugal businesses.

What's most interesting about cloud computing is that you access cloud services, such as storage and data access services, using well-defined APIs, typically RESTful Web Services. Clouds are typically designed to be service oriented, they mesh well with the use of SOA approaches, and thus they support the architecture principles as defined in this book.

In other words, we're able to combine the proper use of SOA with the emerging value of cloud computing, with the ability to better define a software solution that addresses most existing and future business requirements. This is a convergence of concepts that have the power to change the way we think about software and finally bring IT back to a place of productivity and value.

This is a revolution. It's a revolution in how we think about architecture. It's a revolution in how we think about software development. It's a revolution in how we think about IT supporting the business. Also, it's a revolution in how we think about leveraging new platforms such as cloud computing.

We must begin to think differently. What we do today is just not working. Hopefully you all will grasp the value of the concepts defined in this book and begin the journey out of the software factories to systems that finally meet the needs of business.

David S. Linthicum,
Cloud Computing and SOA Thought Leader,
Author, Blogger, and Consultant

PREFACE

Agility requires a fundamental change in IT, and that change is on its way.
—Jason Bloomberg and Ronald Schmelzer, *Service Orient or Be Doomed!*

Remember the dot-com days; what we now call Web 1.0? It was a wild time: Companies with no clue how to make money commanding outrageous valuations, stock prices in the stratosphere, recruiters looking for anyone—anyone!—who had half a clue about the Internet, and lest we forget, the hubris of the *New Economy*. The Internet changes everything, even the laws of economics! Change happening so fast we can hardly keep up!

You ain't seen nothin' yet.

In retrospect, of course, the whole mess was merely a speculative bubble, another example of selling tulip bulbs for more than houses. And while we may argue that today's tech-driven frenzy—*Facebook! Groupon! Pinterest!*—may itself be a bubble ready to burst, there's something more fundamental going on.

Something *truly* revolutionary.

The pace of change is once again accelerating, only now the context for such change is multifaceted and far more complex than the simpler, one-dimensional dot-com days. In fact, so much change surrounds us that we often lose sight of it altogether. It becomes the background noise of our lives.

Such is the nature of true revolutions. It's hard to tell you're in one until after it's done—often many years afterward. But the evidence of revolution is all around us, if we only have the insight to identify individual trends and tie them together into a single story of transformation.

It's human nature when faced with a chaotic environment, however, to filter out much of the noise in order to focus on a single trend. The resulting illusion of stability gives us a context we can understand. But it's still an illusion. The reality is that there are many different, interrelated trends—areas of change that impact us as well as the other trends. There are also discontinuities: sudden shifts that force us to rethink our assumptions.

This book tells the story of just such a revolution. We don't only identify many of the interrelated trends, but we also provide practical advice for leveraging the change in our environment to achieve business success.

You might think from the title of this book that it's about technology, and you'd be correct—in part. The trends we'll be discussing are all technology related. But in reality, this is a *business* book. Technology in the business context is *always* a means to an end—the end being the priorities of the organization. In other words, making and saving money, keeping customers and shareholders happy, and for public sector organizations, the mission priority, whatever that happens to be.

But don't get us wrong—there's plenty of technology in this book as well. Part One focuses on architecture, and connects the dots between Service-Oriented Architecture and the revolutionary concept of enterprise as a complex system. Part Two places the discussion of architecture in the broader context of change impacting enterprise IT, and with it, business in general. Part Three then focuses on implementation, with an in-depth consideration of Cloud Computing and Representational State Transfer (REST). We then tie the threads of the story together to make the case that we face an Agile Architecture Revolution.

Writing a business book about technology is nothing new for us. In 2006, Ron Schmelzer and I published *Service Orient or Be Doomed! How Service Orientation Will Change Your Business*, about how organizations must leverage Service-Oriented Architecture (SOA), not just as a set of technical best practices, but also as *business* best practices for running agile organizations. In many ways, The *Agile Architecture Revolution* is the sequel to *Service Orient or Be Doomed!* Like the earlier book, the one in your hands focuses on *enterprise information technology (IT)*—with the emphasis on *enterprise*, where IT plays a critical, but inherently supporting role. This book isn't about the technology. It's about how the business—that is, *people*—use technology to meet changing business needs.

Some background: Ron and I were the moving force behind ZapThink, the leading industry analysis, advisory, and training firm focused on SOA during the first decade of this century. Ron founded the company in 2000 to focus on XML. I joined in 2001 and expanded the focus to include Web Services, with a consistent emphasis on architecture that led to our thought leadership position in the SOA marketplace. Then in 2007, we shifted our focus from helping vendors with their marketing to helping enterprise practitioners get the architecture right—through advisory as well as our licensed ZapThink Architect SOA course and associated industry credential.

We then sold ZapThink to Dovel Technologies, a U.S. government contractor, in 2011. Ron moved on to his next adventure, while I remain as president of ZapThink. This book represents the best of ZapThink thinking from the time of the publication of *Service Orient or Be Doomed!* to today. As a result, Ron contributed bits and pieces here and there, but I'm responsible for the vast majority of content and insight, for better or worse. This book, therefore, is written from the perspective of ZapThink.

Today, ZapThink's focus has expanded beyond SOA with the release of our *ZapThink 2020* poster, which you can download at www.AgileArchitecture Revolution.com. A small version of the poster appears here, but you really need to download the full version or pick up one of the printed ones, either by finding us at an event or by ordering them from our Web site (we only charge for postage). We've given away tens of thousands of copies of the poster, which illustrates the many different threads that make up the *Agile Architecture Revolution*. You can think of it as a road map to this book.

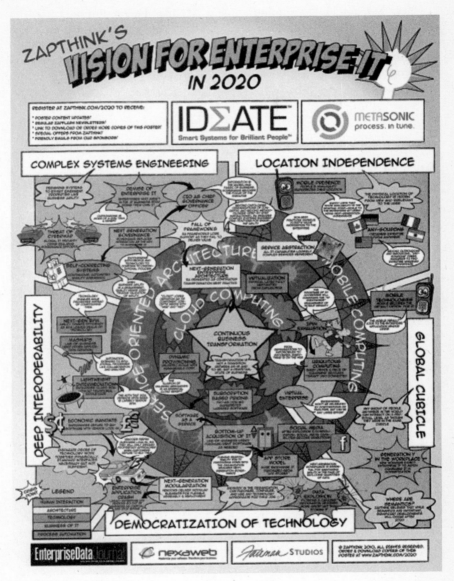

The ZapThink 2020 Vision
Source: ZapThink.

Yes, SOA, Cloud Computing, and Mobile Technologies circle the center of the diagram, and we will unquestionably spend time on these topics. But as the poster illustrates, there are many more trends to discuss. By the end of the book, you'll have a clear grasp of what the *Agile Architecture Revolution* is all about. Hold on to your hats! You're in for a wild ride.

Jason Bloomberg
September 2012

THE AGILE ARCHITECTURE REVOLUTION

PART ONE
Enterprise as Complex System

In the past the man has been first; in the future the system must be first.
—FREDERICK WINSLOW TAYLOR, THE PRINCIPLES OF SCIENTIFIC MANAGEMENT

CHAPTER 1

Introducing Agile Architecture

*A*gile. *Architecture*. *Revolution*. Them's fightin' words, all three of 'em.

Agile—controversial software methodology? Management consulting doublespeak? Word found in every corporate vision statement, where it sits collecting dust, like your grandmother's Hummel figurines?

Architecture—excuse to spend too much on complicated, spaghetti-code middleware? Generating abstruse paperwork instead of writing code that actually works? How to do less work while allegedly being more valuable? (Thanks to *Dilbert* for that last one.)

Revolution—the difference between today's empty marketing drivel and yesterday's empty marketing drivel? Key word in two Beatles song titles, one a classic, the other a meaningless waste of vinyl? What the victors always call wresting control from the vanquished?

No, no, and no—although we appreciate the sentiment. If you're hoping this book is full of trite clichés, you've come to the wrong place. We're iconoclasts through and through. No cliché, no dogma, no commonly held belief is too sacred for us to skewer, barbecue, and relish with a nice Chianti.

We'll deconstruct Agile, and rebuild the concept in the context of real organizations and their strategic goals. We'll discard architectural dogma, and paint a detailed picture of how we believe architecture should be done. And we'll make the case that the Agile Architecture Revolution is a *true* revolution.

Many readers may not understand the message of this book. That's what happens in revolutions—old belief systems are held up to the light so that people can see through them. Some do, but many people do not. For those readers who take this book to heart, however, we hope to open your eyes to a new way of thinking about technology, about business, and about change itself.

Deconstructing Agile

Every specialization has its own jargon, and IT is no different—but many times it seems that techies love to co-opt regular English words and give them new meanings. Not only does this practice lead to confusion in conversations with non-techies, but even the techies often lose sight of the difference between their geek-context definition and the real world definition that "normal" people use.

For example, ZapThink spends far too long defining *Service*. This word has far too many meanings, even in the world of IT—and most of them have little to do with what the rest of the world means by the term. Even words like *business* have gone through the techie redefinition process (in techie-speak, *business* means *everything that's not IT*).

It comes as no surprise, therefore, that techies have hijacked the word *Agile*. In common parlance, someone or something is agile if it's flexible and nimble, especially in the face of unexpected forces of change. But in the world of technology, *Agile* (Agile-with-a-capital-A) refers to a specific category of software development methodology. This definition dates to 2001 and the establishment of the Agile Manifesto, a set of general principles for building better software. The Agile Manifesto (from agilemanifesto.org) consists of four core principles:

1. **Individuals and interactions over processes and tools.** Agile emphasizes the role people play in the technology organization over the tools that people use.
2. **Working software over comprehensive documentation.** The focus of an Agile project is to deliver something that actually works; that is, that meets the business requirements. Documentation and other artifacts are simply a means to this end.
3. **Customer collaboration over contract negotiation.** Customers and other business stakeholders are on the same team, rather than adversaries.
4. **Responding to change over following a plan.** Having predefined plans can be useful, but if the requirements or some other aspect of the environment changes, then it's more important to respond to that change than stick obstinately to the plan.

In the intervening decade, however, *Agile* has taken on a life of its own, as Scrum, Extreme Programming, and other Agile methodologies have found their way into the fabric of IT. Such methodologies indubitably have strengths, to be sure—but what we have lost in the fray is a sense of what is particularly agile about Agile. This point is more than simple semantics. What's missing is the fundamental connection to agility that drove the Manifesto in the first place. Reestablishing this connection, especially in the light of new thinking on business agility, is essential to rethinking how IT meets the ever-changing requirements of the business.

How do techies know what to build? Simple: Ask the stakeholders (the "business") what they want. Make sure to write down all their requirements in the proverbial requirements document. Now build something that does what that document says. After you're done, get your testers to verify that what you've built is what the business wanted.

Or what they used to want.

Or what they said they wanted.

Or perhaps what they *thought* they said they wanted.

And therein lies the rub. The expectation that the business can completely, accurately, and definitively describe what they want in sufficient detail so that the techies can build it precisely to spec is ludicrously unrealistic, even though such a myth is inexplicably persistent in many enterprise IT shops to this day. In fact, the myth of complete, well-defined requirements is at the heart of what we call the "waterfall methodology, illustrated in Figure 1.1.

In reality, it is far more common for requirements to be poorly communicated, poorly understood, or both. Or even if they're properly communicated, they change before the project is complete. Or most aggravating of all, the stakeholder looks at what the techies have built and says, "Yes, that's exactly what I asked for, but now that I see it, I realize I want something different after all."

Of course, such challenges are nothing new; they gave rise to the family of iterative methodologies a generation ago, including the Spiral methodology, IBM's Rational Unified Process, and all of the Agile methodologies. By taking an iterative approach that involves the business in a more proactive way, the reasoning goes, you lower the risk of poorly communicated, poorly understood, or changing business requirements. Figure 1.2 illustrates such a project.

In Figure 1.2 the looped arrows represent iterations, where each iteration reevaluates and reincorporates the original requirements with any further input the business wants to contribute. But even with the most agile of Agile

Waterfall Software Project

Figure 1.1   Waterfall Software Project

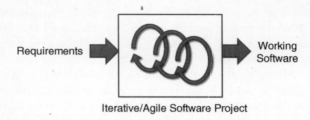

Iterative/Agile Software Project

Figure 1.2   Iterative/Agile Software Project

development teams, the process of building software still falls short. It doesn't seem to matter how expert the coders, how precise the stakeholders, or how perfect the development methodology are, the gap between what the business *really* needs and what the software *actually* does is still far wider than it should be. And whereas many business stakeholders have become inured to poorly fitting software, far more are becoming fed up with the entire situation. Enough is enough. How do we get what we *really* want and need from IT?

To answer this question, it's critical to understand that inflexibility is the underlying problem of business today, because basically, if companies (and government organizations) were flexible enough, they could solve all of their other problems, because no problem is beyond the reach of the flexible organization. If only companies were flexible enough, they could adjust their offerings to changes in customer demand, build new products and services quickly and efficiently, and leverage the talent of their people in an optimal manner to maximize productivity. And if only companies were flexible enough, their strategies would always provide the best possible direction for the future. Fundamentally, *flexibility* is the key to every organization's profitability, longevity, and success.

How can businesses aim to survive, even in environments of unpredictable change? The answer is *business agility*. We define business agility as *the ability to respond quickly and efficiently to changes in the business environment and to leverage those changes for competitive advantage*. The most important aspect of this definition is the fact that it comes in two parts: the reactive, tactical part, and the proactive, strategic part. The ability to respond to change is the reactive, tactical aspect of business agility. Clearly, the faster and more efficiently companies can respond to changes, the more agile they are. Achieving rapid, efficient response is akin to driving costs out of the business: It's always a good thing, but has diminishing returns over time as responses get about as fast and efficient as possible. Needless to say, the competition is also trying to improve their responses to changes in the market, so it's only a matter of time til they catch up with you (or you catch up with them, as the case may be).

The second, proactive half of the business agility equation—leveraging change for competitive advantage—is by far the most interesting and powerful part of the story. Companies that not only respond to changes but actually see them as a way to improve their business often move ahead of the competition as they leverage change for strategic advantage. And strategic advantages— those that distinguish one company's value proposition from another's—can be far more durable than tactical advantages.

Building a system that exhibits business agility, therefore, means building a system that supports changing requirements over time—a tall order. Even the most Agile development teams still struggle with the problem of changing requirements. If requirements evolve somewhat during the course of a project, then a well-oiled Agile team can generally go with the flow and adjust their deliverables accordingly, but one way or the other, all successful software projects come to an end. And once the techies have deployed the software, they're done.

Have a new requirement? Fund a separate project. We'll start over and include your new requirements in the next version of the project we already finished, unless it makes more sense to build something completely new. Sometimes techies can tweak existing capabilities to meet new requirements quickly and simply, but more often than not, rolling out new versions of existing software is a laborious, time-consuming, and risky process. If the software is *commercial off the shelf* (COTS), the problem is even worse, because the vendor must base new updates on requirements from many existing customers, as well as their guesses about what new customers will want in the future. Figure 1.3 illustrates this problem, where the software project represented by the box can be as Agile as can be, and yet the business still doesn't get the agility it craves. It seems that Agile may not be so agile after all.

The solution to this problem is for the business to specify its requirements in a fundamentally different way. Instead of thinking about what it wants the software to do, the business should specify how agile it expects the software to be. In other words, don't ask for software that does A, B, C, or whatever. Instead, tell your techies to *build you something agile*.

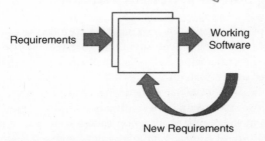

Figure 1.3   Not-so-agile Updates to Existing Software

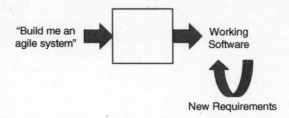

Figure 1.4   What Agile Software Should Really Look Like

We call this requirement the meta-requirement of agility—a *meta-requirement* because agility applies to other requirements: "Build me something that responds to changing requirements" instead of "Build me something that does A, B, and C." If we can build software that satisfies this meta-requirement, then our diagram looks quite different (see Figure 1.4).

Because the software in Figure 1.4 is truly agile, it is possible to meet new requirements without having to change the software. Whether the process inside the box is Agile is beside the point. Yes, perhaps taking an Agile approach is a good idea, but it doesn't guarantee the resulting software is agile.

Sounds promising, to be sure, but the devil is in the details. After all, if it were easy to build software that responded to changing requirements, then everybody would be doing it. But there's a catch. Even if we built software that could *potentially* meet changing requirements, that doesn't mean that it actually *would*—because meeting changing requirements is part of how you would *use* the software, rather than part of how you *build* it. In other words, the *users* of the software must actually be part of the agile system. The box in Figure 1.4 doesn't just represent software anymore. It represents a system consisting of software *and people*.

Architecting Software/Human Systems

Such software/people systems of systems are a core theme of this book. After all, the enterprise—in fact, *any* business that uses technology—is a software/human system. To understand Agile Architecture, it's essential to understand how to architect such a system.

Software/human systems have been with us as long as we've had technology, of course. A simple example is a traffic jam. Let's say you're on the freeway, and an accident in the opposing direction causes your side to slow down. Not because you want to, of course. You're saying to yourself that you really don't care to rubberneck. You'd rather keep moving along. But you can't, because the person ahead of you slows down. And they're slowing down because the person ahead of them is.

What's going on here? Each vehicle on the freeway is a combination human/technology system: driver and car. The drivers are humans, each making their own choices about how to behave, within the confines of the rules of the road. The traffic jam itself is also a system—what we call a *system of systems*. The traffic jam appears to behave as though it has a mind of its own, independent of the individual decisions of each driver.

Subtract the people from this system and you don't have a traffic jam at all. You have a *parking lot*. And parking lots behave very differently from traffic jams (although sometimes it seems they're one and the same!). Similarly, change the technology, and you have a very different system. Say instead of cars you have trains in a train yard. Train yards might experience traffic jams as well, but they behave very differently from the traffic jams on freeways.

We're not interested in traffic jams in this book, of course. We're interested in *enterprises*. Enterprises are systems of systems as well. We can change the behavior of an enterprise by changing the technology, or by changing human behavior—or some combination of both. Our challenge, then, is *architecting the enterprise* in order to achieve business agility. That's what we mean by Agile Architecture.

The Agile Architecture approach we most frequently talk about is *Service-Oriented Architecture* (SOA). With SOA, IT publishes business Services that represent IT capabilities and information, and the business drives the consumption and composition of those Services. In mature SOA deployments, *policies* drive the behavior of Services and their compositions. If you want to change the behavior, change the policy. In other words, SOA is governance-driven, and governance applies to the behavior of both people and technology.

Agile architectural approaches like SOA, therefore, focus on implementing governance-driven technology/people systems that support changing requirements over time. The challenge, of course, is actually *building* such systems that meet the business agility meta-requirement. Where in this system do we put the agility? It's not in any part of the system. Instead, it's a property of the system as a whole—what we call an *emergent property*. Business agility is an emergent property of the combination technology/human system we call the enterprise.

An emergent property is simply a property of a system as a whole that's not a property of any part of that system. Just as the behavior of a traffic jam consists of properties of the traffic, not of the individual cars, business agility is a property of the enterprise, but not of any of its component systems. We don't look to individual people or technology systems for business agility. We want the organization itself to be agile.

In other words, we started by deconstructing the notion of Agile and ended up with Enterprise Architecture (EA), because what is Enterprise Architecture but best practices for designing and building the enterprise to better meet changing requirements over time? This is not the static, framework-centric EA from years past that presupposes a final, ideal state for the enterprise. We're talking about a new way of thinking about what it means to architect technology-rich organizations to be inherently agile.

Meta Thinking and Agile Architecture

ZapThink has long bemoaned the Agile Manifesto paradox: that the point to the Manifesto was to be less dogmatic about software development, but today people are overly dogmatic about Agile, defeating its entire purpose. In fact, this paradox has found its way into what is perhaps the most popular of the Agile methodologies: Scrum. Not to worry, all you Scrum aficionados out there; we're not going to teach you how to do Scrum. Instead, we hope to help you think about a broad set of problems in a particular way, starting with *Scrum Buts*.

The notion of a Scrum But arose when it became clear that thousands of organizations were attempting to follow Scrum for their software development projects, but many of them were having problems with one or another of its tenets. As a result, they would say things like:

> "We use Scrum, but Retrospectives are a waste of time, so we don't do them."

or:

> "We use Scrum, but we can't build a piece of functionality in a month, so our Sprints are six weeks long."

Retrospectives and Sprints are well-known Scrum best practices (examples from scrum.org). Note that both of these statements follow the same "We use Scrum, but X so Y" pattern, hence the term Scrum But.

The question with Scrum Buts, of course, is what to do with them—or more specifically, how to think about them. There are two schools of thought:

1. Scrum Buts are simply excuses not to do Scrum properly, and if you're not doing it properly, then you're not really doing it at all.
2. Resolving Scrum Buts when they come up in order to achieve the desired result (software that meets the stakeholders' needs) is actually a part of the Scrum methodology. As a result, Scrum Buts are expected and even welcomed.

From our perspective, option #1 is an example of taking a dogmatic approach, which is inherently non-Agile. Option #2 basically says that you can modify the rules if necessary (one of the four principles of the Agile Manifesto), even the rules of Scrum itself.

In other words, option #2 is self-referential—which may be more Agile to be sure, but people have problems with self-reference. It brings up uncomfortable visions of the liar's paradox: "Everything I say is a lie," or in more modern terms, the first rule of Fight Club ("You do not talk about Fight Club.") How can we make sense of the world or anything in it if we have to deal with self-reference paradoxes? If a rule of Scrum is "You can change the rules of Scrum," then couldn't anything and everything be Scrum? What use is that?

Fortunately, such problems of self-reference have a straightforward, if subtle solution. Instead of thinking of such statements as referring to themselves, think of them as actually two separate but related statements, where one relates to the other. We call this meta thinking.

In the case of Scrum Buts, we have the Scrum methodology and the Scrum meta-methodology. A meta-methodology is a methodology for creating methodologies. Remember, the Scrum methodology is a methodology for creating software. The Scrum meta-methodology is a methodology for creating or improving the Scrum methodology. So when someone says:

> "When you say, 'We use Scrum, but we can't build a piece of functionality in a month, so our Sprints are six weeks long,' my recommendation is to try three 30-day Sprints before extending the length of the Sprint."

That entire statement is a Scrum meta-methodology statement. Furthermore, without such statements, your methodology wouldn't be Agile. The obvious conclusion is that all Agile methodologies are actually meta-methodologies. Otherwise they wouldn't be Agile!

We're sure one of you wise guys out there is thinking, what about methodologies for creating meta-methodologies? We'd call those meta-meta-methodologies, of course. And what about methodologies for creating those, *ad infinitum*? We call this the *hall of mirrors problem*, because you only need to have two mirrors facing each other to get the infinite tunnel effect.

Simple answer: We don't need a methodology for creating meta-methodologies. Instead, an informal approach will do. In general, we only want to go to the meta-meta step if there's a bona fide reason to do so, as with Model Driven Architecture (MDA), when they talk about meta-meta-models. But even the brainiacs at the OMG (the standards body that shepherds MDA) don't spend much time thinking about meta-meta-meta-models—at least, we hope not!

Another meta that is central to ZapThink's thinking is the *meta-requirement*. In particular, we're talking about the meta-requirement of business agility as a fundamental driver of SOA, and by extension, Agile Architecture in general. When the business asks for an agile system, they are asking for a system that can respond to changing requirements—which is what makes such agility a meta-requirement.

Finally, at the risk of belaboring the point, let's talk about *meta-architecture*: What does it mean to architect an architecture? Yes, we've been spending a lot of our brain cycles on meta-architecture as well. We've been putting our stamp on how best to do SOA for several years now. Our students may be architecting their organizations and their component systems, but ZapThink has been architecting SOA itself. And now that we can stick a fork in that, it's time to work on architecting Cloud architecture, and more broadly, Agile Architecture.

Defining Architecture: Worse Than Herding Cats

Now that we've explained what we mean by *agile*, let's tackle a toughie: *architecture*. The problem with defining architecture is, well, we're leaving it to architects to come up with the definition. ZapThink loves to point out that the collective term for *architect* is an *argument*. As in a flock of seagulls, a pride of lions, or an argument of architects. Put enough architects together in a room, and sure enough, an argument ensues. Furthermore, architects love nothing more than to argue about the definitions of terms—because after all, definitions are simply a matter of convention. Bring up the question as to what *architecture* means—well, you might as well go home. No more work will be done today!

To avoid such an argument of architects, we're going to use a widely accepted, standard definition of architecture: the Institute of Electrical and Electronics Engineers (IEEE) definition. IEEE defines architecture as *"the fundamental organization of a system embodied by its components, their relationships to each other and to the environment, and the principles guiding its design and evolution."* As you might expect, because architects come up with these definitions, there are actually several standard definitions of architecture. But the IEEE's is perhaps the best known. It's concise, and it contains all the elements of what we think of as architecture.

We will make one tweak to the IEEE definition, however: We're going to interpret it in the plural. So for the purpose of the book, architecture is *the fundamental organization of systems embodied by their components, their relationships to each other and to the environment, and the principles guiding their design and evolution.*

Let's take this definition apart and focus on its key elements to make sure we're all on the same page:

- **Organization of systems.** In other words, architecture is something you do with systems. You organize them. Architecture is something you *do*, not something you *buy*.
- **Environment.** If you look at the enterprise as a system, what is the environment of its component systems? The *people*—the *business itself*. Many architects get this point wrong when they think of the systems as consisting of technology, where the people *use* the technology, as though they were separate from the architecture. In fact, the people are *part* of the system.
- **Evolution.** *Change* is built into the definition of architecture. If you think of an architecture as some diagram you can put on your wall, be it your data architecture, Java architecture, security architecture, or what have you, you're missing the big picture. Such a diagram is at best a *static snapshot in time* of your architecture. To accurately represent an architecture, you must include the principles for the evolution of that diagram.

These fundamental elements of the definition of architecture go beyond IT architectures and Enterprise Architectures. Consider where we got the word *architecture* from: the process of designing buildings and other structures. In fact, the word comes from the word *arch*, because the first architects were the people who knew how to design arches. After all, there's a trick to building an arch: You must provide a temporary support for the arch until the keystone is in place. The first architects were the people who knew this trick.

So, what do building architects actually design? Yes, they must design walls, floors, electrical and plumbing systems and the like—but these are all means to an end. What the building architect actually designs is the *space* defined by those elements, because the space is where the people work or live—in other words, how people get value from the component systems.

Just so with the architecture we're considering in this book. Yes, you have to design the applications, middleware, networks, and so on—but those are all simply means to an end. It's how people *use* those components to achieve the goals of the business that is the true focus of the architect.

Why Nobody Is Doing Enterprise Architecture

There are many flavors of architecture—technical architecture, solution architecture, data architecture, Service-Oriented Architecture, the list goes on and on—but the type this book is most concerned with is *Enterprise*

Architecture. The practice of EA has been around for years, but even the most seasoned practitioners of this craft rarely agree on what EA really is. What's the story? It doesn't help matters that many techies have co-opted the term *Enterprise Architecture* to mean some kind of technology-centric architecture or other. Look up *Enterprise Architect* on a job board and chances are four out of five positions that call themselves "Enterprise Architect" are entirely technology focused. In spite of this confusion, if there's one thing Enterprise Architects can agree on, it's that Enterprise Architecture is not about technology, or at least, not *exclusively* about technology. Sure, every enterprise these days has plenty of technology, but there's more to the enterprise than its IT systems.

Unfortunately, there's little else Enterprise Architects agree on. Some of them point to ontologies like the Zachman Framework, in the belief that if we could only define our terms well enough, we'd have an architecture. Others point to methodologies like the Architecture Development Method (ADM) from The Open Group Architecture Framework (TOGAF), figuring that if we follow the general best practice advice in the ADM, then at least we can call ourselves Enterprise Architects.

Hence, an argument of architects. If you're an architect, you probably already disagree with something we've written. See? What did we tell you?

The problem is, neither Zachman nor TOGAF—or any other approach on the market, for that matter—is truly Enterprise Architecture. Why? Because *nobody is doing Enterprise Architecture.*

The truth of this bold statement is quite obvious when you think about it. Where does Enterprise Architecture take place today? In enterprises, of course. That is, *existing* enterprises. And you don't architect things that already exist. Architecture comes *before* you build something!

Can you imagine hiring an architect *after* building a bridge or a building? I can hear that conversation now: "We built this bridge organically over time, and it has serious issues. So please architect it for us now." Sorry: *too late!*

Most forms of technical architecture don't fall into this trap. A solution architect architects a solution before that solution is implemented. A Java architect or a .NET architect does their work before the coders do theirs. You don't build and then design, you design and then build. Even if you take an Agile, iterative approach, none of your iterations has build before design in it.

Enterprise Architecture, on the other hand, always begins with an existing enterprise. And after working with hundreds of existing enterprises around the world, both private and public sector, we can attest to the fact that every single one of them is *completely screwed up.* You may think that your company or government organization has a monopoly on internal politics, empire building, irrational decision making, and incompetence, but we can assure you, you're not alone.

Enter the Enterprise Architect. The role of today's Enterprise Architect is essentially to take the current enterprise and fix it. OK, maybe not the whole thing, but to make some kind of improvement to it. Go from today's sorry state to some future nirvana state where things are better somehow.

If you're able to improve your enterprise, that's wonderful. You're providing real value to your organization. But you're not doing architecture. Architecture isn't about *fixing* things, it's about establishing a best practice approach to *designing* things.

Okay, so if nobody is doing Enterprise Architecture, then who actually architects enterprises, and what are they actually doing?

The answer: *nobody.* Enterprises aren't architected at all. They are *grown*.

Every entrepreneur gets this fundamental point. When entrepreneurs first sit down to hammer out the business plan for a new venture, they would never dare to have the hubris to architect an organization large enough to be considered an enterprise. There are far too many unknowns. Instead, they establish a framework for growth. Plant the seeds. Water them. Do some weeding and fertilizing now and then. With a bit of luck, you'll have a nice, healthy, growing enterprise on your hands a few years down the road. But chances are, it won't look much like that original plan.

Does that mean there are no best practices for growing and nurturing a startup through all the twists and turns as it reaches the heights of enterprise-hood? Absolutely not. But most people don't consider such best practices to fall into the category of architecture.

What's the difference? "Traditional" Enterprise Architecture—that is, take your massively screwed organization and establish a best practice approach for improving it—follows a traditional systems approach: Here's the desired final state, so take certain actions to achieve that final state.

Growing a business, however, implies that there is no specific final state, just as there is no final state for a growing organism. An acorn knows it's supposed to turn into an oak tree, but there's no specific plan for the oak tree it will become. Rather, the DNA in the acorn provides the basic parameters for growth, and the rest is left up to *emergence*.

Such emergence is the defining characteristic of *Complex Systems*: systems with emergent properties of the system as a whole that aren't properties of any part of the system. Just as growth of living organisms requires emergence, so too does the growth of organizations.

Perhaps it makes sense to call the establishment of best practices for emergence *architecture*. After all, if we can architect traditional systems, why can't we architect complex ones? If we have any hope of figuring out how to actually architect enterprises, after all, we'll need to take a Complex Systems approach to Enterprise Architecture.

Complex Systems: At the Heart of Agile Architecture

Complex Systems are poorly named. In fact, many Complex Systems are quite simple. A Complex System is simply a system that exhibits emergent properties. Complex Systems Theory is particularly fascinating because it describes many natural phenomena, from the human mind to the growth of living creatures to the principle of friction. Furthermore, if you assemble a large enough group of people, they become a Complex System as well, which explains simple emergent properties like a stadium of people doing the wave, to more subtle ones like the wisdom of crowds.

It's important to realize that Complex Systems are actually *systems of systems*. The individual elements of a Complex System are themselves systems, which in turn may be Complex Systems in their own right. However, the individual component systems do not exhibit the emergent properties that the larger Complex System will offer.

Although a large enough group of people will constitute a Complex System in its own right, for our purposes we're looking for innovation in Complex Systems that include some software subsystems. The subsystems are not all software, because people must also be a part of the Complex System we're looking to create. In fact, understanding this basic principle is at the center of the Agile Architecture Revolution.

Traditional software innovation focuses predictably on traditional systems, as opposed to Complex Systems. To design a traditional system, start with the requirements for that system and build to those requirements. As a result, the best you can expect from a traditional system is that it does what it's supposed to do.

The emergent properties that Complex Systems exhibit, however, may be unpredictable—at least, before we build the system to see what behavior emerges. The stickiness property of Velcro, for example, is familiar and predictable to us now, but it took a great leap of innovative imagination to look at the little hooks and loops that make up Velcro and see that enough of them put together would give us the stickiness that makes Velcro so useful. The behavior of stock markets, in contrast, is inherently unpredictable, although it does follow certain patterns that give technical analysts something to base their models on. But if technical analysis accurately predicted market behavior, there would be a lot more billionaire technical analysts in this world!

The wrong approach, therefore, is to build to a set of fixed requirements that will tend to eliminate emergent behavior rather than encourage it. This limitation gives start-ups an advantage, because most traditional IT solutions follow traditional systems approaches that limit their flexibility. For example, traditional integration middleware follows a "connecting things" approach that leads to reduced agility over time, whereas SOA (properly done, not the fake

SOA peddled by the middleware vendors) follows a Complex Systems approach that yields emergent properties like business agility and business empowerment.

So, how do you avoid the wrong approach? Don't build anything that does what it's supposed to do. Instead, build something that will lead to surprises. Not every surprise will be useful, to be sure, so you may have to try a few times before you find an emergent property that people will actually appreciate. Also, remember that any system of systems that has component systems that consist solely of technology will most likely be the wrong approach, as the only surprises you're likely to end up with are bad ones: namely, that the system doesn't even do what it's supposed to do.

The key to successful Agile Architecture is to realize that humans are part of the system, not just users of the system. Although people are unpredictable individually, they are always predictable en masse. Your architecture, there- fore, must work at two levels. You must think about individual human/ technology subsystems as well as the complex human/technology systems that emerge when you have enough of the subsystems in place. Remember, you can influence human behavior at the Complex Systems level by introduc- ing technology at the component system level. To generate emergent proper- ties at the Complex Systems level, then, you must introduce some element of unpredictability at the component level.

A perfect example of this phenomenon is Twitter. At the component level we have users entering up to 140 characters at a time into a large database that is able to display those tweets based on various search criteria, the default being your own tweet history. However, if that description were all there was to Twitter, it would never have become the sensation it did. It was the fact that people could follow other people, and that people realized they could use hash tags to designate keywords and "at" people with the "@" symbol that intro- duced an element of unpredictability into the behavior of the individual user/ Twitter subsystems. Scale that up to millions of users, and you have the emergent properties inherent in Twitter trending and other aspects of the Twitterverse that make Twitter such a fascinating tool.

Other examples of successful Complex Systems innovations include:

- **SOA governance.** Human activity–centric governance processes sup- ported by a metadata-driven infrastructure enable SOA implementa- tions to exhibit the business agility emergent property. We'll discuss governance in more depth in Chapter 3.
- **Viral marketing.** One person uses a viral marketing tool to tell his or her friends about something cool in a way that encourages them to do the same, leading to the emergence of popularity across large populations.

- **Semantics tooling.** Our computers aren't smart enough to understand the meaning of data, so to effectively automate semantic integration requires human/software subsystems, which leads to the emergence of automated semantic context, at least in theory.
- **Crowdsourcing.** Ask a random person to do something or provide information and there's no telling what you'll get. But use a crowdsourcing tool to ask enough people, and you'll get the emergent property of the wisdom of crowds, where the crowd is able to arrive at the correct answer or solution.
- **Anything with the network effect.** One fax machine or Facebook when it had one user are entirely useless. Two fax machines or Facebook with two users are almost entirely useless. Up the number to three, four, five . . . still pretty damn useless. But at some point, there's a critical mass of users that makes the solution valuable, and you get the emergent property that more people want to join all of a sudden, where before they didn't.

Complex Systems are self-adapting. They are always in a state of change. How would we ever expect to architect a Complex System like an enterprise if we didn't take an Agile Architecture approach that worked at the meta level to deal with change? In fact, the lack of a Complex Systems approach to traditional Enterprise Architecture—architectural approaches that presume a final to-be state—is why all such approaches are inherently flawed.

Our previous Scrum But example is an illuminating illustration of what we mean by an Agile Architectural approach. You could look at a list of Scrum Buts and say, this team is doomed to failure. They've taken the good bits to Scrum and stripped those out, and now they're screwed. Alternatively, you could look at the same list and say, with a few bits of advice about how to deal with the Scrum Buts (in other words, the right meta-methodology), this team might be successful after all.

This admittedly oversimplified scenario has two outcomes: Team crashes and burns, or team is successful in spite of their Scrum Buts. In Complex Systems theory, these outcomes are called _attractors._ Given a set of circumstances, the end result will usually follow one of a set of patterns, in spite of the fact that different people are involved, each with their own skills and preferences. The system is subject to perturbations (the Scrum Buts, in our example), as well as constraints (the advice that makes up the meta-methodology), and the various identities of the people.

Without the appropriate advice, the attractor that is most likely to describe the outcome is the failure attractor. Clearly, the more Scrum Buts you have, and the more serious they are, the more likely your project will fail (although failure is still not certain). But with the proper meta-methodology, you can steer the project toward the success attractor, in spite of all the Scrum Buts and the various people on the team, who may be disgruntled, incompetent, over-worked, or whatever.

Note that the success attractor is not a final state in a traditional sense. Rather, it allows for the fact that perturbations, constraints, and identities are always subject to change. Generalize our Scrum meta-methodology example to the level of the enterprise, and you can get a sense of what we mean by Agile Architecture. Can we design the Complex System of the enterprise, a system consisting of human and technology subsystems, to move toward desirable attractors through the introduction of appropriate meta-policies, meta-processes, and meta-methodologies? That's the million-dollar meta-architecture question.

If you're looking to architect a Complex System, then, our core advice is to come up with a simple tool that is simple when you put it in front of individual users, but yields some kind of unpredictable behavior that when scaled up to large numbers of people delivers an emergent property that people will value. Keep in mind, however, that you hope to be surprised by the result. It may or may not be an emergent property that people will end up wanting, and thus may not be the basis for a viable business model. There is an inherent element of experimental innovation involved, which makes product development inherently risky. On the plus side, however, that risk gives you a barrier to entry, especially against large vendors who sell predictability.

The Complex Systems we're describing are inherently collaborative, because you're including people in the system, and the unpredictability you seek results from allowing them to interact in some way. But remember, the converse is not necessarily true: Not all human/technology systems are Complex Systems. Any multiuser application in the enterprise, for example, combines people and software on some level, but if the vendor didn't build the right unpredictability into it, then it won't exhibit emergent properties.

CHAPTER 2

Shhh, Don't Tell Anyone, but Let's Talk about Service-Oriented Architecture

The last chapter introduced Service-Oriented Architecture (SOA) as a type of Agile Architecture. So, what is SOA anyway? Whether or not what you're doing is actually SOA is somewhat of a pointless question; after all, what matters is whether what you're building actually solves a business problem. It doesn't really matter if you can call it SOA or not. But be that as it may, there's still widespread confusion and ongoing misinformation in the marketplace as to what actually qualifies as SOA, so this question is more relevant than maybe it should be. Here, then, is how we go about making the line between SOA and non-SOA clear.

The first point to remember is that SOA is *architecture*; in other words, a set of best practices for the organization and use of IT to meet business needs. This criterion, however, sets the bar quite low, because virtually any implementation follows some sort of organizational principles. Whether those principles are best practices, furthermore, is open to interpretation.

The second point, then, is the fact that SOA is an architecture oriented toward *Services*, and thus the definition of "Service" and whether the implementation follows an architecture that is oriented toward such Services becomes the critical question. The problem here, though, is that the word "Service" has several different meanings, even in the context of IT—and defining a criterion that SOA must be oriented toward the sort of Services that we mean in the context of SOA is a circular tautology. We need to be more specific about what we mean by Services.

The next question might be whether Web Services have anything to do with the definition of SOA. Does SOA require Web Services? Absolutely not. In fact, SOA is both technology and protocol neutral. We could implement SOA using

Common Object Request Broker Architecture (CORBA) if we like, or we could even create a completely proprietary environment—proprietary networking protocol, proprietary messaging protocol, proprietary infrastructure, the works—and we could still implement SOA with it if we really wanted to.

In fact, we mean something more by Service than a Web Service, or even a Service interface of any kind. The essence of a Service in the SOA context is the *business abstraction*—that is, a representation of functionality and/or data presented in a business context. For an implementation to be a SOA implementation it must include at least one abstracted Business Service. Whether a Business Service is *sufficient* to identify an implementation as SOA, however, is another question.

Our necessary criteria for SOA are actually more notable for what they're missing more so than what they contain. For example, we don't include the following:

- Whether there is an Enterprise Service Bus (ESB) or not, or any other particular piece of infrastructure or other technology, for that matter.
- Whether there's any eXtensible Markup Language (XML) in use. You could implement SOA with File Transfer Protocol (FTP) and Comma-separated value (CSV) files if you wanted to, and it would still be SOA—not very good SOA, maybe, but still SOA.
- Whether you're able to compose Services. True, one of the primary goals of building Business Services is to support Service composition, but we don't want to set the bar that high for the purposes of our definition. You can still be implementing perfectly good SOA without getting to the point that you're able to compose your Services to support business processes. Alternatively, your requirements may simply not include composition; for example, when the business only requires data-centric Services.
- Any mention of the design or planning work separate from the implemented Service. Drawings on a page, no matter how good, don't qualify as an implementation of anything. This absence is in line with the Agile principle of working software over documentation.
- Any reference to integration. If you can build a Business Service without having to integrate anything, that's fine. If you're not solving an integration problem, that's fine as well. In many ways, integration and SOA have been too closely associated, perhaps because so many vendors in the SOA space are actually integration vendors. Clearly, you can do integration without SOA, and furthermore, you can do SOA without integration.

The bottom line, however, is that the question as to whether what you're doing is SOA is far less important than whether what you're building solves business problems. What qualifies as SOA is an important question, though, for situations where an organization has deluded themselves into thinking that they're building SOA, when actually they aren't doing any such thing. Such situations are still quite prevalent, and when such implementations fail, they can undeservedly give SOA a bad name.

Rumors of SOA's Demise . . .

You may be asking yourself why SOA belongs in this book at all. After all, many organizations spent millions of dollars on their SOA initiatives with little benefit to show for their investment. SOA now has a tarnished reputation as a promising approach that failed to live up to its potential.

Hey, it's even worse than that. Isn't SOA dead?

Okay, everyone, calm down. SOA isn't dead; in fact, it isn't even sick. Thousands of organizations are showing real success with SOA around the world, and more are ramping up their SOA efforts every day. Plenty of smart organizations realize the cost savings and agility benefits of SOA warrant continued investment in the approach, even in tough economic times.

So, why the consternation? Where did this *SOA is dead* meme come from anyway?

The story dates to early 2009, when Anne Thomas Manes from the Burton Group (now Gartner) wrote a wonderfully insightful blog post discussing the misperceptions of SOA in the marketplace at that time. In fact, ZapThink agreed with most everything in the post.

The problem with the post was the title. You see, the more senior managers are in an organization, the shorter their attention spans. At some level, the attention span is three words long.

Now, the full title of Manes's blog post was "SOA Is Dead; Long Live Services," with a focus on building Services properly. But aforementioned attention-deficit executives read the blog post, which meant they read the first three words of the title, and completely freaked. "SOA is dead! Why are we spending all this money! Get the chief architect in here! They have some explaining to do!" Quite a firestorm in the blogosphere, one that lasted for months.

What amazed us at ZapThink most of all about the "SOA is dead" controversy is that there was nothing new there. In fact, the core themes of both Manes's comments and the reactions to those comments have been ZapThink themes for several years, and form an essential part of the discussion in this book:

- Calling a project SOA isn't as important as solving real business problems. In fact, the term "SOA" often gets in the way. Instead, both business and technical people should work to communicate using a common language of Service Orientation that's neither entirely business-centric nor technically oriented.

- SOA is part of a larger trend toward location-independent, loosely coupled computing—a trend that includes Cloud Computing.
- SOA is a loose collection of best practices, and as organizations more broadly adopt these best practices as SOA becomes mainstream, then people will talk about SOA less.
- SOA has a clear, specific definition, even though there's still confusion on this point, in large part because vendors are sowing misinformation.
- SOA is especially important in tough economic times, as long as you're able to realize the cost savings and agility benefits short term. Furthermore, numerous organizations are succeeding with SOA, and, as a result, realize the importance of continuing their SOA investment.

The most important thread that winds its way around all of these principles is the perspective that SOA consists of *best practices*. Best practices are slippery things, for a few reasons. First, they describe human behavior. Second, among all the various practices an organization might undertake, only a relatively small subset are the *best* ones, and which ones are best changes over time as people figure out new ones.

There is no hard and fast rule as to which best practices are SOA, and which are not, because best practices are problem dependent, not terminology dependent. In other words, which business problems you're trying to solve will in large part determine which practices are best for that particular situation: a classic example of the right tool for the job. SOA best practices don't solve all problems, and for any given problem that SOA might be appropriate for, there's a good chance that some of the best practices that the situation calls for aren't specifically SOA best practices.

One way of looking at this situation is that there are best practices for how to apply best practices—yes, *meta-best practices*. Just because your SOA textbook says you should do something doesn't mean that you should do that thing in every situation. On the contrary, what distinguishes a good architect is the knowledge of when *not* to apply a particular practice, even if that practice might be a best practice in a different situation. When we list SOA best practices—leveraging the intermediary pattern to build loosely coupled Services, governance best practices like those for Service versioning or reuse, and so forth, we're not expecting everyone to apply all of them in every situation.

In fact, the belief that to do SOA right you have to do some fixed set of things every time is a fallacy. Belief in this fallacy, unfortunately, is still quite prevalent, and turns SOA into a straw man. Virtually all failed projects with the name "SOA" failed because the organization didn't properly apply best practices. In other words, they weren't really doing SOA at all, because

SOA consists of best practices, and what they were doing consisted of practices that clearly weren't the best.

This point brings us back to the *SOA is dead* meme. Solving business problems the best way available isn't dead, of course, and never will be. But misapplying practices under the name of SOA can't die soon enough. Organizations simply cannot afford to waste money doing things they think are SOA, but aren't.

So, should you call your initiative "SOA"? If you are following best practices, then using the "SOA" label is, yes, a best practice if there's a good reason to do so. For example, if there's understanding and support for SOA among business stakeholders, then calling the initiative SOA will help firm up that support. Such stakeholder understanding is by no means guaranteed, however. In many cases, the best name for your SOA initiative is a name that ties the project to the business problem you're addressing. Some of the most successful SOA projects go under names like "Sarbanes Oxley compliance initiative" or "improved customer visibility" or some other phrase that ties the effort to the solution it promises to deliver.

If your organization isn't following best practices, however, then calling your project "SOA" isn't going to help—but then again, you have bigger problems. These are the situations where the SOA moniker is a straw man: "I was doing X, I called X SOA (even though it wasn't, because it wasn't best practices), and it failed—therefore SOA failed." Well, we don't have the time or money to play such games any more. SOA isn't dead—what's dead is the fake SOA straw man.

Though some architects were no doubt taken aback by the "SOA is dead" conflagration, my guess is that far more of them looked on with more of a sense of bemusement. After all, we talk to dozens of architects every month who are showing real successes with their SOA initiatives, and no blog post will cause them to rethink their architecture. Sure, there are challenges, but nobody is trying to tell you to stop doing what you are doing if it's working for you.

We're so used to all the hype around SOA that now that SOA is becoming mainstream, the decrease in the hype is both refreshing and possibly worrying. After all, shouldn't we all be working on the next big thing, be it Cloud Computing or something else? The fact of the matter is, the answer is no! We should seek to have a laser focus on addressing business needs, and we shouldn't let hype, or the absence of it, steer us astray.

The "SOA is dead" meme, in fact, might be thought of as a kind of "anti-hype"—which is just another kind of hype, of course. If SOA really were dead, then either SOA isn't best practices (the straw man), or best practices are dead, which is just plain silly. Focus on the business problems at hand, apply true best practices to those problems, and ignore the hype, and you will inevitably be successful in your endeavors—regardless of what you call them.

Thinking Outside the SOA Box

In spite of all the SOA is dead nonsense, SOA has turned the corner in many ways: We're now focusing more on consuming Services than building them, governance challenges have risen to the fore, and organizations are finally working through the complexities of SOA quality.

But perhaps the most interesting sign that SOA has reached a new level of maturity are the indications that the focus on SOA as something separate from the rest of IT is waning as Service-oriented best practices gradually become accepted more broadly as general IT best practices. The fact that the spotlight of hype has shifted from SOA to greener pastures like Cloud is actually an indication that SOA best practices are becoming ubiquitous. Ironically, the more ubiquitous SOA becomes, the more it fades from view.

This trend is still in progress, however. Today, most SOA thinking remains "inside the box," in that we're still thinking of SOA as a set of activities and best practices separate from the rest of IT. Such inside-the-box thinking helps us understand what is still a new approach to organizing IT capabilities and leveraging them as flexible business resources. But there is a problem with this limited thinking: The business just doesn't care about the SOA box. After all, business managers care about solving the various problems the business faces on a day-to-day basis; when they require IT to help solve those problems, they generally don't care if the particular solution IT brings to the table is Service-oriented or not. In a fundamental way, therefore, inside-the-box SOA thinking places limitations on SOA's relevance to the business.

Retiring the SOA box is an important step in providing value to the business, and the first step in getting rid of the SOA box is in recognizing its existence. Inside-the-box SOA thinking affects all corners of the greater IT community, including IT end-users, consultants, and vendors. It behooves all these parties, therefore, to recognize the aspects of the SOA box that limit their thinking, in order to think outside the SOA box.

Such inside-the-box thinking also introduces skepticism about SOA across the organization. Fortunately, thinking outside the box is only difficult when no one is doing it; once people realize that existing patterns of thought are too limiting and begin to expand the context of their understanding, then the box breaks down. Here are some notable examples of indications that people are finally starting to think outside of the SOA box:

- Companies are generally not asking their consultants for SOA by name. Instead, businesses are asking for solutions to their business problems, and consulting firms are increasingly leveraging SOA best practices to address those needs, even though those projects aren't "SOA projects."

- The more narrow definition of SOA Governance consists of applying governance practices to SOA implementations; for example, making sure that developers are following reuse policies, and ensuring running Services conform to policies around security and service levels. Increasingly, however, people are defining SOA governance more broadly, thinking about how to tackle broader governance challenges in the context of SOA, once they have SOA in place.
- Many organizations are setting up SOA Centers of Excellence in their organizations, which are essentially teams of architects who create a set of guidelines for the adoption and implementation of SOA across the enterprise. Many of these Centers of Excellence, however, are extensions of existing Integration Competency Centers, and in many cases, they are acting as Enterprise Architecture Centers of Excellence, centralizing best practices for architecture more broadly than just SOA.
- IT shops are finally separating the notions of SOA and Web Services, gaining a clearer understanding of the differences between the two as well as their relative independence. A large part of this trend is away from Web Services toward RESTful approaches to SOA. We'll be covering Representational State Transfer (REST)-based SOA in Chapter 8.
- As Cloud Computing moves from hype to reality, IT organizations are increasingly realizing how important SOA best practices are for achieving success in the Cloud. Not only are Application Programming Interfaces (APIs) to Cloud resources loosely coupled and abstracted—what we call *Services*—but the broader architectural principles of SOA are essential to achieving the elasticity, fault tolerance, and other critical Cloud benefits. We'll also be covering the Cloud part of the Agile Architecture story in this book.
- Generally speaking, when we talk about Agile Architecture, we think of SOA as an example. Not the product-driven, integration-centric SOA that vendors love to talk about, but the technology-independent, governance-centric SOA that ZapThink has long championed. Our hope is that by focusing on Agile Architecture in this book, we can take the old discussions about SOA and separate the wheat from the chaff: focus on what SOA was supposed to be all along, rather than dwell on some of the wrong turns that many organizations made with the approach.

The common thread that ties these illustrations together is that the older thinking presumes that SOA represents something distinct: a distinct set of best practices or a separate market, for example. But in reality, as SOA matures, people find that SOA best practices are simply best practices, and SOA markets, practices, and projects are becoming indistinguishable from the larger software, hardware, and professional services markets, best practices, and IT projects of which they are a part.

It's possible to misinterpret this trend and incorrectly conclude that SOA is fading in importance. In fact, there's even a "SOA is passé" thread through the industry that supposes that SOA is losing importance because SOA best practices are gradually losing their SOA label. However, nothing could be further from the truth: There's more SOA than ever going on today, only now people are actually doing it more so than talking about it.

Okay, So How Did SOA End Up Dead in the First Place?

SOA's future couldn't have been brighter when it hit the scene in the early 2000s. We all expected it to become the predominant approach to Enterprise Architecture (EA) worldwide. In many respects, however, it succumbed to the pressures of confusion, misdirection, and ignorance that assailed it, and for many organizations SOA became a tired label that signified little more than a set of middleware product features. We saw this sad conclusion before with Enterprise Application Integration (EAI)—once a promising architectural approach, now a euphemism for expensive, inflexible integration middleware.

No one group is to blame for SOA's troubles, however. In fact, the crowd chasing SOA with their torches and pitchforks is quite diverse. Understanding the motivations of the people who assailed SOA, however, is important, because the same forces are even now lining up against the broader Agile Architecture trend impacting organizations today. Here's our take on the parties that ZapThink believes were standing in the way of SOA's success.

- ■ **Middleware and other IT infrastructure vendors.** You're a software vendor with a product line chock-full of proprietary, tightly coupled integration middleware. License revenue is suffering as customers look for more flexible, less-expensive ways of leveraging their diverse IT resources. As a result, they are looking at SOA. Your software, however, does not lend itself to SOA best practices—loose coupling, composable Services, and flexibility in general are all capabilities that you failed to build in to your software. What to do?

   Reinventing your company and rearchitecting your software from the ground up is far too expensive and time-consuming, and after all, you already have the older middleware in the can. The only option is to slap Web Services interfaces on your stuff, call it an ESB, and sell it as SOA middleware. Hopefully your customers won't notice the old wine in new bottles. After all, that's what marketing is for!

Not every integration vendor has taken this route, but many have. You can identify them when their salespeople make statements like "ESBs are necessary for SOA," and when their marketing deemphasizes the more significant SOA infrastructure challenges of governance, quality, and management.

- **Enterprise Architects.** EAs are supposed to have a comprehensive perspective on the business and the role that IT plays in supporting its varied and changing needs. Although many EAs do have the rare combination of business and technical acumen necessary to understand how SOA best practices can drive business solutions, many do not. Time and again, architects who find themselves nominally in the role of EA actually only focus on part of the problem.

  ZapThink frequently interacts with such architects who may be perfectly competent business architects or technical architects, but lack the skills or vision to connect the dots between the two. And yet, SOA is a style of Enterprise Architecture that cuts across business and technology. You can recognize EAs that act as SOA impediments by their lack of understanding of the tight relationship between Business Process Management (BPM) and SOA, or mistaken beliefs that SOA is a technical application architecture, that it requires Web Services, or that the best way to get SOA is by purchasing it from a vendor.

- **CIOs.** You'd think that every Chief Information Officer would be all over SOA. After all, SOA can reduce integration cost, increase business visibility and agility, increase asset reuse, and ease regulatory compliance. What's not to love? For any organization that faces any or all of these problems, SOA is a no-brainer. And yet, the CIO is rarely the SOA champion for the IT organization.

  The reasons for this lack of insight are many and varied. Many CIOs are nontechnical, and as a result don't understand, and often fear, architecture of any kind. Others are so driven by quarterly results that a long-term, iterative initiative like enterprise SOA is out of the question. Still others insist on project-based IT funding to meet the needs of individual lines of business, a funding mechanism virtually guaranteed to slow down any initiative that seeks to reuse assets across the IT organization the way that SOA encourages.

  Fortunately, you can recognize clueful CIOs because they understand the business value architecture can provide, they are willing to fund initial SOA iterations, and as the IT organization delivers value with those early projects, the CIO authorizes more of the same. Unfortunately, however, such executives are few and far between. If you know one, buy them this book!

- **Large consulting firms.** Because SOA consists of best practices, if anyone has the potential of offering SOA to their customers, it's the consulting firms. Add the fact that SOA at least has the potential of being an enterprise-wide initiative, and all the large system integrators (SIs) smell opportunity. As a result, they all built SOA teams, and invested heavily in bringing their SOA offerings to market.

The problem they all faced, however, was a shortage of consultants who truly understood how to plan and implement SOA. The few such architects they had ended up playing a critical sales role, helping to close big deals. Once the paperwork was complete, however, the SOA experts moved on to the next deal, leaving a team of junior consultants holding the bag.

- **Business executives.** Fifty years after the beginning of the Industrial Revolution, there's no question that the titans of industry were entirely comfortable with the complexity and power of the factories they commanded. But today, more than fifty years after the beginning of the Information Revolution, it's still unusual to find CEOs or CFOs who are truly comfortable with the fact that their businesses run on IT. They see IT as a tool and a cost center, but even today, when whole industries like financial services deal with no product other than bits on a wire, these executives remain woefully ignorant of the true power, capabilities, risks, and challenges of IT. Of course, if you're a business executive and you're reading this book, this criticism doesn't apply to you!

For those executives who *aren't* reading this book, however, SOA is too "techie" a concept to understand or pay attention to. It's a losing battle to present SOA as a solution to business problems to the boardroom. The best SOA champions in such organizations can do is try to slip SOA initiatives into budgets under the radar, in the hopes that no one will notice.

It would be wonderful if we could claim that the forces that lined up against SOA were no longer in play, but unfortunately, they continue to block progress. As we'll discuss in Chapter 8, the entire discussion about REST took a similar wrong turn, shifting from an architectural style to a better way to build APIs. Yes, we needed better APIs to be sure, but many people missed the boat on REST.

Cloud Computing also faces similar challenges. Because Cloud is the focus of so much hype, marketers are overly generous with the Cloud verbiage, relabeling every product in their catalog as Cloud this or Cloud that—serving only to confuse their customers. Even for those IT professionals who understand Cloud offerings and their value propositions, however, architecture still remains a challenge. There's a common misperception that the Cloud is a "virtual server in the sky," a place you can put any old legacy app you have lying around and it will automatically become elastic, fault tolerant, and less expensive to maintain. Unfortunately, without the proper architecture, there's a very real risk that Cloud Computing won't live up to its promise, or in some situations, will fail outright.

There is more to this book, however, than simply getting architecture *right*. We're actually taking steps to *reinvent* architecture—a new way of thinking about IT, and a new way to think about leveraging IT to deal better with change. We're not saying it's going to be easy. On the contrary, the shift to Agile Architecture will be enormously difficult. The forces of shortsightedness, confusion, and greed that worked to sidetrack SOA will also impact Agile Architecture to be sure—but those will be the least of our challenges. We're talking a *revolution* here, folks. Expect some bloodshed.

In the meantime, however, we recommend taking Anne Manes's advice: focus on building the right Services. It doesn't matter if you call what you're doing SOA—or even if you call your Services *Services*. And by *right*, we mean *addressing the business need*. Never forget that technology is always a means to an end, not an end in its own right. And when the business says *make me more agile*, you'd better listen.

Services: The Core SOA Lesson

To understand SOA, you must understand Services. Unfortunately, the term *Service* is overloaded, even within the IT context. There's *service* as in Software-as-a-Service, *service* as in IT Service Management, and then there's *Service* as in SOA (following ZapThink's longstanding convention to capitalize *Service* when talking about the SOA kind of Services).

Even within the relatively narrow context of SOA, there are still subtle differences in meaning, because people still often get confused about the level of abstraction of a Service. Basically, there are three levels of abstraction we work on in the context of SOA:

1. **Service implementation.** At this level of abstraction we're talking about software. A Service implementation is made up of running code.
2. **Service interface.** Web Services live at this level, as a Web Services Description Language (WSDL) file provides a contract for the interface, but says nothing about the underlying implementation. Web Services, however, are not the only kind of Service interface, because Service contracts are not always WSDL files.
3. **Abstracted Service.** A representation of a business capability or data that the organization can compose with other such Services to implement business processes. These are the sorts of Services ZapThink focuses on, as they are the core abstraction that underlies SOA.

Building abstracted Services thus becomes the core technical challenge of implementing SOA.

So far so good—but the real question here is how we make an abstracted Service actually work, when the tools at our disposal are the Service implementations and interfaces and all the infrastructure that goes along with them. It's one thing to talk about *representations of business capabilities*, and quite another to string your ones and zeroes together into something that actually provides business value, and furthermore, supports the business agility meta-requirement.

The first critical point to understanding abstracted Services is to understand that there is typically a many-to-many relationship between Services and Service contracts. A Service implementation may support multiple contracts, each of which could correspond to a particular Service interface, for, say, a particular type of consumer. Similarly, there might be several implementations that support a single contract, and hence a single Service interface, for the purposes of scalability or fault tolerance, for instance.

With abstracted Services, however, the relationship becomes what we might call *many-to-many-to-many*: A particular abstracted Service might have several contracts that represent relationships with various consumers, while also representing multiple Service interfaces that themselves might each have one or more Service implementations. This approach might sound overly complex, but it's the key to implementing the abstracted Service.

To illustrate this point, let's work though an example. Let's say we have a Customer Information Service that different lines of business in a large enterprise can consume and compose to provide or update any information about their customers that the lines of business might need. From the business perspective, this is a single Service that any line of business can use as per the policies set out for that Service.

From the IT perspective, however, it makes sense to implement the Customer Information Service as a set of Service interfaces in order to support the somewhat different needs for customer information that the various lines of business might have. Furthermore, each Service interface may represent several Service implementations that the SOA management infrastructure can leverage as necessary to meet the service levels set out in the contracts for both the abstracted Service as well as the Service interfaces, in addition to the policies that may apply to these Services as well as other Services in production.

In this example, the complexity beneath the Service abstraction is necessary to support the loose coupling of the abstracted Service. We say a Service is *loosely coupled* if changing the Service doesn't break existing consumers of the Service, and furthermore, the Service can meet the needs of different consumers—even if those needs vary. For example, the line of business consumers may need different formats for the customer information, or may require different data as part of the response from the Service. To loosely couple such consumers, an intermediary (or set of intermediaries) may perform a transformation that can take the output from any of the Service interfaces and put it into the format the particular consumer requires, as per the contract in place that governs the relationship between that particular consumer and the abstracted Service. Then, either the management infrastructure (or possibly the integration infrastructure) may offer content-based routing of the requests from particular Service interfaces to the underlying implementations, based on run-time policies.

Loose coupling, however, means more than being able to support different consumers with different needs. It also means *building for change*. Because we have a governance and management infrastructure in place that enables this many-to-many-to-many relationship among abstracted Services, Service interfaces, and Service implementations, we are able to respond to those changes in a loosely coupled manner as requirements evolve—in other words, without breaking anything.

For example, if one consumer changed its required data format, we could introduce a new contract that might require a new transformation on the intermediary between the Service interface and the abstracted Service, but wouldn't impact the Service interface directly or any of the Service implementations. Another example might be the need to upgrade or add a new data source to support the Service. Such a change might require a new policy regarding the content-based routing that the management infrastructure performs, or a new implementation of one or more Service interfaces. But if the contracts for those interfaces don't change, then the abstracted Service isn't affected, and neither are the consumers. A third example would be a policy update that would change the content-based routing behavior between the Service interfaces and their implementations. In fact, we see this application of content-based routing as more of a management challenge than an integration task because of this need to support run-time policy changes.

But in the final analysis, the most important thing to remember is that the Customer Information abstracted Service is but a single example. In the general case, the architect must select from a variety of SOA infrastructure patterns depending on the specifics of the problem at hand. The bottom line is that loose coupling presents architectural challenges that are at the heart of planning and implementing the SOA infrastructure. Building the Service abstractions presents a simple representation to the business but requires additional efforts under the covers to make that abstraction a concrete reality. This is the work of SOA: implementing loosely coupled business Services that are at the core of any successful SOA implementation.

Implementing Policy-Driven Behavior

One of the main goals of SOA is to separate the Service interface (represented by the contract and associated metadata) from the Service implementation (represented by the underlying code that the interface abstracts). A Service contract defines the relationship between a Service provider and a Service consumer, and the requirements for engaging in an exchange of information. Although this definition is fairly clear on its face, it's important to understand that any particular Service implementation can have more than one contract associated with it.

In fact, it is a best practice for Services to have more than one contract. For example, suppose that a Service developer at a particular company wishes to develop a loosely coupled Service that exposes customer information to authorized requesters. In one instance, the company wishes to expose only nonprivate data to any requester that queries the Service. In another instance, the company wishes to expose all customer data including private information to requesters as long as they provide an authorized digital certificate. To further add to the value of this example, let us also suppose that we wish for the same quality of service policies (such as expected response time) to apply to both of these Service usages. An illustration of this situation is in Figure 2.1.

In this example, a Service consumer has a choice of binding to one of two Service contracts: one in which they can provide no security information and therefore only get general, public customer data as long as they provide valid information in the `<customerID>` element, and another in which they supply an authorized digital certificate and get all data in the `<customerData>` XML document, including data supplied in the optional `<private>` element. The key is that we only need one Service implementation here. The developer, using contract-first development, would have realized that two contracts specified very similar requirements, and that all the developer would need to do is to check whether or not a valid digital certificate was present, and return the appropriate information—both responses that would have complied with the `<customerData>` XML schema.

One interesting thing to note about this example is that the two contracts look very similar to each other, with one notable distinction. In the one case, Policy #1 applies to the first contract, which implies no security requirements, whereas in the other case, Policy #2 applies to the second contract, which requires stricter security. Another interesting aspect of this example is that there is a *third* policy that applies to both Service contracts requiring that in any case, the Service must not wait more than 30 seconds to provide a response. Thus, we have three policies, two contracts, and just one Service implementation.

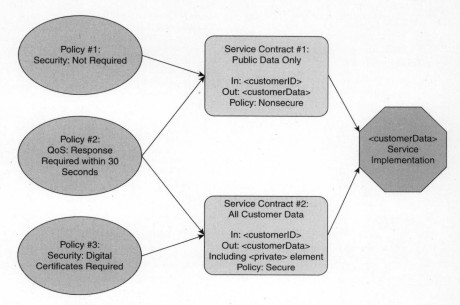

Figure 2.1   Multiple Policies per Contract, Multiple Contracts Per Service

To make this example even more interesting, we can add a third Service contract that responds with a completely different response, providing only the <customerName> field when prompted with <customerID> input, as shown in Figure 2.2. Of course, there's no reason to require another Service implementation, and therefore, we can have at the very least three Service contracts for this one Service, and countless more as long as the Service implementation is appropriate for all such Service contracts. The key to making this example work is that the Service consumer is responsible for choosing the appropriate contract to bind to—knowing full well what the policy requirements are and therefore what to expect from the response.

Another take on the contracts vs. Service implementations question is how a single Service contract can abstract multiple Service implementations. Let us extend the previous example by adding another Service that can respond to the Service contract that provided only the <customerName> data, as shown in Figure 2.3. In this case, this implementation uses a local cache to deliver much faster results to the Service consumer than the more general-purpose customerData Service implementation.

Now, the first question you might ask is *why* would we use two Services to implement a single contract? The reason might be that the infrastructure that implements the Service might decide to utilize the more optimal

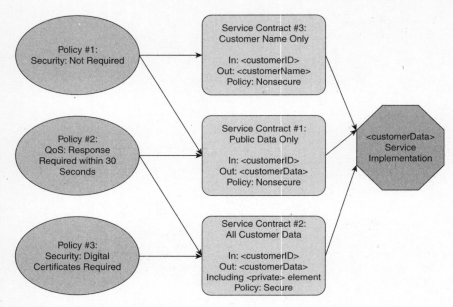

Figure 2.2 Many-to-many Relationship between Policies and Contracts

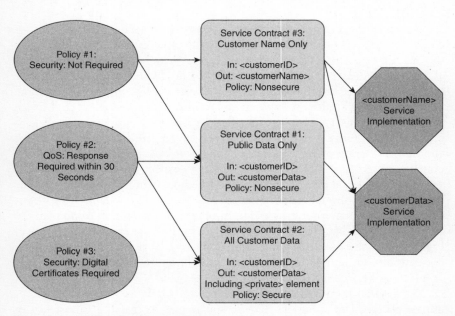

Figure 2.3 Multiple Services per Contract

`customerName` Service when the `customerData` Service is overloaded, or vice-versa, only use the `customerData` Service when implementing Service Contract #1, or perhaps use either on a round-robin basis whenever calling Service Contract #3. Regardless of the implementation mechanism, it's clear that either of the two Service implementations in Figure 2.3 can adequately respond to any Service consumer that binds to the appropriate contract.

To make loose coupling work and to truly separate interface from implementation, we must allow a many-to-many relationship among Service contracts, implementations, and policies that apply to any number of Services. This pattern is quite different from the traditional one-API-per-object interface pattern from the object-oriented world. In a sense, we're extending the principle of polymorphism that applies to methods in Object-Oriented Analysis and Design (OOAD) and extending it to contracts in SOA. However you look at it, the many-to-many relationships among policies, contracts, and Services represent a fundamental aha moment for Service developers.

The other lesson here is the role that metadata play. In this case, we're representing the contracts that specify the various interfaces, as well as the routing policies, as metadata. In general, whenever there is behavior that we wish to externalize because it is subject to change, we want to represent that behavior as metadata, so that we can change the behavior of the software by changing the metadata. For this reason, metadata are an essential enabler of Agile Architecture in general. Remember, we don't only want to build software that meets particular requirements, we also want to build software that can meet *changing* requirements. Metadata are essential to achieving this agility.

Any discussion of change in the context of Agile Architecture, however, must begin with *loose coupling*. As one of the main benefits of Agile Architectures like SOA, loose coupling provides developers the ability to freely change the implementation of a Service without having to change the consumers of that Service, and vice-versa. This loose coupling gives enterprises the benefit of flexibility in the face of IT heterogeneity and change. However, loose coupling doesn't mean that any changes to a Service won't impact other parties. Indeed, loose coupling only applies if the underlying implementations still comply with the existing Service contract. Changes to the Service contract itself, therefore, can lead to real trouble.

A Service contract contains both functional metadata that describe how to interact with a Service as well as nonfunctional metadata that define what conditions and restrictions apply to consumers looking to access Service functionality. WSDL is only one small part of the metadata necessary for adequately defining a Web Service; we also need information on security, process, quality of service, commercial requirements, and other information. Therefore, when a developer decides to make a small change to any contract metadata, such as acceptable security requirements or quality of service, any

Service consumer that makes an assumption about the contract metadata now breaks, and the entire system no longer functions properly.

It seems, then, that loose coupling may be out of reach, at least when following the Web Services approach to SOA. After all, the reality is that just as Service implementations change, so too does the need to change Service contract metadata. So, how can enterprises implement Services in such a way that small changes to Service metadata don't throw a wrench into the works? By making sure that older versions of Service contracts remain valid until an organization can make sure through proper governance that no consumers will ever use those contract metadata again.

What's the Deal with Web Services?

Web Services are only one of many different types of Services. Even within the context of Service interfaces, Web Services aren't the whole story: Sometimes organizations need a richer Service contract than what WSDL and associated Web Services standards—namely XML Schema Definitions (XSD) and WS-Policy—can provide. But even with augmented Service contracts—leading to what you might call augmented Web Services—our problems with Web Services still haven't been entirely resolved.

But we're getting ahead of ourselves. A quick look at the history of SOA and Web Services will help to clarify the distinction between the two. The first indication that SOA and Web Services are separate things is that SOA has been around for longer than Web Services have. Distributed computing approaches from around the early 1990s like CORBA and Microsoft's Distributed Component Object Model (DCOM) were both architectural approaches that abstracted software capabilities in a contracted way that provided a certain measure of loose coupling, providing greater flexibility than architectures that leveraged the tightly coupled interfaces of other approaches—in other words, they were Service-oriented. And though both CORBA and DCOM each had a certain measure of success in the marketplace, DCOM was unabashedly a single-vendor architecture, and whereas CORBA was ostensibly vendor neutral, it was nevertheless vendor specific in practice, as different vendor implementations of CORBA proved to be mostly incompatible with each other.

The SOA story doesn't really get interesting, however, until the late 1990s, when several vendors had two essential realizations: first, that a SOA approach would never provide true flexibility unless it was implementation independent, and second, that the relatively new XML would make an ideal messaging protocol, even though its original purpose was as a document markup language. These insights let to a multivendor standards effort that eventually settled on the core set of specifications that provide the foundation for Web Services: WSDL, Universal Description, Discovery, and Integration (UDDI), and the Simple Object Access Protocol (SOAP, which is now no longer an acronym, as accessing objects is no longer its raison d'être).

The early work on the SOA "find-bind-publish" triangle that these three standards enabled focused on business-to-business (B2B) applications, with early visions of a global "green pages" directory that allowed for automated discovery of, and binding to business Web Services over the Internet. The problem was, nobody wanted to conduct business that way. It's risky enough picking a plumber out of the Yellow Pages as it is, so who would want to automate the process, adding arbitrary interactions between systems? As a result, this early B2B vision for SOA collapsed, as one small part of the broader failure of the "Web 1.0" B2B eMarketplace trend at the end of the dot-com boom.

Meanwhile, although the end of the heady dot-com days and the recession and IT downturn that followed put a damper on many standards efforts, the 2002–2003 period actually marked what we might call the golden age of Web Services. Vendors realized that the only story that had any hope of generating business in tough times was a cost savings value proposition, and Web Services had a great one: *lowering the cost of integration.* Move from proprietary interfaces to standards-based ones, and think of all the money you can save! And though the standards in those days were far from being ready for prime time, the business case was solid enough in any case for investors, who were still reeling from the crash and looking for new opportunities. And thus, the Web Services marketplace was born.

ZapThink, of course, rode this Web Services wave, although we advised vendors in those early days not to talk about SOA, because the market wasn't ready yet for the more complex, business-centric topic that SOA represented. Instead, the buzz centered on Web Services as a standards-based approach to integration.

And yet, we realized back in 2002 one fundamental truth that is every bit as prophetic today as it was then: that although Web Services alone can reduce the cost of integration, only by moving to SOA can an organization reduce the long-term cost of business change. In other words, Web Services get you the ticket to the ball, but you still have to learn to dance.

As the SOA buzz began to grow, Web Services entered their challenging adolescence phase. Support for WSDL, UDDI, and SOAP alone did not guarantee interoperability, and was woefully inadequate to standardize all the complexities of arbitrary system-to-system interactions. These limitations led to various follow-on standards efforts, many of which are now lumped into the term WS-∗ (pronounced *WS star*, where the star is an old Unix term that means *anything and everything*.) These efforts, naturally, took time, and as the various standards bodies consisted mostly of vendors with their own agendas, the entire mess devolved into a complex, political quagmire that for all the noise, had delivered precious little true interoperability to organizations seeking to reduce integration costs. As a result, Web Services never lived up to their potential, and are now an increasingly marginal part of the SOA story.

Meanwhile, by late 2003, we began advising vendors to focus their messaging more on SOA than Web Services. The picture we painted for enterprises was far more challenging than the relatively straightforward adoption of Web Services, because SOA involved rethinking how the business leveraged IT in various ways. Web Services were still part of the story, to be sure, but it became clear that Web Services were not essential for SOA, and furthermore, SOA was not required for Web Services.

One of the most intractable issues with Web Services is their *operations*. Web Service operations are essentially custom: Architects or developers specify them however they like. Furthermore, each vendor deals with operations differently from the next, limiting the cross-product interoperability of the Web Services. Web Services operations also make versioning Web Services into a prickly challenge.

Enter *Representational State Transfer*. Even though REST is an architectural style for building distributed hypermedia applications (as we'll discuss later), challenges with Web Services integration led to the rise of REST as a simplified approach to APIs. REST, however, sports a *uniform* interface. GET, POST, PUT, and DELETE are all you get—for any resource. All your Web Services operation issues have miraculously disappeared! But even though WSDL 2.0 does offer a REST binding (which hardly anybody uses), the notion of a *Service* in the REST context is different than in the Web Services context, as there is no single metadata file representing the Service contract analogous to the role WSDL files play for Web Services.

Implementing REST-based SOA, therefore, is not an elementary task. You can't just switch out your Web Services for REST-based Services and call it a day. Instead, you must take into account the true purpose of REST— building distributed hypermedia applications, remember?—in order to understand how to go about REST-based SOA.

Does REST-based SOA, then, represent the culmination of the evolution of SOA? We'd be unnecessarily shortsighted to come to that conclusion. True, REST does address some of the issues with Web Services, but it introduces some issues of its own. There's no question, however, that if we look back at the history of SOA and Web Services, we can identify a marriage with some interesting twists and turns, because Web Services were critically important at bringing SOA to the fore, even though SOA grew beyond what Web Services could offer.

The Third Conversation

At the heart of SOA is the notion of the *Business Service*, which is an abstraction that provides a representation of a business capability or data that the organization can compose with other such Services to implement business processes. Such Business Services are a level of abstraction above Service interfaces like Web Services and RESTful Services. And yet, even though the notion of a Business Service is critical to understanding SOA, true understanding of the Business Service abstraction remains elusive for most people, even though Business Services promise greater *Business/IT Alignment*.

Wait just a minute. Business/IT Alignment? Don't you just want to *scream* every time you hear that dreaded phrase? It seems that every consultant since the dawn of the computer age has been touting their ability to achieve this visionary concordance, and yet here we are, over half a century since enterprises first began using computers, and the business and IT worlds seem to be less aligned than ever before. Yet, dare we say it, the rise of SOA, especially when we place it in the context of Enterprise Architecture, is yet one more attempt at lining up the suits and the geeks. What is it about this latest technique that promises to make progress where so many approaches of the past have fallen short?

Looking closely at what people actually mean by this tired cliché can begin to shed some light on the problem. From the business perspective, business/IT alignment means getting IT folks to speak the language of business. "If only those techies understood business and could speak my language," the suits say, "then they'd be aligned with the business." The perspective from within the ranks of IT, however, is predictably contrary. "If only the suits could understand the issues of IT," say the tech set, "then they'd be much better able to leverage the technology to meet their needs long term, instead of throwing short-term requirements over the cubicle wall, expecting us to deliver on them in as little time and with as little money as possible." Yet after all these years, neither side has come to speak the language of the other sufficiently well to achieve alignment.

The problem is, neither group is ever going to get what they want if they expect the crowd on the other side of that wall to change their ways and speak the language of the first group. Business conversations and IT conversations come from fundamentally different points of view, even when they are speaking about the same issues. In order to finally make progress on the heretofore unreachable alignment, therefore, everybody in the organization must be able to carry on a different conversation altogether.

Carrying on separate conversations, in fact, is nothing new in the world of IT. From the earliest abstractions like compilers and user interfaces, to today's separation of logical and physical models, an essential technique for conducting simplified conversations about complicated topics has depended on various abstractions. Furthermore, as the IT environment becomes more complex, the need to understand the separations among various conversations becomes an increasingly important tool for dealing with such complexity.

It's also important to note that businesspeople also deal with abstractions every day, even though they may not realize it. After all, *business itself* is an abstraction for the myriad activities that people undertake at work. *Business processes* are also abstractions consisting of sequences of such activities. All of these abstractions provide people with a frame of reference for conducting meaningful conversations where the participants have a good shot at understanding one another.

Regardless of whether the abstractions are business or technology centric, it often falls to the architect to wield the tools of abstraction as a core part of what it means to do architecture. Another important role of the architect is to negotiate between different levels of abstraction. Fortunately, as the practice of architecture matures, separate conversations become more distinct over time. Architecture tools like the Zachman Framework help architects define such separations for the organization. And yet, though Zachman strives to define models for the business as well as for technology, it falls short of providing much meaningful business/IT alignment for most organizations who attempt to use it, often due to the Framework's ambitiousness and complexity.

Instead of the numerous, diverse conversations that tools like the Zachman Framework encourage, therefore, SOA centers on only three: the business conversation, the IT conversation, and the *third conversation*—which doesn't have a formal name, but falls squarely in the overlap between business and technology, what we might call *the Service Orientation* (SO) conversation, for want of a better term. Both businesspeople and IT people can and should be able to carry on an SO conversation, even though this third conversation is, strictly speaking, neither a business nor a technology discussion in its own right.

How do we conduct an SO conversation? Conversations break down into sentences, which consist of words. The three conversations sometimes use different words, while at other times the same terms are used in different ways. Take, for example, the word *Service* itself:

- **Business context.** A Service is a capability the business can draw on to achieve its goals.
- **IT context.** A Service is a contracted interface to software functionality and data that communicates via messages.
- **SO context.** A Service is an abstract representation of an IT capability that the business can compose with other Services into applications that implement business processes.

Note first of all that the first two definitions taken together look like night and day. Put a businessperson who sees a Service as in #1 in a room with a techie who has perspective #2 and they might as well be speaking Greek to each other. Secondly, note that from the business perspective, definition #3 looks rather technical, and yet from an IT perspective, the third definition has a distinctly business-oriented context. That's the fundamental nature of the third conversation: It operates at the overlap of business and IT, and yet falls squarely in neither.

Whereas the previous example deals with the noun *Service*, let's work through a second example that deals with verbs. What actions might someone take to create and use a Service? Here are some ideas:

- **Business context.** Need, decide, order, buy, pay, use, measure, support
- **IT context.** Define, design, analyze, develop, code, test, deploy
- **SO context.** Govern, model, save, render, create, publish, discover, compose

The business, of course, places the acquisition of Services in the context of a business transaction: *Want it, buy it, use it.* You techies out there will instantly recognize #2 as the core verbs in the software development life cycle. The third conversation, however, thinks about Service creation as a set of operations that take place above the Service abstraction: They don't deal with the code-centric issues of the IT perspective, while still providing Services by leveraging IT capabilities.

Today's SOA architect—as well as the Agile Architects they should all become—is part evangelist, part visionary, part therapist, part coach, and part taskmaster. Among all these duties the architect has, let's add one more: *language teacher*. It is this architect who must work with both audiences to explain the new vocabulary of Service Orientation, and with it the new way of thinking about the relationship between business and IT that enables Agile Architecture.

The good news is, you architects out there don't have to worry about teaching technology to a business audience or teaching business to a technology audience anymore. Those of you who have tried either of those Sisyphean endeavors know how often they amount to rolling a stone up a mountain. Instead, leverage your organization's progress with SOA to craft a new language for your organization, one that both constituencies can master. True, the third conversation will seem technical to the suits and "high level" (read: business-centric) to the geeks. But rest assured this new conversation is the key to successfully aligning the two camps.

Even though the goal still eludes us, we've definitely made a certain measure of progress aligning business and IT via previous efforts over the years. In fact, the entire vision of eBusiness in the 1990s was one of improved alignment. And though there's no question that the vision of eBusiness was successful in many ways—when was the last time you traded a stock or bought a plane ticket without using the Internet?—true alignment remained largely out of reach, in large part due to the human communication issues discussed earlier.

Just as eBusiness had only limited success in achieving true business/IT alignment, SOA only had limited success as well. As we move beyond SOA to the broader notion of Agile Architecture, however, it will become increasingly necessary for both sides of the cubicle wall to learn to speak the third conversation. It is only by learning to speak this third conversation that business and IT can finally come into alignment, and only then will Agile Architecture live up to its potential.

Freeing Architecture from the Underlying Infrastructure

We have long advised that beginning a SOA project by purchasing an ESB is starting at the wrong end of the initiative. In fact, purchasing *any* technology, especially an ESB, at the beginning of *any* architecture project is a recipe for failure, which you've been telling anyone who'll listen. But for whatever reason, your organization didn't pay attention to you, and now they've dropped a bundle on an ESB. Maybe your boss golfs with the vendor sales rep, or maybe the powers that be are listening to the wrong analyst firm; who knows? But in any case, you're stuck with that decision, and you're now expected to implement SOA with it.

Fortunately, though purchasing an ESB too early in a SOA project does substantially increase your risk of failure, all is not lost. After all, you're not alone; this mistake is one of the most prevalent SOA snafus in IT shops around the world today, and not all of those projects end up as failures. After all, many of today's ESBs are now mature products, and can be an important part of a fully functional SOA implementation. Understanding the risks that buying an ESB too early in a SOA initiative presents, and dealing with those risks proactively, can turn a bad situation around and get your SOA initiative back on the right track.

Fundamentally, the problem with buying the ESB first is that you might fall into the trap of doing things the way the ESB would like you to do them, in light of the fact that many ESBs are in many ways traditional middleware under the covers. After all, if middleware solved all your problems, then you wouldn't be considering SOA in the first place—and adding Service capabilities to your middleware doesn't change this fundamental fact.

In fact, the pitfalls that the ESB-first approach introduces fall into three broad categories:

1. **Taking an overly integration-centric perspective of the project.** Because most ESB products' heritage is integration middleware, they are generally really good at connecting things—in other words, most ESBs are quite capable integration middleware solutions. The problem is, SOA isn't about connecting things, it's about building loosely coupled Services the business can leverage to meet changing process needs. We want to get away from the "connecting things" approach to distributed computing, and instead move to a "composing Services" paradigm, where integration becomes a result of composition.

2. **The "middleware for your middleware" problem.** If it were practical (or even possible) to take a single piece of middleware and put it all by itself in the middle of your IT infrastructure, that would be one thing, but for most large (and many midsize) organizations, the vision of relying on one piece of middleware to solve all integration problems is an unrealistic fantasy. In reality, organizations tend to have several different pieces of middleware, of different vintages and for different purposes. Introducing one or more ESBs into the mix means that now you have to integrate your ESBs with existing middleware as well as with each other, leading to the requirement of middleware for your middleware. Where will it ever end?

3. **The "good money after bad" fallacy.** Look up "good money after bad" on Wikipedia and you'll see that this fallacy is much broader than IT. People would rather throw money at an approach that's already cost a bundle than to switch approaches to a less expensive, but more effective alternative. If you've been buying middleware from a vendor for years, and now they tell you that you need an ESB, you're likely to take that advice, even if an alternative is lower cost and lower risk, simply because you've already spent so much with that vendor.

Now that you've steered your bus past the pitfalls, let's see if we can point it in the right direction moving forward. The most important thing to remember is that your architecture should drive the technology, not the other way around. Remember that ESBs, like any mature solution, come with a boatload of features—many of which may not be appropriate for your situation. It is often more important to figure out which features *not* to use, rather than the capabilities you should actually use, that is the key to being successful with a product like an ESB.

In particular, it is essential to take a process-driven approach to your infrastructure, instead of an integration-centric approach. Remember that

Service compositions that implement processes typically compose capabilities across multiple execution environments. Furthermore, those compositions are both dynamic and unpredictable—the business process specialist in charge of the compositions may change them around long after you've deployed the Services. *Governance* becomes the key to managing that unpredictability, rather than predefined integrations.

As a result, you shouldn't rely on any one execution environment for your Service implementations, or any one process management environment either, for that matter. ESBs can offer an effective, managed execution environment for some of your Service interfaces, but you rarely if ever want to rely on any one run-time environment for all of your Services. In other words, you should balance the advantages of running your Services "on the bus" with the fact that SOA allows you to leverage heterogeneity both on and off the bus.

So, if you shouldn't think of your ESB as either integration middleware or as a universal Service execution environment, then what role should your ESB play? The answer is a *Service intermediary*. Transformations and content-based routing are the essential capabilities a Service intermediary should deliver, in conjunction with robust security and management. Building the Business Service abstraction depends on transformations and content-based routing, and fortunately, most ESBs offer these capabilities. So, only use the traditional messaging middleware capabilities of your ESB if you really need them, and only leverage the Service run-time your ESB provides when convenient, but configure your ESB as an intermediary to get full value out of it as part of your SOA infrastructure.

Not only does using an ESB as an intermediary enable you to architect the Business Service abstraction, it also resolves the "middleware for your middleware" problem, because intermediaries can intermediate between disparate integration technologies just as well as they can intermediate between Service providers and consumers. If you feel you need to use your ESB's message queuing technology just because it's there, however, then you won't get this benefit.

Yes, you still need security, governance, quality, and management, in addition to the transformation and content-based routing capabilities of Service intermediaries, in order to build an effective SOA infrastructure. But remember, ESBs aren't the be-all and end-all of SOA infrastructure—many ESBs on the market include most of the previous capabilities, but rarely if ever offer everything an organization requires. In fact, XML appliances are likely a better approach to security and policy enforcement, a registry/repository combined with a full-life-cycle SOA quality solution might serve as your design-time and run-time governance tools, while a robust SOA management solution might be a critical part of your infrastructure as well. In fact, many organizations leverage such products in conjunction with existing middleware to build out their SOA infrastructure without having to buy an ESB at all.

The bottom line is to always remember that *the business drives the architecture, and the architecture drives the technology. Don't let the technology drive the architecture!* SOA is particularly adept at abstracting existing technology, which can include recently purchased products in addition to your legacy environment. But knowing which of your existing capabilities to leverage—and which to forgo—can make or break your SOA initiative.

Implementing SOA without an ESB

Whereas traditional middleware-based integration leads to unpredictable spikes in cost when business requirements change, taking a SOA approach to solving integration challenges promises to lead to a flattened cost of change. Implementing SOA means building for change, so the argument goes, so although there will continue to be some ongoing costs, an Agile Architecture will smooth out the ups and downs of IT integration expense.

Today, in spite of ZapThink's repeated warnings about taking an ESB-first approach to SOA, many organizations have bowed to vendor pressure and have undertaken a SOA platform approach to implementing SOA. As the previous section pointed out, it's possible to implement SOA with an ESB, and many organizations are doing just that—but the essential best practice is to leverage the ESB as a Service intermediary, rather than as integration middleware.

We're now seeing evidence of this trend in the marketplace as we shift to Agile Architectures. As organizations attempt to scale their SOA platform-centric SOA implementations, they soon run into problems. Because of the size of today's enterprises, no single platform addresses the SOA infrastructure needs of the entire organization. As a result, they must implement different platforms for different parts of the business.

Herein lies the most dangerous pitfall of the platform-centric approach to SOA: Because it depends on integration middleware, it succumbs to the issues with middleware that SOA was meant to address; namely, the lack of agility and the increasing costs of integration over time. Basically, you'll eventually need more middleware to get your various ESBs running to interoperate or federate with each other. Now, it's still possible to implement SOA in this manner, but if you're unable to achieve either the business agility or cost savings benefits of the new architecture, then why bother?

Fundamentally, integration should be something the business does with the Services, not something IT does to connect one bit of infrastructure to another—a run-time activity rather than a design-time one. The core technical challenge of SOA is building and maintaining the Business Service abstraction, so that the business can build flexible processes by composing those Services. In other words, SOA requires us to move away from a "connecting things" approach to distributed computing to a "composing Services" approach.

The no-ESB approach to SOA may be appealing—but unfortunately, the software-first alternative has always seemed to be lower risk. After all, if you dive into the no-ESB approach and fail, it's your head that's on the block, but if you buy some big package from your favorite vendor and have difficulties, then your job is unlikely to be on the line. And if the big analyst firms (many of whom are in the employ of the vendors, by the way) say that a SOA platform approach is reasonable, then why rock the boat?

Although SOA promises costs savings and greater agility, simply having a SOA initiative doesn't guarantee success. After all, you have to *get it right*. If you implement SOA and fail to achieve its desired benefits, or if you attempt to implement it and fail along the way, that doesn't mean that there's something wrong with SOA. What it means is that you didn't do it properly. When we see enterprises who've taken a SOA platform approach consider purchasing middleware for their middleware to scale their SOA initiatives, oblivious to the fact that following that path will prevent them from achieving the goals of SOA, all we can say is that we'll be placing our bets on your competition—the ones who are taking an architecture-first approach to SOA.

The SOA Marketing Paradox and the Wizard of Oz

It would be reasonable to ask why the vendors in the SOA space apparently got so much wrong. Did all the big middleware vendors maliciously co-opt SOA to their own selfish ends, turning a promising architectural approach into little more than an excuse to buy heavyweight, inflexible middleware? Perhaps. But let's give the vendors a break. Their customers wanted SOA, and clamored for products that would support their architecture efforts. What's a vendor to do?

SOA presented a challenge to software vendors, especially their marketing people, like none other in recent history. On one hand, SOA was the top enterprise software bandwagon to jump on, but on the other hand, many vendors struggled to tell the proper SOA story for their products in a way that led to increased sales and happy customers.

The reason SOA presented such a formidable challenge is at once both subtle and obvious. After all, SOA is architecture, not a set of product features. And therein lies the rub. How do you position your product as a SOA product when SOA consists of best practices, not product features?

For both product management (what features should our products have?) and product marketing (how do we differentiate our products' value propositions in the marketplace?), the focus has always been on product features. Product management meets with customers to elicit requirements, which start with business problems they'd like the product to solve, but invariably end up with a discussion of desirable features. Product management then takes those requirements to engineering, who adds them to the product. Product marketing then takes over, figuring out how best to position the features of the product to gain the attention of prospects, differentiate their products from their competition, and then convince prospects to purchase the products.

This traditional product cycle breaks down, however, when *architecture* is a leading customer driver. Organizations want SOA, but they're not clear on what features they need from software to achieve their SOA goals. Vendor product management ends up crafting a list of features (like Web Services standards support, for example) that should facilitate SOA at their customers. They feed these features into their product cycle, and eventually they end up with a "SOA product" of some sort.

This pattern is an example of what ZapThink likes to refer to as the Tin Woodman pattern. The Tin Woodman wanted a heart, so he went to the Wizard of Oz, who gave him a clock. The clock was clearly not a heart, but it had one salient feature; namely, it ticked. Compare that story to an enterprise who wanted SOA, so they went to their vendor of choice, who gave them a product with Web Services support. Web Services are clearly not SOA, but they offer standards support, the salient feature. The Tin Woodman was happy with this clock. Are you happy with the Web Services support in your SOA software?

The Tin Woodman pattern is virtually ubiquitous in the SOA marketplace. For example, the term *SOA Middleware* has gained some currency as an umbrella term that includes ESBs, Service intermediaries, and other infrastructure software. Other terms include *SOA Stack*, *SOA Platform*, and so on. Well, what does SOA Middleware really mean? Does it mean that if you buy it, you'll get SOA? That's about as likely as the Tin Woodman getting a real heart from the Wizard. Instead, what vendors mean by such terms is traditional middleware that offers a set of features that can potentially help their customers implement SOA. But no, you don't get SOA with your SOA Middleware.

As time went on, vendors continued to improve their products, adding increasingly powerful capabilities to their list of features. But as with any tool, the more powerful it is, the more dangerous it becomes in the hands of someone who doesn't fully understand how to use it. As we move beyond SOA toward Cloud, RESTful approaches, and other aspects of Agile Architecture, this situation only gets worse. If the enterprise customer doesn't have the proper architecture best practices in place, then the more powerful the software they buy becomes, the less likely they'll be able to use it successfully in their Agile Architecture implementation. Adding features, therefore, can actually make the situation worse!

For vendors with SOA-specific point solutions, like many of the governance/quality/management vendors in this space, beginning with SOA best practices and fitting their products into them was straightforward, albeit difficult. For the larger platform vendors, however, this advice went contrary to the whole notion of a SOA platform. Because these larger vendors were seeking to assemble soup-to-nuts suites of software that gave their customers everything they needed to implement Agile Architecture, they believed that architectural best practices must necessarily derive from their platform features, not the other way around. In other words, if you bought into a platform vendor's architecture story, you had to do architecture their way.

The problem is, most platform vendors were heading in the wrong direction. They wanted to be a better Wizard of Oz, so they added more and more features to their clocks. The Tin Woodman got two alarms, a nightlight, and who knows what else with his clock—but of course, he was no closer to getting a heart than if his clock did nothing more than tick. From the enterprise perspective, Agile Architecture best practices involved leveraging heterogeneity to provide business agility. Vendors with point SOA solutions could tell this story—"here are best practices for leveraging heterogeneity, and here's how our products help," but the platform vendors couldn't. Instead, they had to say, "Here are our platform's SOA features, and here's how to use them." As a result, if you look closely at the platform vendor's "SOA" case studies, you'll see that most (or all) of them were not SOA stories at all, but rather examples of how customers implemented the vendor's software.

If the platform vendors have their way, history will regard SOA as a promising architectural approach that ended up being little more than a set of software features—what ZapThink calls "The Great SOA Boondoggle." And yet, it doesn't have to be that way. More and more enterprises are coming to understand the true nature of Agile Architecture, and for those architects that do see the light, they aren't falling for the "architecture as product features" line. Furthermore, an increasing number of vendors are seeing the light as well, and are positioning their products as helping to implement architectural best practices.

The moral of *The Wizard of Oz*, of course, is that the Tin Woodman and his companions possessed what they desired all along. The Tin Woodman didn't need anything from the Wizard at all, and though a clock gave him the ticking, the device was neither necessary nor sufficient for having a heart. Just so with architecture. Organizations who get the architecture right don't need the vendors to give them best practices, because best practices are essentially forms of *human* behavior. Once you have those best practices, the products you purchase can help you implement them, but the products will never be the source of the best practices themselves.

CHAPTER 3

Governance: The Secret to Satisfying the Business Agility Meta-Requirement

F ew topics in today's organizations present such a diverse set of both business and technology challenges as *governance*. Governance consists of establishing chains of responsibility, policies that guide the organization, control mechanisms to ensure compliance with those policies, and communication and measurement among all parties. However, what constitutes a *policy* and what activities, processes, and tools the organization requires for governance are questions that have a broad diversity of answers.

Nowhere are the differences among various definitions of governance more pronounced than in the contrast between lines of business and IT. From the business perspective, top executives as well as government regulators set policies for the organization, which explain in often broad terms how various individuals within the company must act in certain circumstances. From the IT perspective, however, governance covers a range of policies that span the gamut from purchasing and hiring policies all the way to firewall and coding policies and service-level agreements.

In order for organizations to successfully implement Agile Architecture, the IT organization must place increasingly powerful tools into the hands of the business, enabling them to have unprecedented control over their business processes and information. With such power, however, comes responsibility. On one hand, the IT organization has policies it must follow on how it creates, deploys, and secures applications. On the other hand, the business must also follow policies that delineate how the organization complies with regulations, interacts with customers, and operates the business overall. As a result, governance is becoming increasingly important across both business and IT, as organizations struggle not only with increasingly powerful IT capabilities, but with the increasingly complex business world.

Organizational Context for Governance

The concept of governance is drawing substantial attention in corporate boardrooms and technical meetings alike, as companies struggle with complex regulatory compliance pressures, increasing globalization, enhanced competition, and the maturation of their markets. One key differentiator between top performing organizations and their less-successful counterparts is the ability to monitor performance and then evaluate those results and act on the lessons they've learned. As a result, governance can both empower and control. It empowers stakeholders to more rapidly make and implement decisions, while it provides for management controls designed to maintain compliance with corporate policies.

To achieve the balance between business empowerment and IT control—and leverage performance monitoring and decision making without dissention in the ranks—requires effective *corporate governance*, which we define in this way:

- Establishing and communicating the policies that employees must follow.
- Giving employees the tools they need to be compliant with those policies.
- Enforcing policies.
- Providing visibility into the levels of compliance in the organization.
- Resolving and mitigating any deviations from established policy.

There's nothing in the previous five bullets that requires that management involve technology in any way, and in fact, most managers today handle corporate governance in an essentially manual fashion, or where IT serves a secondary support role at best. For example, let's consider the case of a corporate nondiscrimination policy. Corporate council establishes the policy by basing it on the law. They then communicate it to employees via a memo. Next, human resources prepares some instructions on following the policy, which are the tools they provide to employees. The organization then handles enforcement through a formal complaint and investigation process, which also affords management visibility into the levels of compliance with the policy. Finally, the organization institutes a reprimand and dismissal policy for dealing with violations.

Note that in the previous example, technology is not directly involved, but technology likely supported or enabled the governance processes. Perhaps someone sent an email to inform HR about the violation or posted the policy on an intranet. And yet, though a policy like a corporate nondiscrimination policy doesn't lend itself to IT involvement, other policies are better able to take advantage of the resources IT can provide. For example, today's businesses must keep customer and employee information that resides in various databases private and secure. Enforcing confidentiality will then be a combination of manual tasks, like educating personnel, combined with automated processes, like requiring password protection for documents and processes.

IT governance, then, describes how people entrusted with the authority over some aspect of the business will consider IT in their supervision, monitoring, control, and direction of that business entity. And yet, there is more to IT governance than leveraging IT capabilities for corporate governance. It's also important to remember that the IT department is part of the organization, just like any other division, and corporate policies apply to IT as well.

In the case of IT governance, many processes and policies are essentially human based. *Architecture governance*, a key aspect of IT governance, consists of setting up an architecture board who creates and manages policies for the IT organization, including policies for reviews and acceptance, hiring, purchasing, and leveraging existing technology. Architecture, however, serves an additional role by providing best practices for IT governance overall.

Although many governance processes are essentially human-centric, there are certain types of policies that lend themselves well to automation. One challenge for IT governance—and consequently, for SOA governance and architecture more broadly—becomes identifying which policy-based processes are natural to automate and then leveraging the appropriate technologies to automate such processes in a flexible way. In fact, even for the most mature SOA implementations, many governance tasks fall outside the realm of automation. Even so, when architecture drives IT governance, taking a Service-oriented approach to architecture can improve the policy management, flexibility, and visibility necessary for IT governance, and more broadly, corporate governance.

This dichotomy between different perspectives on the nature of policies in the organization presents challenges across the organization as both business and IT managers get a handle on what it means to automate governance. Before SOA, business and IT managers shared little common ground with respect to policy definition and enforcement. SOA, however, helps automate policy activities by treating policies as *metadata artifacts*: policy information represented in a standard, machine-readable format. Once policies appear as metadata, it becomes possible to bridge the gap between the business and IT perspectives on policies by providing an artifact that can drive dialog between business and IT. Note that we're using the term *metadata* broadly to include artifacts external to the application code and the data the applications deal with. The physical representation of a policy might be a document like an XML or JavaScript Object Notation (JSON) file.

The starting point for any governance initiative, therefore, centers on the policies that the organization values and requires, and how they will enforce those policies in order to effectively balance empowerment and control. In order to get a handle on the scope of such an initiative, it is essential to put together a *governance framework*. To create a governance framework, you should answer the following questions:

- Which policies are within the scope of the current iteration? Which policies should you implement first?
- Who in your organization is responsible for creating policies?
- Which policy-related processes are automatable, and which policies are best left for human interpretation?
- How will you create and communicate policies?
- How will you represent policies? In other words, what is the format for your policies?
- How will people within your organization discover policies?
- What tools will people use to follow policies?
- How will management get visibility into policy compliance?
- How will you deal with policy violations? What mitigation approaches will you use?
- What is your process for policy change? Who makes the decisions about changes that impact policies and the people and technology they influence?

This governance framework then becomes an outline of your governance initiatives. In early iterations, it will be a simple document, but in each successive iteration, it is important to flesh it out, delineating in increasing detail how you will define and enforce policies as your governance initiative matures.

Architecture-Driven Governance: Beyond IT Governance

Once your initial governance framework is in place, it soon becomes important to identify the role IT has in implementing the governance initiative. It's important to note, however, that there are several different activities that organizations must undertake to tackle corporate and IT governance, including the following:

- **Communication.** The simple act of communicating policies, either face-to-face, via one-to-one remote communication media like e-mail, or via one-to-many approaches like the corporate intranet.
- **Training.** Formal and informal training on policies and procedures.
- **Human management.** People working with their direct reports to ensure understanding of and compliance with corporate and IT policies.

- **Knowledge management.** Leveraging a centralized repository of policies and associated best practices.
- **Automation.** Taking advantage of IT infrastructure to implement policy enforcement directly.

Of these activities, IT clearly focuses on automation, and may also provide various communication and knowledge management capabilities as well.

As organizations grow, either organically or via acquisitions, their IT efforts tend to decentralize. Such decentralization often leads to redundant, incompatible approaches to solving business problems. On the other hand, IT centralization efforts often run into roadblocks of their own as well. As a result, one of the key goals of IT governance initiatives is to decentralize IT responsibility without leading to redundant or incompatible capabilities, and while maintaining sufficient centralized control. This goal is in addition to specifying the decision rights and an accountability framework for encouraging desirable behavior in the use of IT resources.

Organizations achieve this goal through *architecture*. Architecture is in many ways the cornerstone of IT governance, because it provides the overall organizational guidelines for all of IT. In addition, architectural processes are the best way for the IT organization to implement IT governance. It is also necessary for an architecture board to drive IT governance within the organization.

In fact, it is possible to extend the dual role IT governance has for corporate governance to the consideration of architecture governance as well. After all, not only does architecture drive IT governance, it is also important to govern the architecture initiatives. It is within the context of architecture governance that SOA governance takes place. SOA governance, being a subset of IT governance, puts key IT governance decisions within the context of the Service life cycle. SOA governance addresses aspects of the Service life cycle such as planning, publishing, discovery, consumption, versioning, management, and security of Services. One of the primary goals of SOA governance, therefore, becomes the effective management of this Service life cycle.

SOA governance at its core focuses on establishing a framework for assuring Service quality over the course of the SOA life cycle. To ensure proper SOA governance, organizations must manage Services and Service consumption in the context of specific business, IT, and regulatory policies that apply to those Services and the consumers that interact with them. We can define SOA governance as having three distinct but related parts:

1. Design-time governance that provides rules and policies detailing how Services are created, exposed, and consumed.

2. Run-time governance that stipulates policies that govern the behavior of Services once they are in production and the architecture as a whole as applied to business needs.
3. Change-time governance that details how organizations can effect changes in the overall system with the least disruption to the existing business and its policies.

Fundamentally, however, this core of SOA governance is a narrow view, in that it focuses on governance of Services in the context of the SOA initiative, rather than on IT governance more broadly. As organizations move toward Agile Architectural approaches, however, the broader story is *architecture-driven governance*—not just for the IT organization itself, but for the enterprise more broadly. After all, the point of Agile Architecture is to support the meta-requirement of *business* agility, not IT agility.

SOA governance focuses on the creation, communication, and enforcement of policies that apply both to the design-time aspects of Service artifact creation, publication, and reuse, as well as the run-time aspects of Service operations, including service levels and the management of quality of service (QoS) metrics. It's important for IT shops that implement SOA to govern those SOA initiatives, both at design-time as well as run-time. But even more importantly, as organizations adopt SOA, they are able to leverage the new architecture to implement better IT governance more broadly, and by extension, better corporate governance overall—architecture-driven governance, the essential enabler of Agile Architecture.

Governance is an essential part of any SOA implementation, because it ensures that the organization applies and enforces the policies that apply to the Services that the organization creates as part of its SOA initiative. But more importantly, organizations can leverage Agile Architecture best practices to represent policies broadly in such a way that the organization can achieve better policy management, flexibility, and visibility into policy compliance *across the enterprise*.

SOA is especially useful in dynamic, heterogeneous environments, and can increase business agility in such environments. However, with this increased dynamism comes additional risk; for example, the risk that someone will change a business process in a way that is detrimental to the business. Because Services abstract the underlying complexity of the technology, both changes to business processes or the underlying Services the business processes leverage can place unexpected or excessive demand on the capacity of the underlying information systems, either potentially crashing the system or having an adverse effect on the other processes that the system also supports.

The SOA governance challenge, therefore, boils down to how to maintain adequate control while at the same time providing the flexibility the organization requires from their SOA initiative to foster agility and empower-ment. To this end, SOA governance requires that organizations take business policies, typically in written form, and transform them into metadata-based rules that can help automate the process of validating and enforcing compli-ance with policies in both design-time and run-time environments. Companies must then manage policies through their entire life cycle.

It's important to identify techniques for long-term policy maintenance, as the organization creates, modifies, and retires its policies. In other words, we must define, communicate, and enforce *meta-policies*. A meta-policy, of course, is a policy that applies to other policies. Because the automation of policy-related processes is a core enabler of SOA governance, polices for how an organization performs such automation are quite important—and such policies are meta-policies. An example of a useful meta-policy: "We'll configure our registry/repository's design-time workflow to conform to our existing Service life cycle." Such a configuration means configuring the policies in the tool as a way of automating the corresponding workflow, and thus that statement is a meta-policy.

In this example, the hall of mirrors question focuses more on automation then on the policies themselves. Does it make sense to automate meta-policy-related processes? The answer is basically *no*. It's best to create, communicate, and enforce meta-policies manually, through human communication activities. Yes, you could think of that last statement as a meta-meta-policy, but thinking about it that way doesn't really help you, so don't bother.

The lesson here is that meta thinking about something means more than just thinking about the thing, it means thinking about how the thing might change. The reason we need meta-policies is because policies might change—otherwise we'd just hard-code them into our software and be done with them.

Rethinking Quality

One of the primary reasons why a proper understanding of governance is so important to Agile Architecture is because we must entirely rethink quality in the context of Agile Architecture governance. *Quality*, of course, means far more than simply reducing defects. Fundamentally, quality means building something that meets the requirements of its users, now and into the future. Being defect free is a necessary, but by no means sufficient, criterion for a quality product. Software quality is no different. Though many software quality assurance efforts focus on eliminating bugs, the bug-hunting process is only the starting point for software quality.

The real challenge with software quality, as with any other quality effort, is in guaranteeing that the software meets the requirements set out for it. In an ideal world, quality assurance (QA) personnel would simply take the requirements document, use it to build a test plan, and run tests against that plan. Once the project passes all the tests, it's ready to go live. But in the real world, requirements continue to evolve; both during projects as well as once the projects are complete. And there's nothing worse than evolving requirements for throwing a wrench in the most carefully laid QA plans.

Traditional software quality management essentially consists of design-time and deployment-time activities. Basically, given the requirements, make sure that the software is as defect free as possible given budget and schedule constraints, and then continually monitor the working software to make sure that it meets the requirements set out for it when you deploy it. That basic approach to quality is fine for organizations that know in advance what their requirements are, when those requirements are stable, and when the goal is to build software that meets those requirements.

Such assumptions, however, are frequently false—in many cases, requirements aren't fully developed, they change over time, and the true goal of software is to respond to changes in requirements without extensive additional rework. Hence the need for an Agile Architectural approach like SOA. SOA is particularly effective in such situations, and the broad recognition that the build-to-today's-requirements approach to software is no longer effective is one of the primary motivations for SOA.

After all, a core challenge of Agile Architecture is building for change. If you had good reason to believe today's requirements were permanent, you probably wouldn't bother with the expense and complexity of an Agile Architectural approach. What, then, is your meta-requirement of agility? It doesn't make sense to expect that the IT organization would be capable of building systems that can deal with completely arbitrary change, because such a requirement would be prohibitively expensive to satisfy. Instead, each organization will have to decide for itself precisely how much they can invest in order to achieve the level of flexibility they require.

Although deciding on your agility meta-requirement is an essential part of your architecture planning, even more important for the long-term success of your architecture initiative is ensuring that your implementation conforms to that meta-requirement *over time*. In other words, to guarantee that your implementation meets the needs of the business is a core measure of quality, and as such, quality assurance must address the meta-requirement of agility.

Quality management at run-time is part of the answer, to be sure. Maintaining the quality of service of running software, whether or not it's abstracted as Services, is a key part of the systems management value proposition. What SOA management adds to the picture is run-time management of the Service *abstraction*, which is different from management of the underlying Service implementations. Managing the Service abstraction requires quality assurance for certain kinds of ongoing requirements *changes*; in particular, nonfunctional requirements like performance. Effective SOA management also requires run-time exception management handling in order to reduce the cascading impact of defects and to maintain loose coupling.

Although many existing SOA management tools on the market handle run-time SOA management, it is not the intention of SOA management tools to handle quality management in the face of ongoing requirements changes— at *change-time*. Properly implemented, SOA enables organizations to effect requirements changes via the reconfiguration of Service metadata. As a result, managing quality through such changes means managing the quality of metadata. Such change-time quality management focuses on metadata, and how well those metadata satisfy the requirements that apply during change-time. Such requirements fall into two categories: ongoing, day-to-day requirements that reconfiguration can address, and the broader meta-requirement of agility.

In mature SOA deployments, there are at least three basic types of day-to-day change-time requirements: Service contract changes, policy changes, and Service composition changes. To maintain quality whenever any of these metadata changes requires both assurance that the Service infrastructure can adequately support the changes, as well as assurance that the newly configured metadata meet the requirements that led to the reconfiguration. SOA management tools should address the former challenge, but the latter challenge is potentially intractable.

The intractability of change-time metadata quality assurance results from the open-ended nature of reconfiguration in SOA. If architects fail to fully plan for this problem ahead of time, the sorts of changes users might introduce over time could be entirely unpredictable and unmanageable. Fundamentally, SOA encourages user empowerment, which in the absence of adequate governance can lead to anarchy. The important point to keep in mind is that *change-time metadata quality assurance should be handled as a matter of policy*. Apply Service-oriented principles to change-time quality assurance in order to create, communicate, and enforce policies for metadata-based changes. Then you can treat those policies like other policies that your SOA governance infrastructure deals with.

Considering change-time quality assurance to be a matter of policy enforcement completes the SOA quality tooling picture: testing tools for design-time quality, management tools for run-time quality, and governance tools for change-time quality. But relegating change-time quality to the governance arena suggests the question as to how you should create such policies in the first place. That question takes us back to the meta-requirement of agility.

As your Enterprise Architecture team sits down to plan your Agile Architecture initiative, you should be asking questions about the specific levels of agility your organization requires from the implementation. In particular, you should discover the answers to the following questions:

- What are your business requirements for Service reuse? Is the business looking to achieve a certain cost savings or other metric for reuse?
- What are your requirements for loose coupling? Break this question down into multiple levels: semantic, data, message protocol, wire protocol, and so on.
- What is the user context for your implementation? For example, how many users will your Services need to support? Are they all internal users, or are you allowing users from outside your organization? What users will be allowed to make configuration changes, and under what circumstances?
- What are your meta-policies? In other words, what policies are in place that govern how you should be able to create and enforce policies?

It's important to note first of all that the end product of each of these questions should be a set of policies. Secondly, it's also significant that questions like these don't focus on requirements for specific functionality or behavior of the software you're building as in a traditional project. On the contrary, these questions all dwell on issues of agility—just how agile your organization wants to be, but possibly even more importantly, in what areas is it okay to be *less* than fully agile. Identifying the particular constraints on the architecture initiative that your organization accepts can save substantial money and time, and can also lead to framing the discussion of change-time quality policies.

Introducing the Agility Model

An essential element of quality is the traceability of requirements, including the meta-requirement of agility. As a result, it's essential for your organization to understand the agility requirement in sufficient detail in order to provide adequate testing of that agility. Unfortunately, simply stating the business requires agility does not provide that detail. Remember, however, that business agility is an emergent property of our organizations. So *what* do we test? And *how* do we know what to test?

In other words, how do we *analyze* the agility meta-requirement—what do our business analysts have to do in order to understand precisely what the business wants when they say they want to be more agile, and equally important, how much does the business want to pay for the privilege? What we need is an analysis tool that can break down the agility emergent property into *implementable* requirements that we can analyze and test for. In essence, this tool is what ZapThink is proposing in an Agility Model. An *Agility Model* is a measure of the agility of a particular Agile Architecture implementation against solid measures of flexibility. The idea is to measure the agility against the goals for the business and that project.

Not all projects need to have the same level of agility as others. Some projects require deep levels of loose coupling. Other projects might not need the same amount of loose coupling because each layer of coupling adds flexibility at the potential cost of complexity and efficiency. Good architects should know when to make their solutions loosely coupled enough to meet the business requirements and meta-requirement of agility, but not any more so. Hence, we should consider the agility measure to be a spectrum of sorts, with the desired level of agility matching the business requirement.

As such, companies should shoot for optimal levels of variability where anything outside of those levels is suboptimal. To be specific, if a business is aiming for a specific level of agility, but the projects have been implemented in a way that has made them more flexible than desired, it's quite possible they might have been overengineered. Likewise, projects that don't achieve the desired agility measure are suboptimal and underengineered.

The key question to answer in considering the Agility Model is how does one measure agility? One way to measure agility is to determine various degrees of freedom and variability allowed by the system in question. Considering these agility measures, the fewer degrees of freedom and variability, the less agile the system is as a whole. For example, start with a basic Agility Model that would include the following.

- **Implementation Variability.** Projects at the bottom of this measure of maturity are inflexible with respect to implementation changes, whereas those at the top allow for changes to software elements without impacting other such elements.
- **Infrastructure Variability.** Projects that exhibit poor variability in this aspect of loose coupling are heavily dependent on the current infrastructure, whereas those projects that show greatest variability can accommodate arbitrary changes, replacements, or additions to the infrastructure without skipping a beat.
- **Contract Variability.** Projects at one end of the spectrum don't allow for flexible change to Service contracts, whereas those at the other end are immune to such changes.
- **Process Variability.** Initiatives at the bottom of this variability measure don't allow for dynamic and continual business process change, whereas those at the top can handle any new process change or configuration requirement.

- **Policy Variability.** Projects that exhibit weak variability with regard to policy variability can only handle policy changes through redevelopment, redeployment, or even infrastructure change, whereas those that show greatest variability can handle any policy change or new policy requirement flexibly.
- **Data Structure Variability.** Initiatives that exhibit poor data structure variability cannot accommodate variations to the representation of data, whereas those that show greatest variability can handle such changes without having to refactor individual software elements.
- **Semantic Variability.** Projects at the low end of the spectrum are inflexible with regard to changes to the meaning and semantics of information, whereas those that show greatest flexibility can handle semantic differences between systems without requiring human involvement.

The result of the previous analysis is a heat map diagram, as shown in Figure 3.1. Each project will exhibit characteristics of agility that might be more flexible at one level, though less so at another. The key is not to achieve the highest level of variability for all measures, but to create the Agility Model for the particular project and compare that against a project-specific or corporate-wide Agility Model that acts as a baseline for all subsequent Agile Architecture projects. In this way, companies can use Agility Models for project planning as well as auditing and measurement. Companies can also, if they choose, compare their Agility Models with models of competing firms in the same industry and across multiple industries, but this is certainly not the goal of the Agility Model.

Of course, it's hard to truly summarize the mechanism and methods for determining such levels of variability. If you want to successfully apply the Agility Model to your own company, you should approach it both as an analysis tool as well as an auditing and measurement tool, keeping in mind that the projects might be flexible and agile at one level, but not at another. The idea is

	No Variability	Minimal Variability	Moderate Variability	High Variability
Implementation Variability		X		
Infrastructure Variability	X			
Contract Variability			X	
Policy Variability				X
Process Variability		X		
Data Structure Variability			X	
Semantic Variability		X		

Figure 3.1   Agility Model Diagram

not to achieve some theoretical variability maximum, but rather to achieve an optimal level of variability given your requirements and budget. The secret sauce is determining your optimum and finding concrete ways to measure distributed projects in the enterprise.

Project-specific Agility Models paired with enterprise-wide Agility Models that indicate how the enterprise as a whole will deal with projects at different levels of agility will help to guide Agile Architecture implementations as well as provide an enterprise-wide view of the various projects and how they are contributing to an organization's agility. A good Agility Model will help organizations advance their business to greater degrees of agility on a time frame that matches their ability to invest.

Meta-Policy Governance

Even though considering change-time quality to be a governance issue reduces the risks inherent in empowering users, it's important to keep in mind that governance is not fully automatable. In fact, most governance activities are human: training, organizational management, and other human communications activities. SOA governance streamlines the part of the governance framework that lends itself to automation, and provides better tools for people to handle the rest. But no matter how sophisticated today's Agile Architecture governance solutions become, the human element will always remain.

As an example of this principle, say an organization has a policy that all Service compositions must be reviewed by a manager before going into effect. That policy is clearly a change-time quality policy, especially if there are associated policies that guide what managers should be looking for when they conduct such reviews. A tool can ease the implementation of this policy, but cannot take the manager out of the equation.

A second, more significant example concerns the potential hall of mirrors infinite regression: If metadata quality is a matter of policy, including the quality of the policy metadata themselves, then how can you ensure the quality of those policies that apply to your quality policies? The answer is surprisingly simple: quality at the meta-policy level is up to people to provide. Say you have a policy that all Service contracts must conform to a particular Service specification that your organization has hammered out. Automating the enforcement of that policy is straightforward, but ensuring the quality of that policy is unquestionably a human activity: Read through the meta-requirements list and see if that policy is there, and that people understand it properly. Such activities are simple for people, but prohibitively difficult to automate.

A third example involves Service *versioning*. Security and policy metadata are part of the discussion on Service contract versioning, but changing the

Service contract is only a small part of the policy versioning problem. In the SOA context, a policy is a set of rules that apply to any number of Services. Policies typically govern under what conditions consumers are entitled to access Service functionality. Some policies may be security related, whereas others are time or process dependent. Policies can apply to zero or more Services, and it's important to maintain policies separately from the Service contracts themselves. In many large organizations, the group of people that manages Service policies is separate from the group that manages the Service implementations or the Service contract metadata. As such, policies are likely to change even when the Service contract metadata stay the same.

Independently changing the Service contracts and policies dramatically increases the complexity of the SOA implementation. At any moment, an individual can change a policy impacting an unknown number of Services in ways that can instantly cause them to stop functioning. There are only two ways to potentially prevent unintended consequences from changes to policies: by implementing meta-policies that control who can change policies and when, and by establishing adequate governance to control the creation, communication, and enforcement of such policies.

However, implementing proper governance by itself doesn't solve this metadata versioning nightmare. One potential for chaos is the fact that a large organization might implement multiple governance frameworks to allow independent divisions or subsidiaries to control their own SOA implementations, only to later require sharing of such Services across their organizational boundaries. In these cases, even if proper governance exists to limit the impact of changes to Service contracts and policies, the meta-policies that determine how companies create and establish the governance frameworks themselves might change in ways that have unpredictable consequences. Implementing additional layers of governance might in turn require changes to countless numbers of policies and Service contracts, leading to increased cost and complexity. As a result, the proper establishment of an enterprise-wide governance framework early in an Agile Architecture project is critical for the success of the initiative.

Interrelationships among Governance, Quality, and Management

Companies that are well on the path to SOA adoption know full well that the technical challenges of building and exposing Services are less significant than the hurdles of building truly loosely coupled, business-relevant Services to be leveraged across their continuously changing business processes. Indeed, aside from the even greater challenges associated with organizational and cultural adoption of SOA, the issues associated with managing business-level Services existing in a heterogeneous and continuously changing environment are some of the most significant and tricky for Enterprise Architects to address.

Although SOA simplifies through abstraction the complexity associated with heterogeneous, point-to-point integration and customized, tightly coupled application logic still rife within most organizations today, it introduces a different kind of complexity: the management of distributed, loosely coupled, and dynamically composable Services. There are now a number of approaches for dealing with this new form of complexity: management solutions that isolate failure and provide mechanisms for abstracting end-point differences; quality solutions that provide mechanisms for ensuring changes can be propagated in environments of significant change; and governance approaches that provide oversight into the development of Service-oriented systems, mitigation of change and version management issues, and enforcement of policies central to the operation of the business as a whole.

In order to show that governance, quality, and management are inherently related, it's important to first explore how each of the concepts is connected to the other. One aspect that's becoming increasingly obvious is the connection between run-time quality and SOA management. It makes very little difference if a particular implementation of a Service works if the composition of that Service with others in the environment fails or if some aspect of metadata that impacts the behavior of that Service does so in a manner that adversely impacts the performance of the system as a whole. In essence, the idea of unit-testing an individual Service, or even worse, just the Service interface, to make sure that it works is wholly inadequate to meeting the needs of what's really a composite system of metadata-enhanced Services.

To summarize, the only way to effectively test or ensure quality of an Agile Architecture implementation is to do so continuously, measuring the quality not only of discrete Services, but also all related metadata, composition logic, policy, and underlying schemas. Furthermore, in a mature Agile Architecture environment, it's practically impossible to maintain a useful duplicate of the running system, because Services, configurations, and associated metadata continually change. As a result, maintaining a parallel QA environment rapidly becomes an exercise in futility.

The solution to this quality conundrum is to test new and changed Services and Service configurations in the *live, production environment*. The only way to ensure that all aspects of the new configuration continue to meet the requirements set out for them is to run test messages through production Services. Now, saying you should test in production is tantamount to proposing rewiring your house with the power on—it's possible, but you have to be especially careful, know what you're doing, and plan ahead. In the case of SOA, planning ahead means that Services (as well as Service consumers) must be able to support a testing mode.

Remember, Agile Architecture describes the business, and because the business is continuously changing, a QA model that requires duplication of the environment will be enormously expensive, impossible to manage, and ineffective in any case. Thus, testing in production (or run-time quality if that makes you feel more comfortable), requires a mechanism to isolate failures from having cascading effects. Furthermore, run-time quality management necessitates implementing test modes as matters of Service contract and policy, and managing messages and side effects of Services in a test mode such that no lingering side effects remain after some change moves from tentative to live.

This idea of policy-driven test and run-time enforcement of quality curiously overlaps with many of the ideas of run-time Service management. Many SOA management solutions provide a mechanism for policy enforcement, exception management, failure recovery, and root-cause analysis. Thus, pairing the capabilities of run-time quality tools that facilitate the process of versioning with solutions that minimize the impact of those changes seems to be a natural fit. Furthermore, there is a natural *management/quality feedback loop* that exists between tools and approaches to management that provides visibility when things are failing or tending toward an undesirable state, and there are tools and approaches that allow for incremental testing of parts of the infrastructure, thus guaranteeing the quality of the system as a whole.

The challenge of maintaining continuous quality in a continuously changing system is, in effect, a challenge of maintaining effective governance, and as such, the combination of SOA governance and quality tooling and approaches serves to make that problem more manageable. SOA quality tools provide feedback to governance systems by indicating how policies and changes impact the overall system, and likewise, governance systems and approaches feed into the quality life cycle by providing continuously changing constraints that impact Services at design and run-time.

Companies have put too much emphasis on Service development, run-time execution environments, and inter-Service messaging alone as the basis of their SOA infrastructure. In reality, that is the fairly trivial part of making SOA work. Indeed, that sort of infrastructure can build tightly-coupled Web Service APIs on top of legacy integration middleware just as readily as they can facilitate the building of loosely coupled, composable Services. Because companies are looking for the latter and not the former as the raison d'être of SOA, we must shift the focus of SOA infrastructure to the technologies and approaches we're discussing in this section. We're not saying that SOA infrastructure of the ESB kind is never necessary, but rather that it is not sufficient to guarantee the Agile Architectures that companies desire.

Four Stages of Agile Architecture Governance

At the core of governance, even in the IT organization, is how governance typically involves human communication-centric activities like architecture reviews, human management, and people deciding to comply with policies. We point out this human context for governance to contrast it with the technology context that inevitably becomes the focus of SOA governance. There is an important technology-centric SOA governance story to be told, of course, as long as it's placed into the greater Agile Architecture governance context.

One question we haven't yet addressed in depth, however, is how these two contrasts—narrow vs. broad, human vs. technology—fit together. Taking a closer look, there's an important trend taking shape, as organizations mature their approach to SOA governance, and with it, the overall architectural effort. Following this trend to its natural conclusion highlights some important facts about Agile Architecture, and can help organizations understand where they want to end up as their SOA initiative reaches its highest levels of maturity.

Whenever faced with two orthogonal contrasts, the obvious thing to do is put them in a grid. Let's see what we can learn from Figure 3.2.

First, let's take a look at what each square contains, starting with the lower left corner and moving clockwise, because as we'll see, that's the sequence that corresponds best to increasing levels of architectural maturity.

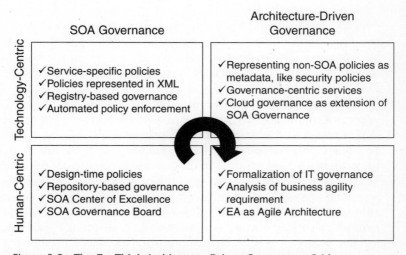

Figure 3.2   The ZapThink Architecture-Driven Governance Grid

- **Human-centric SOA governance.** As organizations first look at SOA and the governance challenge it presents, they must decide how they want to handle various governance issues. They must set up a SOA governance board or other committee to make broad SOA policy decisions. We also recommend setting up a SOA Center of Excellence to coordinate such policies across the whole enterprise. These policy decisions initially focus on how to address business requirements, how to assemble and coordinate the SOA team, and what the team will need to do as they ramp up the SOA effort. The output of such SOA governance activities tends to be written documents and plenty of conversations and meetings.

  The tools architects use for this stage are primarily communication-centric; namely, word processors and portals and the like. But this stage is also when the repository comes into play as a place to put many such design-time artifacts, and also where architects configure design-time workflows for the SOA team. Technology, however, plays only a supporting role in this stage.

- **Technology-centric SOA governance.** As the SOA effort ramps up, the focus naturally shifts to technology. Governance activities center on the registry/repository and the rest of the SOA governance gear. Architects roll up their sleeves and hammer out technology-centric policies, preferably in an XML or JSON format that the gear can understand. Representing certain policies as metadata enables automated communication and enforcement of those policies, and also makes it more straightforward to change those policies over time.

  This stage is also when run-time SOA governance begins. Certain policies must be enforced at run-time, either within the underlying run-time environment, in the management tool, or in the security infrastructure. At this point the SOA registry/repository becomes a central governance tool, because it provides a single discovery point for run-time policies.

- **Technology-centric architecture-driven governance.** The SOA implementation is up and running. There are a number of Services in production, and their life cycle is fully governed through hard work and proper architectural planning. Taking the SOA approach to responding to new business requirements is becoming the norm. So, when new requirements mean new policies, it's possible to represent some of them as metadata as well, even though the policies aren't specific to SOA. Such policies are still technology-centric; for example, security policies, data governance policies, or Cloud policies. Fortunately, the SOA governance infrastructure is up to the task of managing, communicating, and coordinating the enforcement of such policies. By leveraging SOA, it's possible to centralize policy creation and communication, even for policies that aren't SOA-specific.

Sometimes, in fact, new governance requirements can best be met with new Services. For example, a new regulatory requirement might lead to a new message-auditing policy. Why not build a Service to take care of that? SOA is in place, so when a new governance requirement comes over the wall, we naturally leverage SOA to meet that requirement.

- **Human-centric architecture-driven governance.** This final stage is the most thought provoking of all, because it represents the highest maturity level. How do we take an architecture-driven approach to governance across the entire organization in order to achieve the business agility meta-requirement? Clearly, XML representations of technical policies aren't the answer here. Rather, it's how implementing Agile Architecture helps expand the governance role architecture plays in the organization. It's a core best practice that architecture should drive IT governance.

  How this architecture-driven approach impacts Enterprise Architecture is also quite significant. It is at this stage that part of the architecture-driven governance value proposition benefits the business directly, by formalizing how the enterprise represents capabilities consistent with the priorities of the organization.

The big win to moving to the fourth stage is in how leveraging Agile Architecture approaches to formalize EA governance impacts the organization's business agility meta-requirement. In some ways, business agility is like any other business requirement, in that proper business analysis can delineate the requirement to the point that the technology team can deliver it, the quality team can test for it, and the infrastructure can enforce it. But as an emergent property of the implementation, business agility is a different sort of requirement from more traditional business requirements in a fundamental way.

A critical part of achieving this business agility over time is to break down the business agility requirement into a set of policies, and then establish, communicate, and enforce those policies—in other words, provide business agility governance. Only now, we're not talking about technology at all. We're talking about transforming how the organization leverages resources in a more agile manner by formalizing its approach to governance by following Agile Architecture best practices at the EA level. Organizations must understand the role SOA governance plays in achieving this long-term strategic vision for the enterprise.

Architecture-Driven Governance and the Butterfly Effect

The Butterfly Effect is a principle of chaos theory that states that small differences in the initial conditions of a system can lead to dramatic variations in the future behavior of that system. As there is little in this world as chaotic as today's IT-dependent enterprises, it should come as no surprise that small variations in the decisions of the business can lead to dramatic, unexpected effects in the world of IT. As long as the lines of communication between IT and business remain within the largely manual sphere of phone calls, faxes, and e-mails, the Butterfly Effect rarely presents a problem. However, the more effectively IT provides business decision makers with the tools they need to make and communicate decisions in an *automated* fashion, the more likely it is that some inadvertent action on the part of an unsuspecting business manager will lead to unexpected, potentially dangerous effects on IT.

Agile Architecture approaches like SOA enable the business to be better able to take advantage of those resources in a flexible, essentially automated fashion—an approach that manifestly increases the chances of the Butterfly Effect. The possibility that increased business agility might actually lead to new risks presents an interesting irony. After all, we frequently caution architects about the risks of implementing SOA *poorly*, but the Butterfly Effect suggests risks inherent in implementing Agile Architecture *properly*. Fundamentally, architecture done right gives people greater power and flexibility, and as a result, an increased risk that they're really going to muck things up.

Let's explore an example of the Butterfly Effect in action. Say, for an example, that an executive reviewing sales reports requires data that are more current than any available through the company's CRM system. In the old days, the executive might call a data analyst in the IT department and ask for a current report using more recent data. The data analyst knows that the analytics software that generated the report uses queries against a data warehouse that only contains summary data as of the previous Saturday. However, the executive doesn't care about how the technology works and simply needs the report to make critical business decisions. In this case, the data analyst then figures out how long it will take to create, test, and run an *ad hoc* query against the transactional systems, and translates this information into a request for additional funds and time to perform the request. The executive must now make an informed business decision about whether the report is important enough to warrant the time and expense to generate it.

Now, let's segue to the Agile Architecture scenario. In this case, the executive in the same situation has a policy management tool accessible via a corporate portal. The executive is none the wiser about the technical details; all managers need to know is that they have the authority to change certain corporate policies via the corporate portal. As such, the exec can go into the portal and adjust the service-level agreement (SLA) for corporate reporting that includes the required report, changing the turnaround time for corporate data from "up to one week" to "up to one day," through the click of a button.

Now IT has a problem, as the Butterfly Effect takes its toll. Will the IT infrastructure be able to respond to the executive's change automatically, or will it require manual intervention by the IT staff? Will IT simply fail to satisfy the new SLA? Even worse, what if different executives have entered more than one policy change during the same period of time? Which one should IT address first? It used to be that the lack of automation required humans in the loop on changes that affected IT, so there was always the possibility that human judgment could be brought to bear in the case of business changes with unexpected consequences. As architecture-driven governance leads to more automated policy management, however, companies run the risk of automating human discretion out of the policy implementation process, to their peril.

Fortunately, once companies become aware of the Butterfly Effect problem, the solution is relatively straightforward. Clearly, there must be a distinction between the policy changes that the business may implement on their own, and policy changes that must require (manual) IT approval. In other words, architecture-driven governance not only requires the management of policies, but the management of meta-policies. Such meta-policies might be boundary conditions on allowed policy changes. For example, a meta-policy might state that authorized business managers may change a policy threshold value up to 10 percent in either direction without requiring IT approval, but any changes greater than 10 percent must go through a particular IT manager first.

As a result, there's no such thing as a fully automated governance framework. At some point, humans must directly manage policy change. This limitation doesn't constitute a policy shell game, however, as effective governance tools will provide greatly increased automation and flexibility in how companies create, communicate, and manage their policies. But as with any powerful tool, people must know what they're doing when they use it, and wield it carefully. Another important lesson that the Butterfly Effect teaches is that IT must have the appropriate managing authority in place to make the necessary judgment calls on meta-policies. After all, if the IT manager responsible for approving a policy change doesn't understand the implications of that change, then the core problem remains.

When a company has implemented Agile Architecture, the IT managers responsible for approving policy changes must have a broad understanding of the interdependencies of the various elements of the architectural implementation. In the previous pre-SOA example, only the data analyst had to understand the cost and time implications of ad hoc data queries. In the Agile

Architecture world, however, a policy change might impact multiple applications, data sources, and legacy systems. As a result, an analyst is unlikely to be the right person to make the call as to whether a particular policy change has unintended consequences. The correct person not only must have that broad understanding of IT, but also must be able to speak in business terms about the costs and benefits of complex policy changes. As a result, the Enterprise Architect—in the context of Agile Enterprise Architecture—may be the best person for the job.

CHAPTER 4

The Enterprise as Complex System

Perhaps the biggest aha moment on the road to Agile Architecture is when you realize that implementing such an architecture isn't traditional systems engineering (TSE) at all, but rather a fundamentally different approach to dealing with complexity in the IT environment. Needless to say, this realization is an especially big wake-up call for people with TSE backgrounds! The fundamental shift in thinking is this: TSE focuses on building big systems out of small components, where the behavior of the resulting system depends directly on the properties of the components. Essentially, TSE boils down to a "connecting things" way of thinking about distributed computing, where integration is the central activity, and what you end up with when you're done with all the integrating is at best what you expected to build.

Agile Architecture, on the other hand, calls for an entirely different approach—*Complex Systems Engineering (CSE)*. In this context, we focus on building and maintaining the Business Service abstraction, which supports inherently unpredictable behavior as the business composes Services to support fundamentally dynamic business processes. Essentially, with Agile Architecture we're building for change, whereas with TSE, we're building for stability. The problem with stability, of course, is it only takes the business so far—if the organization requires business agility, then it's much better off implementing Agile Architecture.

Engineering the Enterprise with Complex Systems Engineering

Complex Systems theory is especially fascinating because it describes how many natural phenomena occur. Whenever there is an emergent property in nature then that system is a Complex System. Everything from the human mind to the motion of galaxies is an emergent property of its respective system.

Fair enough, but those are all *natural* Complex Systems, and we're charged with implementing an *artificial*, human-made Complex System. How we take the lessons from nature and apply them in the IT shop is a question that engenders the perplexity we see on architects' faces.

There is a fundamental flaw in this distinction. Making such a distinction between natural and artificial systems is basically a TSE way of thinking because it separates people from their tools. In a traditional IT system, people are the users, but are not inherently part of the system. In many Complex Systems, however, people aren't just *part* of the system, they *are* the system.

Too often in the enterprise, people confuse Complex Systems with collections of traditional systems, which is just as big a mistake as confusing a parking lot full of empty cars with a traffic jam. In fact, architects are often the first to make this mistake. Of course, it's certainly true that some architects are too focused on the technology, leaving people out of the equation altogether, but even for those architects who include people in the architecture, they often do so from a TSE perspective rather than a CSE approach. But no matter how hard you try, designing better steering wheels and leather seats and the like won't prevent traffic jams!

In traditional systems thinking, then, we have systems and users of those systems, where the users have requirements for the systems. If the systems meet those requirements then everybody's happy. In Complex Systems thinking, we have systems made up of technology and people, where the people make decisions and perform actions based on their own individual circumstances. They interact with the technology in their environments as appropriate, and the technology responds to those interactions based on the requirements for the Complex System as a whole. In many cases, the technology provides a feedback loop that helps the people achieve their individual requirements, just as brake lights in a traffic jam help reduce the chance of collisions. The feedback loops between people and technology at the component level enable the overall system to continue to meet requirements as those requirements change—the essence of business agility.

If you still find yourself perplexed by this whole Complex Systems story, it might help to point out that Complex Systems aren't necessarily complicated. In fact, in a fundamental way they are really quite simple. Traffic jams may be difficult to understand, but individuals driving cars are not. Best practices like metadata-driven governance, the Business Service abstraction, and infrastructure and implementation variability, to name a few, are well within reach of today's architecture initiatives. And the great thing about Complex Systems is that if you take care of the nuts and bolts, the big picture ends up taking care of itself.

For organizations who don't take a Complex Systems approach to architecture, however, the risks are enormous. As traditional systems scale, they become less agile. Ask any architect who's attempted to hardwire several disparate pieces of middleware together in a large enterprise—yes, maybe you can get such a rat's nest to work, but it will be expensive and inflexible. If you want to scale your implementation so that it continues to deliver business agility even on the enterprise scale, then the Complex Systems approach is absolutely essential.

Complex Systems of systems have unique characteristics that distinguish them from traditional monolithic systems, including higher levels of complexity, flexibility, and emergent behavior. Such characteristics result from the operational independence of their constituent parts, from independent evolution, and from the nature of emergent effects, whereas traditional monolithic systems depend on central control, global visibility, hierarchical structures, and coordinated activities. As a result, such traditional systems are unable to exploit the advantages of emergent behavior like business agility.

Complex Systems theory recognizes that a result of tightly coupled systems is the fact that accidental failures of individual subsystems lead to cascading failures across the entire system—a familiar happenstance in many traditionally architected enterprise IT environments. The core architectural principle of loose coupling, on the other hand, leads to the system of systems requirement of autonomous systems. Furthermore, systems of systems depend on interoperation among systems, rather than integration, where integration of subsystems leads to a unified system, whereas interoperation among systems is the combination of autonomous systems into a system of systems.

Interoperation in systems of systems demands a node-centric perspective, where each constituent (a Service provider or consumer, say) views the system from its own individual perspective. For each node, a node-centric perspective describes the interactions with its immediate neighbors based on available metadata. In this view, the behavior of the overall system of systems depends on the interactions between Service providers and consumers. An individual constituent node need have no knowledge of the details of other nodes that it doesn't interoperate with. We'll see the same node-centric perspective when we discuss REST later in the book.

To achieve the necessary interoperation, systems of systems should be interdependent with other systems beyond their boundaries, where it's impossible to predict the resulting outcomes of the architecture. Furthermore, requirements for systems of systems that interoperate are constantly changing and imprecisely known, as they typically are for SOA implementations. Interoperation also encourages distributed control, which aligns nicely with the business empowerment benefit of SOA as well as the decentralized nature of the Web that RESTful applications exhibit.

It seems, therefore, that an Agile Architectural approach that leads to loosely coupled, autonomous, interoperable Services in response to dynamic business requirements is a perfect example of a system of systems. However, it's essential to manage an Agile Architecture implementation's emergent behavior in order to achieve the benefits that systems of systems exhibit. ZapThink hammers home this point whenever we talk about business empowerment. If we mistakenly conclude that the sole point of SOA, for example, is to build all these flexible Services and then simply turn them over to the business to compose willy-nilly, then it's true we'd never be able to achieve the business agility benefit, because such a haphazard lack of control would lead to immediate chaos. Avoiding this chaos is why we say that the key to the business empowerment benefit of Agile Architecture is governance—a set of organizing principles that tempers the emergent properties of the architecture, thus providing the essential management of emergent properties that such architectures require for us to consider their implementations to be Complex Systems.

There is an important insight here: For Agile Architecture to be successful, organizations must take a CSE approach to their implementation, *including the implementation of architecture-driven governance itself*. Our natural tendency would be to take a TSE approach to governance, where we hammer out organization-wide policies and put in place a systematic governance infrastructure to enforce those policies. Though such an approach might be integral to a traditional architecture that we've implemented with TSE approaches, taking such a heavy-handed approach to architecture-driven governance will stifle the implementation's emergent properties, most notably business agility. We call this situation the *big brother effect*, where excess governance can lead to the failure of the architecture initiative.

Instead, it is essential to take a CSE approach to Agile Architecture governance. Represent policies as metadata, and leverage SOA governance infrastructure to manage and enforce those policies in the context of Services. As the SOA implementation matures, leverage Agile Architecture governance best practices to support overall IT governance, and, in turn, corporate governance. This approach to governance not only improves the organization's governance overall, it is also essential to promoting the emergent properties of the architecture implementation.

Best-Effort Quality and the Agile Architecture Quality Star

The first question people often ask us when we explain the CSE approach to architecture is *How do you make sure the software is always doing what it's supposed to?* Sure, you have policies in place that govern the behavior of the software, but how do you ensure its *quality*?

In fact, maintaining quality of an agile system is a complicated challenge—not only because we have policy-driven behavior, but because we must also test for the agility meta-requirement itself. And the more time we spend on quality, the less agile we are.

We ran into this trade-off in one of ZapThink's recent courses for a U.S. Department of Defense (DoD) contractor, when we were discussing SOA Quality. We pointed out that as a SOA implementation matures, it becomes increasingly important to manage quality continuously over the full Service life cycle, as the agility requirement for SOA reduces the practicality of focusing quality assurance solely on predeployment testing activities. The students then pointed out that the DoD requires that they put any new software implementation through six months of rigorous acceptance testing before deployment. Clearly, these two views of quality are at odds. So, which has to give? Does the DoD or any other organization implementing SOA have to sacrifice either agility or quality in order to obtain the other?

The answer is no, such organizations don't have to sacrifice quality to obtain agility, but rather, they must rethink what they mean by quality in the Agile Architecture context. The agility meta-requirement vastly complicates the quality challenge, because functional and performance testing aren't sufficient to ensure conformance of the implementation with the business's agility requirement.

To support this agility requirement, therefore, traditional predeployment acceptance testing is insufficient and impractical, as the acceptance testing process itself impedes the very agility the business requires. Instead, quality becomes an ongoing process, involving continual vigilance and attention. Quality itself, however, need not suffer, as long as the business understands the implications of implementing an Agile Architecture.

An intriguing analogue to this shift in perspective that Agile Architecture quality requires appears in the telco world's move to the mobile phone network. In the old circuit-switched, plain old telephone service (POTS) days, the carriers sought to deliver eponymous *carrier grade* quality of service, delivering the proverbial five nines (99.999%) availability. However, the new cell phone network was entirely unable to deliver carrier-grade availability— and even to this day, as we move to fourth-generation mobile networks and beyond, we still live with dropped calls, dead zones, and more. Does that mean that today's mobile phone networks are essentially of lower quality than POTS? The answer is no, as long as you define quality in the context of the new environment, what the telcos call *best effort*. After all, the components of this network—cell towers, mobile phones, and so forth—have all been tested thoroughly, and the network overall delivers the quality the telcos promise and that we're willing to pay for. As long as the infrastructure delivers its best effort to complete and maintain our phone calls, we're happy.

Just so with Agile Architecture quality. If we exclude the agility requirement from the quality equation, we'll never be happy with the result. But if we build agility into our quality approach, then the resulting implementation is within reach of both. Nevertheless, there is still a trade-off between agility and quality, but that trade-off depends on more than two variables. As a result, there's more to this story.

To understand the agility/quality trade-off question, we have to reach back into the ancient history of software development (say, more than 10 years ago) and brush off the venerable Software Development (SD) Triangle, which states that any SD project has three key variables: *cost*, *time*, and *scope*. It's possible to fix any two of these, but the third vertex of the triangle will vary as a result. For example, if you fix the cost and schedule for a project, you may or may not be able to deliver on all the requirements for the project, and so forth.

Restricting the relevant variables to these three, however, assumes a fixed level of quality. In other words, if an SD stakeholder attempts to fix all three corners of cost, time, and scope, then all that's left to give way is the quality of the resulting deployment, which is rarely if ever acceptable. We might say, therefore, that the SD Triangle is really a *square*, with quality being the fourth vertex.

Agile Architecture projects, though, vary this relationship in a fundamental way: They add agility to the equation, turning this square into a star (or a pentagon, if you will), as shown in Figure 4.1, where the lower three vertices form the traditional SD Triangle.

Now, it's tempting to posit that this Agile Architecture Quality Star exhibits a fundamental five-way symmetry, where we might fix any four

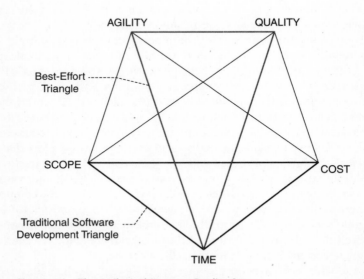

Figure 4.1   The Agile Architecture Quality Star

vertices at the expense of the fifth, but if we take a closer look, the situation isn't quite so simple. In fact, there is a second triangle embedded in the star that illustrates some important fundamental principles of Agile Architecture Quality. This triangle that connects agility, quality, and time we'll call the *Best-Effort Triangle*, because it illustrates the problem the DoD faced in the story: The more agile an implementation becomes, the more time is required to ensure quality, and as a result, it isn't long until quality activities become so time consuming that the agility of the implementation is at risk.

Combining the SD Triangle and the Best-Effort Triangle into the Agile Architecture Quality Star, then, doesn't lead us to the conclusion that we can fix any four vertices by varying the fifth, because the maximum agility we can achieve is limited by the time it takes to obtain the required quality. As a result, the only two vertices we might leave unfixed are the two that are not on the Best-Effort Triangle, namely scope and cost. In other words, if we're able to specify the required agility, quality, and time for a particular project, within the context of the dependencies the Best-Effort Triangle expresses, then either we can set the cost of that project by adjusting the scope, or set the scope of the project by allowing for additional cost.

The conclusion of this analysis is clear: The only way to obtain the balance between agility and quality the business requires is to take an *iterative* approach to an Agile Architecture initiative, where each iteration is bounded either by scope or cost. As a result, such projects differ from traditional SD projects in that with an Agile Architecture project, time-boxed iterations (that is, those with the time vertex fixed) are impractical, because time boxing doesn't take into account the effect of the agility requirement on quality. Instead, the time vertex depends upon the agility/quality balance that characterizes best-effort quality.

Perhaps the most important lesson here is the contrapositive: "Big bang" architecture projects that attempt to roll out broad, enterprise-wide initiatives in a noniterative fashion inevitably sacrifice the agility/quality balance, essentially because the time it would take to adequately test such an implementation would severely curtail the agility of the result. Only when agility is not a requirement at all would such a big bang project be even theoretically feasible—but if that met your requirements, then why would you be reading this book?

You could even say that an ostensible architecture project with no agility requirement is in truth an integration project, as there would be no need for loosely coupled Services in the first place. Unfortunately, we see evidence of such projects all the time: organizations that think they want to implement SOA for one reason or another, but instead purchase an ESB or other integration middleware first and deliver what becomes a large-scale, big bang integration project instead. The end result is business stakeholders scratching their heads over the resulting lack of agility and wondering why they didn't get the business value from the initiative they expected and thought they were paying for. Taking an iterative approach to architecture is the first step in avoiding this undesirable result.

Best-Effort Quality in Action

When Thomas Edison was in quest of inventing the electric light bulb, he didn't get it right the first time. In a well-documented exchange, Edison was told that he had failed 700 times in his attempts to make the breakthrough he sought. In response, he said, "I have not failed 700 times. I have not failed once! I have succeeded in proving that those 700 ways would not work!" What we can learn from the king of perseverance is that failing often, and quickly, is one of the best ways to increase the likelihood of success, and do so sooner.

However, most developers and architects, especially those building Services, want to minimize the number of times they spend rebuilding anything— and for good reason. Development is expensive. Architecture takes time. So, doing things over is rarely an option. Indeed, though we often hear the refrain, "I don't have time to do it right, but I have time to do it over," we tend to shake our heads in disdain. Yet, perhaps there is a kernel of truth in that refrain. From the Edisonian perspective, trying to get things right increases the penalty for failure. If you can only afford to do things once, it had *better* be right or you just wasted a lot of time, money, and resources.

On the contrary, one of the fundamental ideas inherent in Agile Architecture is the notion that things keep changing. If it's not the business and their requirements, processes, policies, or metadata that change, it's the underlying technologies, implementations, and schemas that do. The enterprise is constantly shifting, much like the Earth's crust (except at a much faster pace)— continually changing due to erosion, tectonic forces, and the presence of humans. Yet, despite these changes, life goes on, and so, too, must the business. In this reality, how can one even hope to get it right the first time when the assumptions that presuppose that correctness are guaranteed to be wrong within a short period of time?

Yes, there's no point to trying to get the Services right, get the infrastructure right, build the right governance, quality, and management systems and processes, and associated metadata, and trying to lock them down so that they can't change. If you know that they will change in advance, why spend months (or sometimes years, as we have observed) trying to build the perfect solution when the business's tectonic forces promise such change as will ruin your plans? Beat the urge of perfection by focusing on failing your way to success. When things keep changing, there's no way you can always be right. So fail often to succeed sooner. And to do that, you need to reduce the cost of failure so that failures are just successful proofs of how *not* to do things.

When we advise people that it's not important for them to get things right at the start, we often get significant resistance and pushback. In response, we often tell them that of *course* they need to build working solutions using the best practices available to them. Clearly, any technology you deploy has to *work*, otherwise it's not meeting any business requirements.

The point is that we need to see our attempts to meet those requirements as simply that—attempts. The implementation might be wrong in its optimal approach to meet the requirements. The business might be wrong in its definition of its requirements or business process. Or they both might be right—for now, before things completely change in a shorter time frame than expected.

And there's so much that can go wrong. You built something you thought would last, and you made it such that redoing things is now impossibly expensive and time consuming. Things have changed; your solution doesn't work. Whose fault is it? Yours. Because you didn't design to fail. *You designed to make failure expensive.*

Agile Architecture rethinks this proposition. Instead of making failure expensive, focus on reducing its costs. There are four primary ways to reduce the cost of failure, or in other words, increase the overall likelihood of success for any system that is continually changing:

1. **Allow for ambiguity.** One of the hardest things for developers and architects to do is to design for unknown requirements. Certainly no one can be asked to do a task that the requesters themselves don't understand. But we are often asked to do tasks that are ill defined. Many times a business unit wants to see an implementation so that they can know *better* what they actually want. That's what prototypes are all about.

   Design *all* the aspects of your implementation to be prototypes, and you'll be allowing for ambiguity. Why bother spending 12 months implementing a $5 million middleware product when you don't even know what functionality you'll need down the road? Start with a prototype infrastructure solution. Start with a best guess for the capabilities you think you need, realizing that any aspect of your prototype is subject to change. Show the business the results so that they can use it to better define their requirements. Prototype faster, cheaper, and better, and you will be successful sooner.

2. **Design for flexibility.** When you see a part of the technology or business change often enough, you start realizing that you need to

accommodate the possibility for that change when you design the system in the first place. From an Agile Architecture perspective, we allow for this variability through the power of abstraction. Keep things abstracted and build for flexibility, and you won't be disappointed when things change.

3. **Behave iteratively.** Design and implementation are not enough to guarantee success in the face of ongoing change and ambiguity. You have to also align your organization, methods, practices, and even budget to enable continual change. We have long advocated the movement away from waterfall styles of development to more iterative styles, because iterative styles naturally force organizations to plan for change both in technology as well as in process and budget.

4. **Measure frequently.** Allowing for ambiguity, designing for flexibility, and being iterative aren't enough to guarantee success—you need to make sure you are heading in the right direction! Measure every iteration and implementation against success criteria. Those criteria might be functional as well as a nonfunctional. They might be relevant to business metrics such as profitability or technology metrics such as performance. And remember, even your success criteria may change over time. Only by knowing what to measure can you know what to manage, and in turn, know that you are failing your way to success.

We think we would be misleading you if we told you it would be easy to accomplish all the previous steps. There's so much in the Business-IT environment that conspires against the "fail your way to success" approach to architecture. For one, IT budgets are still rooted in the "get it right or else" style of pay-and-pray implementation. There's simply no leeway in the budget, schedule, or resources to keep doing things over. Our answer: Change your budgeting, time scheduling, and resource allocation, because you'll keep doing it over anyway.

Remember, the whole point of Agile Architecture is to enable agility through the abstraction of IT capabilities. The more that we can enable change without having a high penalty cost for that change, the more we enable business agility. If you agree with this viewpoint, then it should be obvious that *getting things right* at the start is simply not an appropriate goal for an Agile Architecture effort. In fact, the goal might be just the reverse—build capabilities that you know won't be right and then make sure the architecture enables you to change them without breaking anything.

If you find that changing your solution breaks things at a wide range of levels of abstraction, then you know there's a flaw in your architecture. To prove that you can implement Agile Architecture, you must prove that things can change without breaking.

Resilience: The Flip Side of Agility

Resilience is the property of an entity to absorb energy when it is impacted by some change, but then rebound from that change back to its original condition. The concept of resiliency is a self-righting tendency that allows the system to retain its overall structure without lasting impact even when affected by significant change. And if we primarily want to enable the sort of change that Agile Architecture purports, then certainly the solutions we build, infrastructure we implement, processes we model, and systems we enable should have some measure of resilience.

In many ways, the concept of resilience is similar to that of agility. Both agility and resilience deal with change in its various forms, but there are distinct differences that inform the way in which we architect, engineer, and design our Complex Systems. One way to understand the difference is to compare the concept of resilience with that of flexibility. Flexibility is another word frequently used to describe one of the desired benefits of agility. If systems can stretch and bend to meet new needs, then we don't need to continually reengineer them as things change.

However, resilience is not the same concept as flexibility. The best way to understand the difference is to look at the antonyms of each of the words. *Rigidity*, often couched in terms of *robustness*, is the antonym of flexibility, and it implies the inability or resistance of an object to change. However, *fragility* is the antonym of resilience, and it implies that the given entity will break when a sufficient force is applied. There's clearly a relationship between flexibility and resilience because things that are flexible have a higher tolerance for force, but flexible systems can still be fragile.

Things can also be flexible and not resilient, in that many systems can be changed but never regain their original shape. However, if that happens often enough, you are left with a system contorted beyond its original intention. Indeed, you want resiliency and agility, not just flexibility and robustness. Even more so, it is much easier to build systems for robustness than it is to build them for flexibility. The general thinking goes that you should build systems big, strong, and thick, and you can *withstand* change. But who wants to or even can withstand the inevitable force of change? Wouldn't you rather avoid colossal failure when the inevitable force of change does occur? Wouldn't you rather capitalize on change?

Systems are fragile when you change them beyond their *elastic limit*—that point where balloons pop and rubber bands snap, even though they are elastic. From this perspective, things that are rigid have a very low elastic limit, and are thus very fragile. Things that are flexible have a high elastic limit and are resilient up to a point.

Elasticity is measured by variability, and we can plan ahead with regard to this variability by thinking about how much we expect things to change and how much force there is when they change. As you might guess, in a system that's continually undergoing rapid and often unpredictable change, resilience provided through robustness provides neither flexibility nor emergent properties of agility. The only form of resilience that works is that which is based on flexibility. In this way, we can think of resilience that we plan into our systems as variability, and resilience that emerges unplanned in our systems as agility.

The idea of measuring flexibility by planning for variability is the point of the Agility Model. The Agility Model provides architects with three key capabilities: a method for planning Services and processes with regard to their expected variability, a means for business users to express their desires with respect to variability, and a means to measure developed systems and Services for their actual variability. Having variability provides flexibility, which in turn provides a measure of resilience, and contributes to agility as an emergent property. Specifically, planning for variability requires you to think beyond how a particular aspect of that Service is designed for today. What could change in the future? What is the cost/benefit trade-off for designing that variability into the system now, rather than just acknowledging its inflexibility? Now you're thinking like an Agile Architect!

But there's more to the resilience picture. In reality, architects can provide for resilience in one of two ways: by either building the system rigid enough to resist the change or building it flexible enough to absorb change without permanently changing the system. We often handle these resilience issues through a few key mechanisms: redundancy, distribution, failover, load balancing, clustering, and an enforced "no single point of failure" rule. With those mechanisms in mind, it doesn't matter how flexible a particular Service might be if it can unexpectedly become unavailable at a moment's notice. And we shouldn't come to depend on systems to provide this sort of resilience either. Systems management software, ESBs, and other infrastructure can introduce more brittleness through a single point of failure. We can't depend on infrastructure to solve architectural resiliency issues. We have to design resilience into the architecture, regardless of the current technology in use.

Just as we can plan for flexibility at a variety of levels using measures of variability in the Agility Model, so, too, can we plan for resilience at those levels. For example, in a SOA deployment, Services that are resilient cannot only handle a wide range of request types, but also significant numbers of Service requests without tipping over into failure. Although it is possible for ESBs and other Service infrastructure to handle such Service availability resilience, the best practice is for architects to consider Service availability as part of resilient Service design. For example, architects should consider failover Services, clusters of Service implementations, or load balancing by having multiple Service interfaces and Service endpoints defined in Service contracts. In this way, the architect doesn't have to depend on specific infrastructure to handle variable Service loads. In fact, this approach is fundamental to architecting for the Cloud as well, as we'll discuss later.

Yet, resilience at the Service level is not enough to guarantee overall resilience of the Enterprise Architecture. Just as we need failover, redundancy, load balancing, and just-in-time provisioning for Services, so, too, do we need them for the business processes implemented as compositions of those Services. Consider failover processes that provide an alternate execution path for business logic, redundant processes that channel interactions across alternate invocation mechanisms, and methods to create ad hoc processes when other processes are on the verge of tipping over.

Perhaps the easiest form of resilience can be achieved at the infrastructure level. Infrastructure should be able to handle a wide range of usage loads and invocation methods, but to depend on a single vendor or single implementation to provide that guarantee is foolhardy. Rather, good Enterprise Architects count on resilience of infrastructure by having redundant, load-balanced, and alternate run-time engines, and by using distributed, heterogeneous network intermediaries instead of single-vendor, proprietary, single point of failure ESBs. Organizations should also implement distributed caching, federated registries with late binding, and network gateways that handle security and policy enforcement away from the Service endpoints. Resilience at the infrastructure level is much more doable when you count on high levels of reliability and throughput without counting on one vendor's implementation to pull all the weight.

But why stop there? Organizations seeking SOA resilience also need to make sure to have resilient Service policies. This resiliency requires not just redundant policy enforcement mechanisms, but also failover policy definition points and even redundant, failover, and load-balanced Service policies. When you're using policies at run-time to determine binding to Services, having unexpected outages of Service policy definition availability can cause just as much havoc as if the Service itself were not available.

Similarly, SOA implementers should have resilience at the Service contract and schema level. Having redundant Service implementations makes no sense if they are all sharing a single Service contract file that is in danger of disappearing, especially if it is sitting on an unprotected file server. Protect your metadata by locking them behind a policy-enforced registry/repository, but also make sure to have redundancy, failover, and load balancing to avoid shifting a single point of failure. Apply the same principle to all Service metadata, process metadata, data schemas, and semantic mappings that might be necessary to allow for proper functioning of the system.

Yet, all this work doesn't matter if the most important part of Enterprise Architecture, namely the architect, is him/herself not resilient. Are you the only EA in your organization that understands Agile Architecture? Even worse, are you the only EA in your organization, full stop? What happens if your job changes, or you get laid off, or the organization otherwise changes its feelings on EA? Will that kill the whole Agile Architecture project? What about budgets and funding? Are you operating your projects on the edge, just awaiting a single nudge to push them into project oblivion? If so, you need architectural and organizational resilience. Make sure you have a broad base of support (redundancy). Distribute the workload and responsibility for architectural activities and make sure that there is a team of architects, not a lone crusader (failover and clustering). Provide visibility to the rest of the organization of the benefits of your activities and make sure you provide closed-loop interaction on how specific EA tasks result in specific business benefits, preferably iteratively, on a short time schedule, and frequently.

If some of the so-called benefits of SOA were to disappear (namely, standards-based integration), but we remain with agile, resilient EA, we have achieved the main objective of Agile Architecture Enabling the business to operate in a continuously changing, heterogeneous environment without breaking, necessitating significant cost, or high latency requires Enterprise Architects to think, act, and plan for resilience as well as agility.

The Flash Mob Enterprise

You shouldn't be surprised that this admittedly technical section concludes with a discussion of organizational best practices. After all, Agile Architecture means architecting people as well as technology. Here's a story that will help clarify this point. In 1973, science fiction author Larry Niven wrote *Flash Crowd*, a novella that explored the consequences of inventing an instantaneous, practically free teleportation booth that could take you anywhere on Earth in the blink of an eye. An unexpected consequence of this technology was that whenever anything newsworthy occurred, tens of thousands of people would immediately descend on the location of the news, leading to disorder and confusion.

A modern analogue to a flash crowd is the *flash mob*, which is a group of people who assemble suddenly in a public place, perform an unusual and pointless act for a brief time, then disperse. Notable examples include pillow fights and dance sequences. In the case of Niven's novella, both the teleportation as well as global instantaneous news are technology enablers of the phenomenon. Flash mobs, however, only require coordinated communication. The Internet clearly simplifies the formation of flash mobs, but a simple phone tree would also work almost as efficiently. We see similar patterns on all large social media platforms. Ad hoc, self-organizing activities are now quite common on Facebook and Twitter, for example.

There are many differences among various examples of such activities, along two axes: goal-oriented vs. pointless, and centrally planned vs. viral. But they all have one essential property in common: They are all *self-organizing*. Once the underlying framework for the action and the enabling technology are in place, then the overall behavior of the people involved takes on a life of its own. This self-organizing behavior of crowds is the essential commonality among these various patterns.

From our perspective, the most fascinating aspect of this behavior is the unpredictable impact of technology. Flash mobs may have been possible using only telephones, but today's ultraconnected city dweller is far more likely to participate. Furthermore, we are only now beginning to scratch the surface of the power of massive social networks. With self-organization comes unpredictability.

The fact that technology-enabled social networks self-organize in interesting ways, however, is itself predictable, even though the resulting behavior may not be. Such self-organization can therefore serve as a powerful tool, although as with most powerful tools, it is also dangerous in the wrong hands.

Self-organization, of course, is a fundamental behavior of Complex Systems. In fact, technology-enabled Complex Systems like the enterprise will self-organize whether you want them to or not. They will exhibit unpredictable behavior, regardless of anything the participants or an outside controller might do to stop or control the behavior. Fighting such self-organization is a futile exercise. Instead, we must learn to understand it and leverage it to achieve our intended goals.

On one hand, this self-organization can be a threat to the enterprise. Bernard Madoff's massive Ponzi scheme is one obvious example. A scheme like this one cannot work if only a handful of people participate. The entire premise of such a scheme is predicated on the participation of hundreds or thousands of people, interacting with each other and leveraging technology to facilitate communication and other aspects of business, all while being oblivious to the fraud.

But on the other hand, the self-organization of social networks is also an opportunity. How can your organization leverage this principle to achieve its goals? Can the people in your organization self-organize by leveraging technology, but instead of scheduling an impromptu pillow fight, actually work to address a strategic challenge your organization faces?

For the architects in our audience, this thought exercise should prompt a fundamental question: How should you architect your enterprise to capitalize on the self-organizing power of your organization, while mitigating the risks inherent in such behavior? If you think of yourself as an Enterprise Architect but you haven't yet asked yourself or your team this question, then you have yet to take the first step on the road to implementing Agile Architecture.

CHAPTER 5

Agile Architecture in Practice

Enterprises around the world are facing a momentous transformation, as they move away from traditional, inflexible approaches to leveraging IT resources to a more agile way that helps to improve *business processes*. But what is a business process, anyway? The traditional definition is *a sequence of activities that leads to a business result* or something similar. The implication from that definition is that business processes are repeatable and formally defined, as though we were programming a robot, only we may be programming people instead.

ZapThink believes that such a definition is too limited to be of much use today. Instead, we define a business process as *anything a business does*. Such a process might be automated, or fully manual, or some combination. It might be highly repeatable, different every time you do it, or somewhere in between. It may be formally defined and documented, or completely ad hoc.

We understand that this definition is broader than most, but we've defined business processes this way on purpose—because we're going to consider how technology can help us automate or otherwise streamline the full breadth of business processes, from the most mundane, repeatable sequences of activities, to the most fluid, dynamic endeavors. After all, Agile Architecture presupposes that business processes (defined broadly) will often be dynamic.

From the technology perspective, however, the more dynamic a process is, the more difficult it is to automate. Our traditional integration-centric approach to automation is inherently inflexible. In this chapter we're going to move away from that approach to a *composition-centric* approach to automation in order to put Agile Architecture into practice.

This transition from an integration-centric view of technology, which leads to brittle assemblages of heterogeneous assets, to the composition-centric view, which positions IT resources as flexible Services that the business can compose together to support and manage flexible processes, heralds a new era of value to organizations. The first step in this transition is the move to Service-Oriented Architecture (SOA), which provides best practices for organizing IT resources to enable organizations to better leverage business change.

The Composition Vision for IT

The twenty-first century business environment is tougher than ever before. Enterprises are facing pressure through competition, globalization, and consolidation. And yet, IT has largely lagged behind in solving the ever-changing business problems such pressure creates. In the 1970s, IT focused on building core systems, and in the 1980s through 1990s, enterprise application vendors like SAP and Oracle offered standard software that required expensive, time-consuming customization to meet business needs. And yet, such applications were never more than part of the story; every enterprise required multiple systems and applications from multiple vendors, resulting in complex aggregations of technology.

Every time an organization aggregates technology, however, they end up with a heterogeneous IT environment that increases in complexity and brittleness as time goes on. Before long, the lion's share of the IT budget goes to keeping such aggregations working, and CIOs are able to devote less and less time and money to new capabilities that lead to increased business value. Now that we're in the twenty-first century, many IT shops are reaching a critical point, where the business simply cannot afford to continue to support such increasingly inflexible IT organizations.

Fortunately, change is on the horizon—and for many of the world's most progressive enterprises, change is already here. Instead of aggregation of technology, IT organizations are supporting composition of IT capabilities and information, known as *Services*. Furthermore, IT is empowering the business to handle the tasks of composition themselves, so that they can implement and manage business processes. Instead of supporting a grab bag of heterogeneous technology, therefore, IT is increasingly focusing on implementing such Services and supporting the composition capabilities that businesses require.

It is critically important, however, for IT to take into account the interdependencies of Services and various requirements for those Services, because the business wants to be able to compose Services to implement business processes without worrying about whether those Services will behave as expected. SOA is an essential enabler of this goal, because done properly, it pulls together governance and business process management (BPM) to support the composition of Services as the business requires. By basing their BPM efforts on SOA, organizations seek to expand and enable dynamic changes in their business processes in the future.

This combination of architecture, governance, and BPM is supposed to support the fundamental goal of Agile Architecture: technology implementations that deliver on the meta-requirement of agility. However, the devil is in the details. SOA alone has not fully capitalized on this vision of agile business process. Nevertheless, understanding how close we were able to come to implementing Agile Architecture following SOA, and then understanding what's missing from the SOA approach, forms the essence of understanding the Agile Architecture Revolution.

Today, organizations require a way to separate the process layer from the underlying applications, so that the business can own and control their processes directly, providing the desired flexibility and reliability. As today's businesses move to achieve this agility goal, however, they struggle with a massive dilemma: Formalize your business processes to the level where everything is well defined, and you end up with a rigid, uncompetitive corporation that's unresponsive to change; don't formalize your processes, and end up with an uncontrollable mess that wastes money and pleases customers only by accident, if at all. Clearly, we need to identify some way out of this dilemma in a way that's both controllable and flexible.

Furthermore, this new vision of composition-driven business processes that SOA enables must include collaboration, self-healing, and governance. People are part of virtually every business process, and therefore the composition environment must support people and the way they wish to work. In addition, for people to be able to rely on the composition of Services, those Services as well as the compositions must be able to adjust dynamically to any underlying technical issues—in essence, to be able to heal themselves.

And finally, organizations require governance to balance the otherwise competing needs of business empowerment and IT control. After all, IT is responsible for making sure everything operates as required, and yet this composition vision for business process places unparalleled power in the hands of business users. Governance is the key to bringing these needs together.

The history of BPM tells the story of transition from an aggregation-centric to a composition-centric approach to achieving business value with IT. This tale begins with the business process re-engineering (BPR) push in the early 1990s. At that time, rigid systems and IT architectures built on aggregation hindered BPR and made it difficult for IT departments to keep up with the advances the business side wanted to make in improving their processes.

The process measurement tools and strategies that methodologies like Six Sigma provided didn't take into account tightly coupled, hard-coded, monolithic IT systems that supported the organization's processes. Making a change on a paper-based process map seemed simple, but implementing that change on the IT side might equate to thousands of person-hours and hundreds of thousands of dollars.

BPM promised to make a significant impact on the way organizations ran. Technology advancements improved the IT landscape, making it much more process-innovation friendly. As a result, software vendors introduced many process-definition, execution, and optimization tools that connected with IT systems to align business and IT strategies, closing the gap somewhat between innovative process design and implementation.

Today's BPM engines, however, have their limitations. In many cases they implement static versions of a process, or dictate to the business how they should run their processes, rather than vice versa. In other cases, there are many versions of a single process: one in the BPM engine, another in the documentation, and still a third in how the process actually works. Another equally challenging drawback is that BPM engines do not provide sufficient information for the business to give feedback on changes to the process, in order to improve it.

But the most significant missing link with many of these BPM engines is that enterprises implement them without an architecture that provides for business agility in the face of heterogeneous IT environments. Without such an architectural approach, BPM yields inflexible processes that constrain the business, preventing it from responding efficiently to changes in the business environment. In fact, this need for flexible business processes is the primary benefit of SOA for many organizations.

In properly architected SOA, therefore, companies must build business Services that represent the data available to the business and the core func-tionality of the underlying systems—in other words, they must build the *right* Services. Businesspeople then must be able to drive the composition of those Services to implement agile business processes and configure those composi-tions based on the applicable business rules, even as the business requirements for those processes change over time.

The important point to understand is that in an Agile Architecture deployment, the compositions should contain all of the new business logic in the enterprise, while existing legacy applications typically become a vital part of the underlying implementation. Certain programming logic remains in the software infrastructure that supports the business Services available to the enterprise, and the business puts most new business logic at the process layer. Business users will create, configure, and compose Services to implement processes without traditional programming languages, but instead use tools appropriate for those users.

What makes a Service useful is not simply its machine-processable interfaces, but also interfaces that humans can use. Furthermore, Services must be composable not only in theory, but in practice. Clearly, it doesn't matter how useful a composition appears to be if the software that consumes the composition prevents users from taking advantage of the flexibility that building the application as a composition of Services promised in the first place. No enterprise, however, would risk allowing any of its employees to assemble and reassemble business processes without controls in place to ensure that the resulting compositions followed corporate policies. In other words, Service compositions require governance.

In fact, such governed service compositions provide a new type of business application. Rather than simply connecting directly to the back-end systems and providing visual islands of information, a new generation of such applications is poised to provide a process-driven approach to assembling logical flows of information from disparate data and information sources, providing a role-based, personalized presentation layer on top of those flows. In this way, compositions close the loop on business process challenges by providing powerful tools to the lines of business (LOBs). No longer is IT getting in the way of business process; instead, IT serves as a critical enabler of business agility.

The first step to implementing business processes in an enterprise is to create a representation of a business process that human and/or machine-based systems can execute. However, historically there has been little way to connect these meaningful diagrams to flexible applications that help automate them. With the advent of Service compositions, users should actually be able to execute their abstract business process representations. Because business-oriented users will rarely become programmers, these users are expecting visual representations to be the primary way in which they can build compositions that will implement their process flow desires.

The second step to building compositions is to identify the Services that are available to the enterprise. Once the organization has a visual representation of their business processes and clear definitions of the Services available, what remains is to tie the business requirements to the functionality of the architecture in an agile way. The technology work is done at this point—all that remains is the human side: issues of governance, change management, and responsiveness to customer needs.

The real work of building and running compositions, then, rests in the hands of the business. The business should be in charge of dynamic business processes, whereas IT takes a supporting role, hidden behind the scenes as enablers of the Services and compositions that make business processes work. This is the true vision of the composition-driven Agile Architecture: business empowerment through governance, architecture, and composition.

Vision to Reality: Rethinking Integration

The vision we just delineated is sound: abstract IT capabilities as Services that empower the business to manage and innovate their business processes through governed compositions. But vision has a habit of differing from reality. In reality, achieving this seamless business empowerment goal with SOA has generally been out of reach. Instead of supporting the Complex Systems approach to satisfying the business agility meta-requirement, many SOA initiatives focus on *integration:* helping to connect bits of technology together, rather than supporting agile business processes. The controversy rages even to this day. What is SOA's fundamental purpose: to solve integration problems, or is it more of a business transformation approach centered on implementing agile business processes?

In some circles, SOA means little more than middleware-based integration that leverages Web Services; in other words, ESB-based integration. The problem with this definition is that much of the ESB-based integration today is in organizations that haven't implemented SOA. ZapThink may be fighting an uphill battle here, pointing out that ESB-based integration without SOA is really not SOA at all. Be that as it may, arguments over definitions of terms are usually a waste of time, as the more useful arguments are over how best to solve problems.

In other cases, however, pushing for a redefinition of a term is an insidious way of influencing public opinion. SOA is too difficult, some vendors say, so buy my ESB instead. Though there's broad agreement that many SOA initiatives focus on solving integration-related challenges, no one who's put any thought into this issue would actually say SOA and integration are the same thing.

All of these arguments over SOA, however, really miss the key point here, which is *how* SOA can help organizations with their integration challenges. Because SOA is supposed to be Agile Architecture, it should consist of best practices for organizing IT resources to better meet the changing needs of business. In other words, SOA requires us to rethink how we approach the problem of integration altogether, in the context of an architecture oriented toward Services rather than toward tightly coupled interfaces. Instead of taking a "connecting things" approach to distributed computing, therefore, we need to take a "composing Services" perspective. The difference between these two approaches goes to the heart of SOA, and represents our first big step on the road to Agile Architecture.

In the traditional, integration-centric world, the enterprise IT environment consists of a heterogeneous mix of resources that don't automatically talk to one another. As a result, IT must devote substantial resources to connecting those resources to each other in order to provide value to the business. In other words, integration is something the techies do *before* the business can get the value they want out of the complex IT environment.

SOA, on the other hand, focuses on building and using Services. Deployed Services, in essence, are *ready to be integrated*; if the organization implements the Business Service abstraction properly, then it's possible to compose the

Services to implement business processes. Furthermore, whereas specific process requirements often drive the initial design of the Services, reusability of those Services is also a design priority for some of those Services.

Remember, however, that Service reuse means composing Services into new compositions that implement other business processes, often in ways that the original designer of the Services did not predict. Furthermore, business process requirements drive such compositions. When the business composes Services to meet such requirements, they are actually performing the act of integration. Only now, integration is a result of composition that takes place after the Services have been deployed, rather than something IT does to connect systems in order to deliver business value in the first place.

Once you understand that the core technical challenge of SOA is in building the business Service abstraction that allows the business to compose such Services to support changing process needs, then the question of whether SOA is for integration or business process becomes moot. Instead, the focus of integration becomes Service composition. IT focuses on building and supporting Services, rather than connecting things.

One important caveat: Part of the "building Services" challenge is in integrating existing legacy assets. After all, SOA is much more about leveraging legacy systems than it is about building greenfield applications. As a result, legacy application integration and data integration are essential parts of the SOA implementation story. What's changed here is the role such integrations play in the architecture. In SOA, they play a supporting role, part of the hard work that goes into building Services properly. In contrast, such integrations play a leading role in ESB-based integration. If you think that connecting things to your ESB gives you SOA, then you've fallen for the SOA straw man that gave rise to the "SOA is dead" meme. From ZapThink's perspective, such integration isn't SOA at all.

Thinking of integration as a result of Service composition supports not only the business agility driver for SOA, but also the business empowerment benefit that SOA promises. Because true SOA is business process–driven, it enables LOBs to take greater responsibility for such integration. If the IT organization has abstracted all of its capabilities as composable business Services, then the LOBs can drive the integration of those Services via their BPM efforts. And though LOB users will still likely call on IT personnel to create the compositions themselves, they will be doing so at the behest of business process specialists who are focusing on solving process-centric business problems.

Of course, this process-centric view of Services raises the bar for the IT organization, because building the Business Service abstraction is a far more difficult challenge than simply implementing Web Services, or even implementing an ESB. If there's one thing all the SOA pundits can agree on, it's that

SOA is *hard*. Nevertheless, if you're able to get the architecture right, then you'll be able to shift the focus of integration from the tightly coupled, technology-centric world of connecting systems to the loosely coupled, business-centric world of composing Services, and you'll be well on your way to an Agile Architecture.

Aligning Agile Architecture with BPM

Because we're not talking simply about making technology work better with technology, it makes sense that Agile Architectural approaches like SOA must be aligned with the needs of the business. The needs of the business are reflected primarily in the organization's business processes, and thus SOA must have a business process–centric perspective. But all too often, the conversation ZapThink has with end-users, consulting firms, and technology vendors focuses not on those business processes, but rather on the underlying technology platforms, standards-based interfaces, and system-to-system communication. Indeed, the story of business process has been at times so buried within the discussion of SOA that to the business, SOA itself has no business relevance. And yet, if there is any hope for a long-lasting impact and benefit of Agile Architecture, it must indeed be business relevant, and thus business process–driven.

The fact that many IT folks are unable to justify a business case for a SOA investment signals that there must be a disconnect between the problems the business wants to solve and the promise of SOA as a solution. People with BPM skills are not typically part of the SOA discussion, and as such their knowledge and connection to the business has not transferred to the organization's separate efforts.

Historically, IT treated the worlds of integration and business process separately. The IT environment has been so complex over the past thirty to forty years of computing that simply getting things to communicate and interact with each other is a significant challenge for IT. Technology offerings and approaches such as EAI; Extract, Transform, and Load (ETL); and Enterprise Information Integration (EII) are squarely focused on solving the integration problem without needing much of a business context in which to justify their value. And yet, by focusing just on the technology problems of integration, the business placed little emphasis on requiring integration technologists and specialists to understand the business context or process in which those integrations form a part.

At the same time that integration efforts were under way, the business sought a means to address their continually changing business requirements in the context of IT. BPM evolved to reduce the amount of time it took to distill the needs of the business into implementable, automatable parts. Increasing productivity in the process improvement cycle is one of the greatest of BPM's value propositions, and organizations usually achieve this value by reducing design-to-deployment time frames through an integrated approach to both team management and technology. Successful BPM adherents point to methodologies and technologies that let them quickly develop and test process models, create and deploy user interfaces to those processes, and then connect those interfaces to existing systems.

One definition of BPM is *a natural and holistic management approach to operating business that produces a highly efficient, agile, innovative, and adaptive organization that far exceeds that achievable through traditional management approaches*. This definition brings two things to mind. First, this definition of BPM sounds rather close to the vision of Agile Architecture, and perhaps melding this perspective of BPM with Agile Architecture would lead to a more business-relevant perspective on SOA and a more architecturally grounded perspective on BPM. In fact, the idea of starting with a business process representation and rapidly iterating on that model to create the required logic necessary sounds much like a top-down, model-driven best practice. Yet, enterprises are still stuck building Services from the bottom up, starting not with business processes, but rather with underlying systems.

The BPM and SOA communities are more separated than they should be. But even more worrisome is the fact that many IT people who now champion SOA are not conversant in the language of business process. They often lack skills to do proper business process modeling and have not been involved enough in the organization's BPM efforts to learn the benefits and pitfalls of various BPM approaches. After all, traditional integration experts are not the same as business process experts.

At first blush, some might see the efforts of BPM and SOA as opposed to each other: Business process experts on one hand try to build the perfect model and the technologists on the other try to expose the perfect Services. And yet, there really is no such diametric opposition. In any environment of change, the business processes will continue to result in the need for new and different Services, and the technologies will likewise change with such regularity as to complicate the efforts of anyone trying to realize a particular process. In the business reality of continued and simultaneous evolution, companies need to take an Agile Architecture perspective on BPM and a business process perspective on architecture.

Taken as a starting point, business process models detail at an abstract level the various activities and relationships between activities to result in some sort of outcome. For many people, these models serve as a requirements document that guides development. However, from an Agile Architecture perspective, such models are insufficient. On one hand, SOA demands that compositions of

Services be defined via metadata that are both executable as well as a human-understandable. Therefore, business process models are *run-time* artifacts, not simply design-time requirements documents. On the other hand, such models, if seen solely as design-time artifacts, serve only to complicate things by trying to define every bit of process detail beforehand, resulting in excessive complexity and "analysis paralysis" that impedes any forward movement on process enablement.

In fact, proper process-driven SOA considers BPM to be the top-down portion of any iterative SOA methodology, with the result of well-defined Service contracts and a methodology that enables continual, iterative definition of both the processes and their representative Services. Furthermore, well-established BPM techniques don't consider the life cycle to be complete once the process team has completed their modeling. On the contrary, effective BPM requires simulation and walkthrough of existing business processes to identify optimization and improvement as well as continued feedback from attempts to implement activities and Services. Good BPM creates effective teams who can see how a business process will perform before they actualize it via Services at run-time.

However, before we can wrap up this topic, it's important to note that BPM + EAI + Standards does not equal SOA, let alone Agile Architecture. Too many software vendors consider their SOA efforts to merely be the collection of their process, integration, and standards-based middleware toolsets without realizing that the core motivation is the reduction of complexity by helping transform existing business processes through the use of agile Services. Agile Architecture is an approach to organizing IT assets as well as considering business processes and changing requirements. In this light, rather than piling formerly unrelated products together under the new banner of Agile Architecture, companies should carefully *reengineer* their process and infrastructural tools to be inherently agile and process driven.

Business Modeling and Agile Architecture

Anybody who has ever attempted to teach computer programming to a room full of tech novices knows that some people easily get it, whereas others simply don't. There's something about the basic "do this, make a decision, then do that" execution flow of any program that comes naturally to some folks, whereas other people simply don't seem to be wired in such a way as to make sense of such algorithmic thinking. As it happens, the algorithm-resistant population is every bit as clever as the programming friendly group; it's just that they think differently about the behavior of systems and thus choose to represent them in different ways than their more technical peers.

The underlying observation here is that human beings are marvelously adept at representing arbitrarily complex concepts with a wide range of different kinds of models. In fact, our innate ability to model reality is so pervasive in our day-to-day lives that the modeling process tends to fade from our awareness. Nevertheless, whether in business or in any other aspect of our lives, we are actively dealing with the complexity that surrounds us by building internal models that represent various aspects of reality. Furthermore, the types of models we use are amazingly diverse, as each of us leverages different types of models for representing the full spectrum of experiences we encounter in our lives.

As organizations look to Agile Architecture to offer best practices for leveraging IT to provide agile resources for the business, the ubiquitous, varied, and subtle nature of the human ability to model complex situations becomes a central concern. After all, abstractions like Services that represent IT capabilities and information to the business are models themselves, as are all the ways that people think about using Services in their business processes. Furthermore, the dichotomy between people who are comfortable thinking algorithmically and those who aren't resonates well beyond the classroom, with the algorithmically inclined leaning toward careers in IT, while people who prefer other types of models gravitate toward business roles.

This natural division of aptitude presents a challenge for any organization implementing Agile Architecture, because such an approach brings together these disparate ways of thinking about modeling, and requires IT to support the variety of models that businesspeople prefer. Indeed, technical approaches to business modeling have fallen short of addressing the needs of business-people who tend to think in nontechnical terms. As a result, learning how to accommodate the different ways that people in the organization think about both business and technology is a critical best practice in the architect's tool belt. Without this understanding, the business is unlikely to achieve the value and flexibility that they desire.

Ask an average nontechnical cubicle-dweller to break down what they do every day into its most basic elements, and you're likely to solicit a list of human interaction–based activities that move information around: conversations, meetings, sending and receiving communications, reading and writing, and the like. Knowledge workers might throw in activities like analyzing or evaluating. Few businesspeople, however, will reply that they spend their days *executing business processes*.

From the IT perspective, however, if you define a business process broadly as *what a business does*, or more narrowly as *a set of activities intended to achieve a business goal*, then all the various activities that our cubicle crowd undertake fall into the category of executing business processes. In fact, the Agile Architecture approach to business process calls for flexible processes that respond to the way humans work, rather than processes that constrain humans to work the way the systems want them to work. The problem is, the various models IT uses to represent business processes—flowcharts, graphs, defined flows, etc.—are only a small subset of all the useful models that businesspeople might use to represent the way they understand how the business actually works.

In fact, businesspeople have a rich, varied set of models for representing how they move information around: conversations, messages, documents, spreadsheets, Web interfaces, mind maps, flowcharts, agendas, schedules, calendars, and other loosely structured forms of information representation. To be truly successful with Agile Architecture, therefore, IT must support these multiple approaches for representing and exchanging information, instead of shoehorning business operations into an IT-centric representation of how techies think the business is supposed to work.

There is an essential lesson for the architect here: Design is an outward-in process, not inward-out. All good architects begin with humans and what they want from the systems the architects are designing. Because Agile Architecture requires an enterprise perspective on the interactions between business and IT, it's essential for the architect to be able to wear the hat of a business architect, and consider all the various models that the business is apt to use to represent the capabilities both of the business and the IT that serves it.

Furthermore, there is an important lesson here for technology vendors as well: Architecture tooling must be as diverse as the business users who wish to use it. People may utilize any number of different tools that leverage numerous models to take advantage of the capabilities their architecture provides. Gone are the days where tool vendors can manufacture only hammers, and expect their customers to recast all their problems as nails. By abstracting the interaction between business and IT, the business now expects IT to take care of business however the business sees fit, and not vice-versa.

Processes That Satisfy the Meta-Requirement of Agility

It's unfortunate, but today's rigid systems and applications limit agility instead of promoting it. For example, relational database technologies leverage fixed hierarchies, whereas traditional BPM software depends on design-time flowcharts. Such technologies do not adequately respond to the unique and varied conditions and circumstances of individual business activities.

Organizations need a practical mechanism for providing agility to their key business processes without increasing system overhead or latency. In other words, they require an architectural approach that pulls together the human and technology parts of the organization. This approach moves away from rigid structures to human-centric, governance-driven applications that support business agility. The new mantra of the twenty-first century is that the business wants to be agile, so let's deliver a system that responds to change and enables the organization to leverage change for competitive advantage—the essence of business agility. Such systems require a new way of thinking about architecture and governance.

Traditional systems consisting solely of technology components have focused on automation, and therefore lack sufficient support for process variance, innovation, events, and other dynamic, human aspects of business. Relying on middleware and other intermediary approaches introduces performance overhead and limits flexibility. Furthermore, traditional process automation, even in the SOA context, involves modeling system responses in advance. No matter how many conditional paths a process may include, standardization limits responsiveness to individual instances by design.

To address this inherent inflexibility, all agile SOA initiatives depend on governance. Governance pulls together the human and technology systems that make up the system of systems that constitutes the enterprise. However, governance of SOA deployments must span distributed components, introducing additional expense and system latency. And in any case, although Services may provide flexibility, the underlying legacy systems remain inflexible, further limiting the agility of the resulting business processes. It's imperative, therefore, that organizations take an approach that automates business processes in a way that takes into account the human context of the individual processes themselves.

The end results are dynamic processes that have no predetermined flow. Instead, the people involved in the process begin with the goal for the process and then the technology supports the interactions among the people in order to achieve the goal. The interactions among the people involved with the process actually help define the process. The questions CIOs should ask, therefore, are what dynamic processes must we support, and how best to support them.

This need for dynamic processes emphasizes one additional benefit that Agile Architecture provides organizations that is fast becoming one of the most important: *business empowerment*. The concept of business empowerment begins where the notion of user empowerment leaves off; focusing more on the teams of people we call Lines of Business (LOBs) and how technology both directly and indirectly gives them the capabilities they need to succeed at overcoming the business challenges that face them. As a result, business empowerment is fast becoming a central motivation for Agile Architecture, second only to business agility.

User empowerment is a straightforward concept: Give users more powerful tools, and they have a greater ability to accomplish the tasks their jobs present to them. From the perspective of the IT department, those tools are computers, mobile devices, and other bits of technology that people interface with largely on a personal, one-to-one basis. The more capabilities we load on these tools, largely through better, more powerful software, the greater user empowerment we achieve.

SOA, of course, empowers users by offering Services that abstract capabilities and information across the organization and beyond. Now, users in front of their devices have as much power and flexibility as the IT department is able and willing to offer them. With greater power, however comes greater responsibility—and this reason more than any other is why governance is so critical for any SOA initiative. Without effective governance, user empowerment is simply too dangerous.

So far, so good, but taking this discussion to the higher level of *business* empowerment involves two additional dimensions: the collaboration inherent in business and the focus on business process beyond IT. On one hand, lines of business do not depend on technology "users" per se, but rather on teams of people who don't identify themselves by the technology they use. On the other hand, LOBs also do not identify the process these lines of business undergo in terms of the technology that supports them. On the contrary, IT plays a support role, empowering the business as needed to create, manage, and run the processes as the business sees fit.

It's fitting, therefore, that our discussion of the enterprise as Complex System ends with the users—the human beings that are the point of Agile Architecture in the first place. Our next step is to take a deep breath and look more broadly at the people in our equation—more broadly even than architecture per se. To understand the Agile Architecture Revolution, it's important to get a broad, big-picture view of the role of technology in our lives. For the revolution is not solely about architecture, or technology, or even the Cloud. It's about all of those trends, and more—what we call the *ZapThink 2020 Vision*.

PART TWO

The ZapThink 2020 Vision

The crises of our time, it becomes increasingly clear, are the necessary impetus for the revolution now under way.

—THOMAS KUHN

CHAPTER 6

You Say You Want a Revolution . . .

Remember the heady dot-com days circa 1999? We thought we were reinventing business, forming a New Economy, revolutionizing the essential nature of commerce. In our dreams! By late 2001 the bubble had burst, and what we thought was a new *paradigm* for business—the World Wide Web—turned out to be little more than a new *marketing channel*.

Don't get me wrong—I'm not trying to disparage the power and importance of the Web. After all, the Web, and the Internet in general, have deeply affected so many aspects of business today. It's hard to remember the time when you had to talk to a teller to use a bank or a stockbroker to trade stocks! But we were wrong that the Web was a revolution. It wasn't a paradigm shift. Fundamentally, the rise of the Internet was more *evolutionary* than *revolutionary*.

Not wanting to succumb to this delusion again, ZapThink has long held that the rise of SOA was also more evolutionary than revolutionary. We point to many SOA best practices, including abstracted interfaces, encapsulation, loose coupling, and iterative approaches to dealing with changing requirements, among others—all practices that were already well known and favored before SOA came along. SOA moved the ball forward, to be sure, but didn't fundamentally change the way we tackled distributed computing. It wasn't a true *paradigm shift*, because we didn't have to throw out old ways of thinking and replace them with new ways. Instead, we leveraged the existing approaches while tweaking and improving them.

Today, however, we're willing to go out on a limb and proclaim that we now have a true revolution on our hands. A true paradigm shift in the world of IT is afoot, one that is already forcing us to discard old ways of doing things in favor of new approaches, new technologies, and new ways of thinking—what we call the *ZapThink 2020 Vision*. But we still have to answer the question, why does this decade herald a true revolutionary change, when even the dot-com period (a.k.a. Web 1.0) of 1994–2001 didn't qualify?

The most familiar revolutions, of course, are *political*—the American Revolution, the French Revolution, and so on. The author most responsible for extending this definition beyond the political sphere was Thomas Kuhn, whose 1962 book *The Structure of Scientific Revolutions* discussed the nature of revolutions such as the Copernican Revolution or the one leading to the atomic theory of matter. Such revolutions in the process and theory of science represented periods of dramatic change, requiring intellectuals of the day to discard old ways of thinking and replace them with new ones—often over the course of a generation, as the old guard eventually died off. Kuhn also coined the term *paradigm shift* to refer to such upheaval in ways of thinking. (Yes, if you ever wondered where the notion of paradigm shifts came from, it was Thomas Kuhn who came up with the whole idea.)

Kuhn's book was so influential that his notions of revolutions and paradigm shifts expanded well past the realm of the history of science into virtually every area of human endeavor. His insights, after all, applied to fundamental aspects of human thought and behavior: Human endeavors don't progress evenly and gradually, but rather in fits and starts, and occasionally there's a large upheaval that resets the playing field. But not every change represents a paradigm shift, and not every trend is revolutionary.

How, then, do we know we're truly in a revolution, and not simply another period of evolution like the dot-com or SOA eras? Kuhn points out that, well, it's harder than it sounds. People often don't recognize that a revolution has taken place until well after the fact. It's not like one day somebody wakes up and realizes that the way they were doing things is suddenly obsolete. In fact, the prerevolutionary patterns often persist well into the revolutionary period, even though in retrospect it becomes clear their days were numbered.

Another reason why revolutions are hard to identify while in the midst of them is that the changes are numerous, often sporadic, and typically subtle. When Galileo turned his telescope toward the moons of Jupiter, it's not clear that he realized he was helping to change an entire civilization's worldview. When the Catholic Church forced him to recant his discoveries, the church authorities had no idea they were fighting a losing battle. Only in retrospect can we place these events into the proper context of the Copernican Revolution.

A third impediment to identifying a revolution in progress is the clichéd nature of the terms *revolutionary* and *paradigm shift*. It seems that every technology start-up these days touts their new widgets as being revolutionary paradigm shifts. Hell, it seems that every minor improvement in laundry detergent or automobile oil is revolutionary. It's no wonder we've become jaded about the entire subject. If the marketeers tout every minor improvement as revolutionary then *nothing* is revolutionary.

That is, until a *real* revolution comes along.

If we only spotted one trend (like SOA) or one disruptive change (e.g., the Web replacing tellers and stockbrokers), then we might have a hint of a revolution, but more likely than not, we'd be wrong to apply the term. However, there are simply too many different forces of change impacting IT today, and in turn, impacting business in general to consider such changes to merely be an evolutionary trend. We have Cloud Computing, mobile computing, the threat of cyberwarfare, the rise of social media, the app store model for purchasing software, outsourcing, insourcing, Complex Systems engineering . . . the list goes on and on. Any of these trends taken separately may be considered evolutionary, but put them together and there are strong hints of a paradigm shift in progress.

The second aspect of the ZapThink 2020 Vision that indicates a revolution in progress is the potentially disruptive nature of what we call the *crisis points* of the ZapThink 2020 Vision. We'll talk about the Stuxnet worm that disrupted Iranian power plants, but the next professionally designed cyberattack promises much greater disruption. And though buying enterprise-class apps via your phone is novel, it has yet to put one of the big enterprise app vendors out of business. So, we won't really know just how disruptive this paradigm shift will be until after the fact.

Perhaps the greatest indicator of an ongoing revolution is the evolving perspective on *change*, and the role technology has in supporting it. People are simply getting fed up with inflexible technology. We're sick and tired of legacy that slows down our organizations and sucks up our budgets. The need for greater agility drove the move to SOA, but SOA alone doesn't solve our inflexibility problems, in large part because SOA is part of the old paradigm. What we need is a new paradigm for architecture-driven agility that is inherently different from today's architectural approaches. It's the fact that we're already seeing the shift to this new paradigm that is the primary reason we're calling this point in time a revolution.

The most challenging aspect of identifying a revolution is that it's extraordinarily difficult to do so while it's still in progress. We understand this challenge, and realize that we may be wrong about the whole affair. After all, there are still so many unanswered questions. For example, in 20 years when we look back on this time, what will we call the revolution? We can guess, but there's no way to know what the next big thing will be until it's finally here.

Perhaps we can look back at the last revolution for inspiration—the postwar Information Revolution that heralded the Information Age. Starting with Colossus cracking the Nazi's Enigma codes at Bletchley Park, through the rise of digital, programmable computers to the networked world we have today, no one can disagree that the rise of computing disrupted the precomputer ways of thinking and conducting business, leading to an entirely new context for human endeavor writ large. But no single innovation, no single disruption signaled the revolution. Only in retrospect can we consider all the disruptions together and recognize a true paradigm shift.

We're the first to admit, therefore, that we may be completely wrong about what we call the *Agile Architecture Revolution*. And we may not know how right we are for another 20 years or more. But we *can* say that rethinking how we approach agility will be a critical enabler for organizations over the next 10 years and beyond. Whether Agile Architecture heralds a revolution may be too hard to say with any certainty, but Agile Architecture is undoubtedly here to stay.

Five Supertrends of Enterprise IT

Look closely at any revolution in progress and all you see is chaos, characterized by a seemingly never-ending sequence of crises. Look at the French or Russian Revolutions, for example—no calm transition of power, those. They took years as the political ebbs and flows favored one party and then the other, surrounded by the bloodshed and turmoil of war.

Even revolutions like the Scientific and Information Revolutions experience similar chaos, albeit with less literal blood in the streets. So here we are, in the midst of a supposed Agile Architecture Revolution, doing our best to stand above the fray in order to get a better picture of where we are and where we're going. Our challenge: learn from the turmoil around us, but see through it to the greater trends that should lead us to the next paradigm.

Getting our arms around such turmoil, however, is a daunting task, because there are so many threads to the story: Cloud Computing, mobile technologies, advancements in Enterprise Architecture, even the exhaustion of IPv4 as available IP addresses run out in the next year or two. To help organizations deal with this period of change, ZapThink has fleshed out a conceptual framework we call *ZapThink 2020*, which organizes the important trends that are facing enterprise IT today and over the next several years. The point to this exercise is to work through the interrelationships among the various threads, so that no one concept receives more than its fair share of attention. For example, the buzzword du jour is Cloud, but Cloud is a mix of different capabilities that are mostly old wine in new bottles. How will these different capabilities interrelate with everything else going on in the enterprise IT shop, as all the other stories play out and Cloud loses its luster?

In order to organize all the various stories, capabilities, and trends that play a part in the ZapThink 2020 Vision, we'll begin with five broad organizing principles we call *Supertrends*. Here are the five Supertrends of the ZapThink 2020 Vision for Enterprise IT:

1. **Location Independence.** Narrowly speaking, location independence is a SOA principle, where the underlying physical implementation of a Service is abstracted from the Service itself. This abstraction is also fundamental to the virtualization inherent in Clouds, whether they be public, private, or hybrid. But there's more to this story than

virtualization; mobile presence is also a critical aspect of location independence. Think global buddy list, tied together with your mobile device, your instant messaging, and other indicators of your personal availability. If you can tell people you're available no matter where you are, that's part of the location independence Supertrend as well.

2. **Global Cubicle.** The Internet gave us the Global Village. Take that idea to its logical extreme and you have the Global Cubicle. Any two people anywhere in the world can work together, communicate, and socialize as though they were in the same room, or even the same cubicle. This Supertrend is over 100 years old, as the telephone itself gave us our first glimpse of this capability. But now add the location independence from the previous Supertrend, along with ubiquitous computing (where every device is on the Internet, wired or not), combined with the power of social media to bring people together in new ways. Outsourcing and its natural successor, insourcing, become "any-sourcing" as organizations can now find expertise anywhere. And remember, as Generation Y (today's college kids, more or less) hits the workforce, they will expect and demand a work environment aligned with the Global Cubicle.

   The component trends to this Supertrend include the arrival of Generation Y in the workforce, the increase in ubiquitous computing, the maturation of social media, the continuation of the outsourcing trend, and the rise of the virtual enterprise. From the perspective of the IT manager, this trend suggests that the IT employee of the near future will live anywhere, work anywhere, and use whatever technology is at hand to collaborate, communicate, and get their work done.

   But the perspective of the individual contributor is quite different. Gone are the days that IT workers are little more than cogs in big wheels (wheels made up of legacy technology, no less). Instead, we are members of many communities, covering the continuum from purely personal to entirely career-centric, with no clear distinctions among those communities. Furthermore, the old model of "belonging" to the company we work for where we expect our employer to take care of us is long gone. We are all our own individual contributors with our own individual brands, and sometimes we lend our brand to a large organization.

3. **Democratization of Technology.** How do you buy IT in your organization today? Big vendors, big RFPs, big purchases, high-risk deployments, right? Well, look closer. Is anybody in your organization buying IT via a mobile app store? Or how about provisioning an ad hoc Cloud instance using a personal credit card? Or maybe downloading a free piece of software? This bottom-up acquisition of IT is fast becoming the norm as the subscription-based pricing of SaaS meets

open source meets the app store model. Who'll be left out in the cold? The traditional enterprise app vendors.

4. **Deep Interoperability.** Yes, *this* should work with *that*. That's why we have open standards, after all. If everybody supports Web Services or REST or what have you, then we should have product-to-product interoperability. Unfortunately, today's reality falls far short of the promise of open standards.

   What we really want is for *any* two pieces of software to auto-matically negotiate with each other to establish seamless interoperability. We have the technology now to achieve this goal, but the only way vendors will put in the effort to make deep interoperability a reality is if we stop buying software that doesn't offer this capability.

5. **Complex Systems Engineering.** To achieve true agility, organiza-tions must rethink integration entirely. *Governance* now becomes the new mantra instead of integration. Chief Information Officers become Chief Governance Officers. Static Enterprise Architecture frame-works give way to continuous business transformation best practices. Business process management finally leaves the realm of the integra-tion vendors (who never got it right anyway), as organizations begin truly managing their business processes in order to achieve their goals in the context of an ever-changing business environment.

ZapThink 2020 is a multidimensional vision for change, and the five Supertrends are but one dimension. We'll also discuss *crisis points* that promise sudden, transformative change. Also note that SOA and Cloud as well as mobile technologies are not Supertrends in and of themselves, but they weave their way across the five we're discussing here. And perhaps most importantly, the business of IT is a critical part of the ZapThink 2020 story, as how organizations spend money on IT will continue to undergo radical change over the next 10 years. And at the center of ZapThink 2020? *Continuous business transformation*.

Continuous Business Transformation: At the Center of ZapThink 2020

It was the ancient Greek pre-Socratic philosopher Heraclitus who famously said, "You cannot step twice into the same river," indicating that *change itself* is the central principle of the universe. For those of us whose universe is the enterprise, change is also the central principle of our organizations. The forces of change impacting the business are the underlying motivations for Agile Architecture, of course. Business agility, after all, means responding to change and leveraging change for competitive advantage. If it weren't for the constant force of change, all the hard work that goes into building an Agile Architecture wouldn't be worth the time and effort.

Even though the permanence of change drives how we run our organizations, it nevertheless goes against our human nature. People prefer stability. We innately feel that change is temporary, that the point of change is to reach the end of it, when we can finally settle down and enjoy the new state of affairs that results when the change is finally complete. Unfortunately, this new state of affairs is largely an illusion, especially when we're talking about the large organizations we call enterprises. Simply put, there is no such thing as an end state, some kind of nirvana where whatever was changing has finished its transformation.

We find the mistaken belief that there is a stable end state both in business and IT, and perhaps most surprisingly, in the practice of Enterprise Architecture (EA). In each of these realms, if you are faced with a challenge, you may analyze your "as-is" state and your "to-be" state, in order to come up with a plan to move from "as-is" to "to-be." In fact, this end state illusion is core to the definition of EA, according to the Enterprise Architecture Center of Excellence (EACOE):

> Enterprise Architecture is explicitly describing an organization through a set of independent, non-redundant artifacts, defining how these artifacts interrelate with each other, and developing a set of prioritized, aligned initiatives and road maps to understand the organization, communicate this understanding to stakeholders, and move the organization forward to its desired state.

But if business change is constant, *there is no desired state*, and thus this definition is inherently flawed. What, then, is the proper goal for EA? Essentially, EA should move the organization to greater levels of business agility, where being agile is not an end state *per se*, but rather allows for the fact that change is constant, and it is the role of EA to help organizations better deal with that fact, and use it to their advantage.

So whereas the traditional definition of EA involves transformation to a desired state, continuous business transformation forms the core of the ZapThink 2020 Vision. You can think of continuous business transformation as a goal, but the word *goal* connotes an end state, so the word is misleading. Instead, we are looking to move from the current state of inflexibility to an environment where the business is in a continual state of reinvention, responding to forces of change as efficiently as possible, and also introducing change in the form of innovation in order to achieve ongoing strategic advantage. Perhaps a better word is *attractor*, in the Complex Systems sense.

By saying there's no end state we don't mean to imply that there is no best practice approach to continuous business transformation. On the contrary, many executives will continue to struggle with change, but there will be a few who reinvent EA as a best practice enabler of agility, and thus successfully transform their organizations.

But even the word *transformation* presents issues, as we're talking about two levels of transformation. The transition from "as-is" to "to-be," from the screwed-up state we're in now to the fixed, nirvana state of the future is the false transformation we are revealing as specious. Instead, ZapThink is helping organizations transform from a traditional goal-focused mode of thinking to a continuous business transformation mode of thinking—a higher level of transformation that leads to true business agility.

Continuous business transformation drives the entire ZapThink 2020 Vision, including each of the five Supertrends. In fact, the entire point of ZapThink 2020 is to help organizations deal with change more intelligently. There's no question that change is pervasive. What remains to be determined is how well organizations can ride the wave.

Where's Our Deep Interoperability?

An essential enabler of continuous business transformation in the ZapThink 2020 Vision is *Deep Interoperability*, and the starting point for Deep Interoperability is open standards. We like to say that open standards are the bumps on the Legos. The whole point to standards like those in the Web Services family is to provide seamless interoperability between products that support those standards. After all, what fun would Legos be if the bumps were all different sizes? Unfortunately, standards alone never guaranteed interoperability.

So, where's our seamless interoperability? Although the Web Services standards were an important step in the long road to true interoperability, the static interfaces that these standards specify are only part of the story. Contracted interfaces alone can never guarantee interoperability long term.

The story, of course, is one of *change*. The Lego metaphor breaks down, because the bumps have never needed to change. Today's Legos interoperate with Legos from 50 years ago, because our requirements for the plastic blocks are essentially the same as they were back then. But in the world of IT, change is constant, as it is for the business requirements that drive IT. Any fixed set of standards, no matter how robust and detailed, will never solve the interoperability problem for long.

Lest we forget, this story is not a new one. Remember the analog modem market from the 1980s and 1990s? 300-baud acoustic couplers gave way to

1200 baud, then 2400, on up to 56K before newer technologies like ADSL took over. But in the heyday of the analog modem, each box supported multiple standard protocols, and would attempt to negotiate with the modem on the other end of the line using the fastest protocol it knew. If that didn't work, each modem tried the next slower one, and the next, until they were able to establish a connection.

We need the same kind of process now with general product-to-product interoperability, only where the modem interaction story was single dimensional, now we're working in multiple dimensions. As a result, the "modem negotiation" model of interoperability is now orders of magnitude more complex.

Eventually, however, the vendors will figure it out. At that point we will have what we call *Deep Interoperability*. The Deep Interoperability Supertrend suggests that products actively change how they seek to interoperate until they're successful. Modem negotiation on steroids.

Imagine: You buy a new enterprise IT product. You hook it to the network and turn it on. It automatically negotiates with everything else in your environment until it's fully integrated. And when something changes, it negotiates again as needed.

Are vendors working on Deep Interoperability now? It's not clear. Unfortunately, they're not particularly motivated to get interoperability right. After all, proprietary interfaces lead to customer lock-in, and all vendors want that.

So maybe that's why Web Services standards never provided seamless interoperability. Vendors were driving the standards efforts all along, of course. They love paying lip service to standard interfaces, because customers demand them. But if such standards *really* worked—if products *truly* interoperated, in a way that stood the test of time—then you could easily replace a poorer product with a better one.

And what vendor today wants that?

The Crisis Points of the ZapThink 2020 Vision

As Thomas Kuhn attests in the quote at the beginning of Part Two, *crises* characterize revolutions. Fortunately, ZapThink 2020 is as much about risk mitigation as it is about strategic benefit. Every element of ZapThink 2020 is a problem as well as an opportunity. Nowhere is this focus on risk mitigation greater than with ZapThink 2020's six crisis points. Crises, after all, both drive and constitute paradigm shifts. And try as we might, we can't avoid them. We can only live through them, and learn from them.

Of course, life in general, as well as business in particular, are both filled with risks, and a large part of any executive's job description is dealing with everyday crises. A crisis point, however, goes beyond everyday, garden-variety firefighting. To be a crisis point, the underlying issue must both be potentially game changing as well as largely unexpected. The element of surprise is what makes each crisis point especially dangerous—not that the crisis itself is necessarily a surprise, but rather just how transformative the event promises to be.

Here then are ZapThink 2020's seven crisis points, why they're surprising, and why they're game changing:

1. **Collapse of enterprise IT.** Enterprises that aren't in the IT business stop doing their own IT, and furthermore, move their outsourced IT off premise. Why is it that so many enterprises today handle their own IT, and in particular, write their own software? They use office furniture, but nobody would think of manufacturing their own, except of course if you're in the office furniture manufacturing business. The game-changing nature of this crisis point is obvious, but what's surprising will be just how fast enterprises rush to offload their entire IT organizations once it becomes clear that the first to do so have achieved substantial benefits from this move.

2. **IPv4 exhaustion.** Every techie knows that we're running out of IP addresses, because the IPv4 address space only provides for about 4.3 billion IP addresses, and they've all been assigned. IPv6 is around the corner, but very little of our Internet infrastructure supports IPv6 at this time. The surprise here is what is happening now that we've run out of addresses: The secondary market for IP addresses is exploding. As it turns out, a long time ago the Internet Assigned Numbers Authority (IANA) assigned most IP addresses to a select group of Class-A holders, who each got a block of about 16.8 million addresses. Companies like Ford, Eli Lilly, and Halliburton all ended up with one of these blocks. How much money do you think they can make selling them now that the unassigned ones are all gone?

3. **Fall of frameworks.** Is your chief Enterprise Architect your CEO's most trusted, important advisor? No? Well, why not? After all, EA is all about organizing the business to achieve its strategic goals in the best way we know how, and the EA is supposed to know how. The problem is most EAs are bogged down in the details, spending time with various frameworks and other artifacts, to the point where the value they provide to their organizations is unclear, at least to the C-level. In large part the frameworks are to blame—Zachman Framework, TOGAF, the Department of Defense Architecture Framework (DoDAF), to name a few. For many organizations, these frameworks are little more than pointless exercises in organizing terminology that leads to checklist architectures. At this crisis point executives get fed

up, scrap their current EA efforts, and bring in an entirely new way of thinking about Enterprise Architecture.

4. **Cyberwar.** Yes, most risks facing IT shops today are security related. Not a day goes by without another virus or Windows vulnerability coming to light. But what happens when there is a concerted, professional, widespread, expert attack on some key part of our global IT infrastructure? It's not a matter of *if*, it's a matter of *when*. The surprise here will be just how effective such an attack can be, and perhaps how poor the response is, depending on the target. Will terrorists take down the Internet? Maybe just the DNS infrastructure? Or will this battle be between corporations? Regardless, the world post-cyberwar will never be the same.

5. **Arrival of Generation Y.** These are the kids who are currently in college, more or less. Not only is this generation the "post–e-mail" generation, they have grown up with social media. When they hit the workforce they will hardly tolerate the archaic approach to IT we have today. Sure, some will change to fit the current system, but enterprises who capitalize on this generation's new perspective on IT will obtain a strategic advantage. We saw this generational effect when Generation X hit the workforce around the turn of the century—a cadre of young adults who weren't familiar with a world without the Web. That generation was instrumental in shifting the Web from a fad into an integral part of how we do business today. Expect the same from Generation Y and social media.

6. **Big Data explosion.** As the quantity and complexity of available information exceeds our ability to deal with such information, we'll need to take a new approach to governance. But although an essential part of dealing with the Big Data Explosion Crisis Point is a move to governance-driven Complex Systems, we place this crisis point in the Democratization of Technology Supertrend. The shift in thinking will be away from the more-is-better, store-and-analyze school of data management to a much greater focus on filtering and curating information. We'll place increasingly greater emphasis on small quantities of information by ensuring that information is optimally valuable.

7. **Enterprise application crash.** The days of Big ERP are numbered—as well as those of Big CRM and Big SCM and . . . well, all the big enterprise apps. These lumbering monstrosities are cumbersome, expensive, inflexible, and filled at their core with ancient spaghetti code. There's got to be a better way to run an enterprise. And fortunately, there is. Once enterprises figure this out, one or more of the big enterprise app vendors will be caught by surprise and go out of business. Will it be your vendor?

We can't tell you specifically when each of these crisis points will come to pass, or precisely how they will manifest. What we can say with a good amount of certainty, however, is that you should be prepared for them. If one or another proves to be less problematic or urgent than feared, then we can all breathe a sigh of relief. But should one come to pass, then the organizations who have suitably prepared for it will not only be able to survive, but will be able to take advantage of the fact that their competition was not so well equipped.

Big Data Explosion and the Christmas Day Bomber

The real challenge with preparing for such crisis points is in understanding their context. None of them happens in isolation; rather, they are all inter-related with other issues and the broader Supertrends that they are a part of. Remember the airplane bombing attempt on Christmas Day, 2009? Amid the posturing and recriminations following this ill-fated terrorist attack, the underlying cause of the intelligence breach had gone all but unnoticed. How is it that the global post-9/11 antiterrorist machine could miss a lone Nigerian with explosives in his underwear? After all, chatter included reference to "the Nigerian"; his own father gave warning; he was on a terrorist watch list; and he purchased a one-way ticket to Detroit, paid cash, and checked no luggage. You'd think any one of these bits of information would set off alarms, and the fact that the intelligence community missed the lot is a sign of sheer incompetence, right?

Not so fast. Such a conclusion is actually fallacious. The missing piece of the puzzle is the fact that there are hundreds of thousands of monthly air travelers, and millions of weekly messages constitute the chatter the intelli-gence community routinely follows. And that watch list? Hundreds of thou-sands of names, to be sure. Furthermore, the quantity of information that agents must follow is increasing at an exponential rate. So, though it seems in retrospect that agents missed a huge red flag, in actuality there was so much noise that even the combination of warnings taken together was lost in a sea of noise. A dozen red flags, yes, but could you discern a dozen red grains of sand on a beach?

The true reason behind the intelligence breach is far more subtle than simple incompetence, and furthermore, the solution is just as difficult to discern. The most interesting part of this discussion from ZapThink's per-spective, naturally, is the implication for enterprise IT. The global intelligence community is but one enterprise among many dealing with exponentially increasing quantities and complexity of information. All other enterprises, in the private as well as public sector, face similar challenges: As Moore's Law and its corollaries proceed on their inexorable path, what happens when the human ability to deal with the resulting information overload falls short? How can you help your organization keep from getting lost in the noise of Big Data?

Strictly speaking, Moore's Law states that the number of transistors that current technology can cram onto a chip of a given size will increase exponentially over time. But the transistors on a chip are really only the tip of the iceberg; along with processing power we have exponential growth in hard drive capacity, network speed, and other related measures—what we're calling corollaries to Moore's Law. And of course, there's also the all-important corollary to Murphy's Law that states that the quantity of information available will naturally expand to fill all available space.

Anybody who remembers the wheat and chessboard problem knows that this explosion of information will lead to problems down the road. IT vendors, of course, have long seen this trend as a huge opportunity, and have risen to the occasion with tools to help organizations manage the burgeoning quantity of information. What vendors cannot do, however, is improve how *people* deal with this problem.

Fundamentally, human capabilities at best grow linearly. Our brains, after all, are not subject to Moore's Law, and even so, enterprises depend far more on the interactions among people than on the contributions of individuals taken separately. Though the number of transistors may double every 18 months, our management, analysis, and other communication skills will only see gradual improvements at best.

This disconnect leads to what ZapThink calls the Big Data Crisis Point, as illustrated in Figure 6.1.

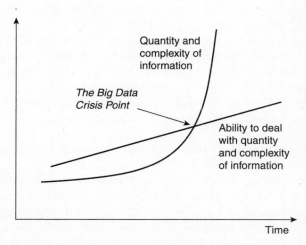

Figure 6.1   The Big Data Crisis Point

Figure 6.1 illustrates the fact that although the quantity and complexity of information in any enterprise grows exponentially, the human ability to deal with that information at best grows linearly. No matter where you put the two curves, eventually one overtakes the other at the Big Data Crisis Point: When human activities are unable to deal with the quantity and complexity of information available.

Unfortunately, no technology can solve this problem, because technology only affects the exponential curve. I'm sure today's intelligence agents have state-of-the-art analysis tools, because after all, if they don't have them, then who does? But the bomber was still able to get on the plane. Furthermore, neither is the solution to this problem a purely human one. We'd clearly be fooling ourselves to think that if only we worked harder or smarter, we might be able to keep up. Equally foolish would be the assumption that we might be able to slow down the exponential growth of information. Like it or not, this curve is an inexorable juggernaut.

Agile Architecture addresses this problem because of its special focus on governance. Neither technology nor human change will solve the Big Data problem, but a better approach to formalizing the interactions between people and technology gives us a path to the solution. In practice, the governance team sorts the policies within scope of the current project into those policies that are best handled by human interactions and those policies that lend themselves to automation.

The question then becomes how the governance team deals with policies; in other words, what are their meta-policies? Working through the organization's policies for dealing with governance, and automating *those* policies, gives the organization a *meta-policy feedback loop* approach to leveraging the power of technology to improve governance overall.

How this meta-policy feedback loop might help intelligence agents catch the next terrorist provides a simple illustration of how any enterprise might approach their own information explosion challenges. First, how do agents deal with information today? Basically, they have an information challenge, they implement tools to address that challenge, and they have policies for how to use those tools, as the following expression illustrates:

Information problem → tools → policies for using tools → governance

Now, the challenge with the previous expression is that it's static; it doesn't take into account the fact that the information problem explodes exponentially, whereas governance best practices grow linearly. As a result, eventually the quantity of information overwhelms the capabilities of the tools, leading to failures like the explosives in the underwear. Instead, here's how the expression should work:

Information problem → tools → policies for using tools → meta-policies for dealing with governance → next-generation governance tools → best practice approach for dealing with information problem over time

Essentially, the crisis point requires a new level of interaction between human activity and technology capability: a technology-enabled governance feedback loop that promises to enable any enterprise to deal with the information explosion, regardless of whether you're catching terrorists or pleasing shareholders.

Okay, so just how *does* Agile Architecture fit into this story? Remember that architecture consists of a set of best practices for organizing and leveraging IT resources to meet business needs, and the act of applying and enforcing such practices is what we mean by governance. Furthermore, Agile Architecture provides a best-practice approach for implementing governance, not just for IT, but for the organization as a whole.

In essence, Agile Architecture leads to a more formal approach to governance, where organizations are able to leverage technology to improve the creation, communication, and enforcement of policies across the board, including those policies that deal with how to automate such governance processes. In the intelligence example, Agile Architecture might help agents leverage technology to identify suspicious patterns more effectively by allowing them to craft increasingly sophisticated intelligence policies. In the general case, such architecture can lead to more effective management decision making across large organizations.

Stuxnet and Wikileaks: Harbingers of Cyberwar

Remember Stuxnet, the computer worm that attacked Iranian industrial equipment in June 2010? The details about this unprecedented attack were chilling. Leveraging a remarkable four zero-day Windows bugs, Stuxnet targeted the control systems in specific industrial equipment, apparently as a way to target Iran's nuclear power infrastructure. This worm was so sophisticated it was in a class by itself. No product of a lone, geeky Xtr3m H4x0r (that's "extreme hacker" to the n00bs in the room), indications were that Stuxnet was the product of a professional, well-funded covert organization within the U.S. intelligence community, perhaps with help from Israel.

James Bond meets William Gibson? Or perhaps Spielberg's *Munich* for the twenty-first century? On the contrary, the Stuxnet story is not a typical spy story set in a post-9/11 world. No, Stuxnet is a warning call, not just for the global political sphere, but for private enterprises as well: the warning call of the *Cyberwar Crisis Point*.

Lest you think that Stuxnet isn't relevant to the day-to-day operations in your own IT department, let's present several questions to mull over. Answer these questions as truthfully as you can.

> Q: Is the expertise that Stuxnet required so difficult to assemble that it's unlikely any other covert organization would be able to create another attack of the same or greater level of sophistication?
>
> A: Not on your life. Now that we know such sophistication is possible, anybody with a sufficient bankroll could gather the expertise needed to create a similar attack—or a better one.
>
> Q: Does the fact that Stuxnet targeted a specific type of industrial control system mean that my mission-critical applications aren't likely to be a target?
>
> A: If anything, Stuxnet's apparent political motivation is more an exception than the norm, as money wasn't the goal of the attack. However, banking systems, credit card processing systems, and other technologies that deal directly with money are far more obvious and lucrative targets.
>
> Q: Stuxnet's use of four zero-day Windows attacks was unprecedented. Is it likely then that another attack that leverages multiple zero-day attacks would be impossible?
>
> A: We're talking about Windows here, right?
>
> Q: Fair enough. That's why our critical infrastructure is Windows-free. Is our Unix/Linux/Mainframe/Apple/"anything else not Microsoft" technology immune to sophisticated attacks like Stuxnet?
>
> A: Remember, Stuxnet leveraged Windows but targeted proprietary SCADA software from Siemens, which means that the Stuxnet team had to possess systems that ran that software in order to develop and test the worm. Getting a copy of Unix or even a mainframe is quite a bit easier.
>
> Q: Now that Stuxnet has been neutralized, are the anti-malware organizations able to prevent attacks of similar levels of sophistication?
>
> A: Perhaps to some extent, but who's to say the next attack won't be even more sophisticated?

The bottom line: There's no reason to believe Stuxnet is unique, either in its sophistication or its target. The global cyberwar has just reached a new level, so you had better be prepared. In fact, even for those enterprises who take Stuxnet-type threats seriously, there is still the question as to what they should do better or differently now that they know that Stuxnet-type attacks are feasible. After all, you're already doing everything practical to secure your systems and networks, right? What else should you do?

There is no easy answer, of course, but the ZapThink 2020 Vision helps organizations address such issues within the context of all the forces of change impacting organizations today. In the ZapThink 2020 context, cyberwar (or the threat of cyberwar) drives a realignment of IT governance initiatives, repositioning governance as the primary mechanism for ensuring that IT meets changing business needs, while conforming to dynamic policies that are important to the organization. This shift away from today's integration-centric IT environments to governance-centric approaches is all part of the Complex Systems Engineering Supertrend.

The threat of cyberwar is not a specific risk, but rather the realization that there is an always-changing set of risks facing the enterprise. Taking the "find a vulnerability fix a vulnerability" approach, though still necessary, becomes only one facet of a more dynamic approach to security. In other words, security must leverage the business agility benefit that Complex Systems provide where traditional, integration-centric systems cannot.

Cyberwar is a catchy term to say the least, but don't let its science fiction flavor fool you. The stakes are as high as with any war, even though there are fundamental differences between cyberwar and conventional warfare. First and foremost, it can be difficult to identify the participants, either the aggressor or the target. Secondly, the participants are more likely to be corporations than governments (even though Stuxnet appears to be government related). And finally, the weapons are inherently dynamic. In many cases, the aggressor knows that they can only use a particular weapon once, so building defenses against all known weapons is inherently inadequate.

Even with Stuxnet's obvious sophistication, it appears that it was a particular aggressor with a specific target. There is no reason to expect that pattern to be generally true. You might find your organization is a target, not because of any specific desire on the part of the aggressor, but simply because you were caught in the crossfire of a shotgun attack.

Just as firms plan for server outages and deployment problems, now every firm must have a contingency plan to deal with the potential outage of their most important online suppliers. If cyberwar seemed to be a benign or irrelevant threat, you might soon experience firsthand why you can no longer afford to ignore the potential crisis that cyberwarfare can have on your organization.

Even if you're not directly targeted in a cyberwar, you can still be dramatically impacted by the skirmishes. In fact, it's the collateral damage of high-likelihood attacks on critical infrastructure that pose much more threat to your business than the relatively less-likely direct attacks on your business. Imagine that you are a small manufacturing business in Costa Rica. Costa Rica is so peaceful that it doesn't even maintain a standing army, and the business is so small and inconsequential to the rest of the world that you barely get any traffic to your site at all, let alone a large enough quantity that downtime would even be noticeable.

You may think you're immune to cyberwarfare, but you're wrong. Your company uses Google for mail, a specialty Software-as-a-Service (SaaS) supplier for its business-to-business (B2B) network that just happens to use Amazon's Cloud Computing infrastructure, and processes its online payments with an Internet-based credit card gateway. The first thing that your company notices is that you can't process payments because the credit card processor is under siege. Then, your B2B network goes down because Amazon is under attack. Finally, you can't even send requests for support to either the card processor or the B2B network because Gmail is down due to a distributed denial of service (DDoS) attack. At this point, your company is effectively knocked off the Net from a business standpoint, even if your Web site is up and operational.

If you think this is all a theory, you're wrong. Remember Wikileaks? In mid-2010, a crowdsourced group of pro-Wikileaks "hacktivists" attacked all the infrastructure providers above, with the exception of Google . . . for now. Even though most of the targeted firms emerged from these attacks relatively unscathed, the fact that some online providers, most notably PayPal and MasterCard, were down for even a short amount of time should leave most IT organizations shaking in their boots. Post Finance, a Swiss bank that shut off Wikileaks funding, was down for over 33 hours.

What if next time these attacks are more successful? How many hours can you afford to be disconnected as collateral damage in a cyberwar? You say you have no contingency plans to deal with direct or consequential damage from malicious attacks? Then you are due for a Cyberwar Crisis Point. It's just a matter of time. Deal with it now or deal with it later, but you *will* have to deal with it.

The more interconnected and dependent on third parties you are for your IT capabilities, the more threatened you will be by these attacks. Disconnecting yourself from your suppliers and the Internet is not an option these days. This means that you must find additional suppliers that themselves depend on different infrastructure to be able to continue your business operations if your current supplier gets knocked off the Net.

You need to not only source backup SaaS and Cloud suppliers, but also alternate modes of communication and payment if you want to be fully secure. Depend on Google for mail? That's fine, just set up a backup e-mail provider. Depend on a single DNS provider? Then set up a secondary DNS source. Require Amazon's Cloud for your primary operations? Then set up a secondary Cloud supplier. You can see where this advice is going.

Having backup plans introduces additional complexity that must be tested, but it doesn't necessarily add a lot of extra cost. Most Cloud providers charge on an as-you-go basis, so having just-in-case capability should not involve double the cost of your existing supplier. The additional cost of "just in case" is your insurance premium against the potential future losses your business might face if your sole infrastructure suppliers become unavailable.

An alternative to leveraging an ecosystem of service providers is to bring all your computing infrastructure in house. However, for most companies, bringing their most critical infrastructure in house is not really an option. Though liability and economics concerns might demand that the most critical suppliers not depend on third parties for most of their critical infrastructure, the argument of taking on the full burden of outsourced infrastructure will most likely bankrupt you in the short term to deal with an unforeseeable problem in the long term.

Cyberwarfare, or even privacy, governance, and security concerns, are no reason to throw out the Cloud Computing baby with the high-risk bathwater. You simply need to actively plan for disruption and have mitigation plans in place that you regularly test. If you can't handle the downtime, then you at least need to degrade gracefully. Find ways to deal with the potential outages of your most critical suppliers with failover plans that involve using people or non-IT processes. Even your worst-case failover should provide some degree of confidence to deal with unknown threats.

If you think the cyberwar threat, Stuxnet, and Wikileaks are isolated incidents that will soon come to an end, we have bad news for you—we're just at the beginning. What's to stop foreign crime syndicates from leveraging this new approach to bring large networks and companies to their knees? What about anarchist online mobs that seek disruption for fun? Indeed, the decentralized nature of these sorts of attacks leaves every company and network a potential threat. The fact that any disgruntled group could crowdsource an attack for any reason should be a major concern. It could be something as innocuous as dislike of a new product. There's just no telling. As such, you should find ways to prepare for the unpredictable.

Contingency planning is essential for dealing with outages that cyberwarfare can cause to organizations, regardless of whether or not they are the target of the attack or simply collateral damage. Attacks on Visa, MasterCard, and Amazon.com over the WikiLeaks brouhaha hammered this point home. But collateral damage or direct target, there is still a broad misperception that such attacks are always centrally planned and coordinated. We are just not accustomed to the possibility that there might be a large-scale attack with no central instigator.

But if we combine the Cyberwar Crisis Point with the social media trend—both elements of the ZapThink 2020 Vision—then chilling, yet fascinating conclusions emerge. Here is a recipe for cyberwarfare in today's social media world. The social media story begins with crowdsourcing. But even crowdsourcing depends on a single instigator, who outsources tasks to a social network. Crowdsourced DDoS attacks are bad enough, but they are still a traditional form of attack in the sense that there is a central perpetrator.

Next up is viral communication processes, whose best-known example is viral marketing. Where viral marketing uses social networks to spread word-of-mouth information about a product or service, the same approach can spread nonmarketing information as well. The essence of a viral process is its self-replicating nature; that is, when somebody receives a particular message, the message motivates that person to pass along the message to several other people.

Combine crowdsourcing and viral communication with the hacker underground—which is actually not particularly far underground. The WikiLeaks-motivated attacks leveraged a hacker tool called the *Low Orbit Ion Cannon* (LOIC). Google this term to find an entrance to the underground, but beware the goofy terminology and occasional booby traps as you explore. What you'll find is an entire subculture with tools that turn DDoS attacks into child's play.

Now add Twitter. Think of cyberwarfare as the planting of bombs and Twitter as the fuses. Coordinating attacks and avoiding countermeasures are as simple as following and tweeting. Next, mix in Ubiquitous Computing (also part of ZapThink 2020). We're not talking about computers in the traditional sense any more. Any device with an IP address can either be part of the attack or part of the target. Mobile phones, yes, but refrigerators, electric meters, automobiles, security cameras . . . virtually anything can be on the Internet these days.

Finally, place this whole mess into the context of the wisdom—or sheer foolishness—of crowds. If you've changed your Facebook profile image to support a cause you know what I mean. Why did you do that? What purpose did it serve? Answers: because other people were doing it, and, well, not really clear on the purpose, are we? So, what if it's just as easy to participate in a DDoS attack against some organization or other who has offended you or your buddies in some way? Knocking a corporation or a government off the Internet can be as easy as making Bugs Bunny your Facebook picture.

Contingency planning through redundancy is only the starting point to protecting yourself from decentralized, viral cyberattacks. The long-term answer requires dynamic approaches to policy enforcement that leverage the same fundamental principles that drive such attacks in the first place; in other words, *Agile Architecture–driven governance*.

Such governance does more than protect organizations from attacks. It is actually an approach that keeps organizations agile over time, even as the complexity of their systems explodes. It won't be easy, but organizations who implement such approaches will achieve lowered risk and increased strategic advantage. On the other hand, companies who are unable to implement such approaches compound their risks dramatically.

Finally, cyberwar is likely to be asymmetric, where the target is unlikely to mount a cyberattack against the aggressor, or at least, a retaliatory response would be quite different from the original attack. In this way cyberwar follows the pattern of terrorism, where a small group of fanatics attacks much larger organizations than their own, and the aggressors are generally immune to similar counterattacks.

Getting ahead of the problem, therefore, is quite difficult, just as it is with terrorism. If you stick with traditional security approaches, expect the next 10 years to be filled with surprise attacks, difficult remediation, frantic adjustments of security protocols, followed once again by surprise attacks. The only way to get out of this vicious cycle is to think differently about how to deal with this inherently dynamic and unpredictable set of challenges and take an Agile Architecture approach instead.

Cybersecurity the Agile Architecture Way

Identity theft, password breaches, viruses and worms, phishing attacks, Stuxnet—the more we rely on technology in our increasingly connected world, the greater the risk that we'll be hacked. Even worse, it seems that the rate at which hacking stories come across the wire is actually *increasing*, in spite of all the hard work at all the various security organizations, both commercial and governmental. The frightening truth is, perhaps the hackers are actually *winning*.

The root cause of our vulnerability, of course, is the Internet itself. When the essential elements of the Internet first rolled out—Transmission Control Protocol/Internet Protocol (TCP/IP), Hypertext Transfer Protocol (HTTP), and Domain Name Service (DNS), to name the most flagrant offenders—no one had any idea how important security would become or just how flawed these enabling technologies were when it came to protecting ourselves from increasingly dedicated and persistent malefactors. Today, that horse has long since left the barn. Maybe we can close the door, sure, but it might not matter anymore.

But let's not lose perspective: We've been using the Internet commercially for less than 20 years. An eternity in what we innocently called Internet Time back in the day, but nevertheless, a mere eyeblink in the course of human history. Better to take the long view. Extrapolating today's trends, can we gain any insight into what the future will hold?

Our crystal ball reveals three possible scenarios. The first: *Cyberpunk*. Hackers continue to gain the upper hand, outstripping any efforts to combat them. By 2100 hackers run the world, which has devolved into feudal tribes of hacker communities battling each other for the remaining scraps of civilization.

The second scenario: *Star Trek*. The forces of order and rationality overcome those of anarchy and evil, and as a result, we have no qualms about trusting our computers with our lives. Computer viruses may still appear, but we can take care of them routinely in less than 52 minutes.

Finally, scenario number three: *More of the same*. Hackers continue to become increasingly sophisticated in their attacks, but the forces fighting them do so as well. The advantage shifts back and forth as new attack vectors rapidly appear and are dealt with equally rapidly.

More of the same may appear to be the most likely scenario, as it lacks the science fiction overtones of the other two. In reality, however, it's the least stable of the three, because it assumes an ongoing balance between hackers and their nemeses—an unlikely situation. The pessimists among us point to *Cyberpunk* as the inevitable course of events. But what we really want, of course, is to steer from more of the same toward *Star Trek*. After all, who wouldn't want our grandchildren to live in the *Star Trek* universe?

Unfortunately, it seems that today's Software Security Assurance is heading toward the *Cyberpunk* scenario. *Software Security Assurance* (SSA) is the process of ensuring that the software we build has adequate security, and is an aspect of *Information Assurance* (IA). SSA involves analysis, review, and testing steps that seek to identify potential weaknesses so that the software development teams can lower the risk of potential security breaches to acceptable levels. Fundamentally, SSA describes the best ways we know to build unhackable systems.

The problem is, it's not good enough. And furthermore, it's dropping further and further behind. After all, if SSA actually *worked*, we wouldn't have to worry about worms and breaches and the rest. Hello, *Cyberpunk*!

The problem with traditional SSA is that fundamentally it follows a traditional systems approach. In other words, divide and conquer: Break up an arbitrarily complicated system into its component elements, analyze the security risks inherent in each component, and take steps to ensure that those risks are very low—where we define "very low" in terms of our acceptable risk profile.

There are two core problems with the divide and conquer approach to SSA. The first is what we call the *lottery fallacy*. If you want to run a lottery with a large jackpot, you want to make sure the chance of any ticket winning is very small. And sure enough, the chance of *your* lottery ticket being a jackpot winner is smaller than your chance of being hit by lightning—*twice*. But the chance we'll have to give away the jackpot is still quite high—and the larger the jackpot, the greater the chance we'll have to give it away.

Dividing up a complicated system into pieces and lowering the chance of hacking each piece is tantamount to selling lottery tickets—except that hackers are smart enough to figure out how to buy millions of them at a discount. In other words, there's a really good chance that any valuable target will be hacked no matter how good your SSA is. Yes, the recipe for our *Cyberpunk* scenario.

Agile Architecture, however, is the secret to the *Star Trek* scenario. In the cybersecurity context, we want to move away from traditional SSA to building systems that can deal with future attacks (even though we don't know what they are yet), and furthermore, enable us to take the initiative to prevent future attacks from occurring in the first place. A tall order to be sure, but not quite the science fiction scenario it might sound like.

There are signs that we've been making progress in both areas. (We say "there are signs" because we suspect much of the work in this area is secret, so even if we knew about it we couldn't tell you.) The first area—dealing with unknown future attacks—is essentially the *zero-day* problem. How do we protect our systems from previously unknown attacks, during the window of vulnerability that doesn't close until we develop a traditional countermeasure? Many approaches to zero-day protection already exist, but they tend to address *known* types of attacks like buffer overflows and the like. In other words, such protection techniques will only work until a hacker comes up with a new type of attack—an example of the back and forth we call the *more of the same* scenario.

The second area—preventing future attacks—is more challenging, but also more interesting. One example is the HoneyMonkey project out of Microsoft Research. Where a *Honeypot* is a passive approach—essentially setting a trap for hackers—a *HoneyMonkey* essentially surfs the Web looking for trouble. The idea is to identify Web sites that install malware before a user happens across them with their browser.

It's not clear whether the HoneyMonkey project led to commercially available security tools, but in any case, it was only a simplistic example of a tool that could actively seek out and prevent potential attacks. But let's put our sci-fi hats back on and extrapolate. How will we ever get to the *Star Trek* scenario unless we take the active prevention approach?

Targeting *Star Trek* is all well and good, but we need to separate fiction from reality if we're ever going to beat the hackers (*Heisenberg compensator*, anyone?). So, let's move away from science fiction into the realm of biology. After all, biological systems are well-known Complex Systems in their own right. How, then, do biological systems like you and me fight off infections?

At the risk of oversimplifying what are admittedly extraordinarily complicated processes, our bodies have three primary mechanisms for preventing infections. The first is our skin. Simply having a tough barrier keeps out many attack vectors. You might think of skin as analogous to traditional SSA: necessary but not sufficient.

The second mechanism, of course, is our immune system. It's what differentiates a healthy body from a few hundred pounds of rotting meat.

What we need to beat the hackers at their own game is an immune system for our software.

But even immune systems aren't perfect. And this biological metaphor begs the question: How do we architect and build an immune system for our software anyway? Again with the biological analogy: How did we develop our immune systems? Through millennia of natural selection, individuals who succumb more easily to infection tend to die off, whereas those with better ways of fighting off the attackers survive to propagate. Rinse and repeat for, oh, hundreds of millions of years, and presto! The human immune system is the result.

The cybersecurity challenge, therefore, boils down to bringing natural selection principles into our security software development processes. The hackers are diverse, persistent, and imaginative. To fight them, our software must be agile, self-innovating, and able to evolve. The devil, of course, is in the details.

Unfortunately, this book is hardly long enough to lay out a revolutionary approach to architecting better security software even if we had all the answers, which we obviously do not. But the point of this section isn't to solve all our cybersecurity challenges. Rather, we're trying to make the case that traditional architectural approaches, including those of Software Security Assurance, are doomed to fail eventually—if not today, than at some point in the all-too-near future. If there's any hope of moving any closer to the *Star Trek* scenario, it's absolutely essential that we take an Agile Architecture approach to cybersecurity.

It won't be easy. And the path from where we are today to where we need to be tomorrow isn't smooth or continuous—that's why we consider the move to Agile Architecture a true paradigm shift. But on the positive side, many elements of this revolution are already in place. The first step is thinking about the problem properly. We can only hope that we figure out how to solve the cybersecurity problem before the hackers take over. Or welcome to your worst *Cyberpunk* nightmare.

The Generation Y Crisis Point

Speaking of nightmares, there's an invasion coming. In fact, it's already under way, and you probably haven't realized that you're about to be taken over. That's right—Generation Y has entered the workforce, and is bound to become the dominant part of your enterprise over the next decade. What does this mean for your organization? How are the needs of Gen Y different from those of existing markets? And why does this discussion have *anything* to do with Agile Architecture? The answers follow, but rest assured, the emergence of Millennials in the workforce is every bit a crisis point for your IT planning as dealing with the downfall of EA Frameworks and cyberwarfare, albeit with most likely a positive ending.

Generation Y generally refers to the "echo boomers" who predictably followed Generation X. These Millennials have birth dates ranging somewhere from the mid-1970s to the early 2000s. Basically, they're baby boomer spawn. Big deal? Well, not necessarily. Without exception, Millennials have grown up entirely in the information age. They don't know a world without computers, cell phones, and MTV. Steve Jobs and Bill Gates were already fighting with each other by the time they were born, and the term *minicomputer* never even entered their lexicon. But what makes the Millennials most relevant for the enterprise is that their experience of IT is primarily with the vast rate of change happening on the consumer side, rather than in the enterprise.

It's not just an inherent technical fluency that separates Millennials from the rest of your workforce. Millennials emerged in a world where instant communication in the form of e-mail, texting, instant messaging, social networks, online gaming, virtual worlds like *World of Warcraft* and *Second Life*, and online sharing platforms such as YouTube were the norm. Because they conducted much of their lives in the public sphere, the notion of personal privacy has eroded. Will Millennials have the same respect for corporate information as that of their less publicly verbose colleagues?

Likewise, Millennials leverage the power of these mass communication and sharing platforms to revolutionize the way marketing and information sharing is done. Viral marketing, flash mobbing, Internet memes, and spontaneous meetups are not only the new social cliques and in-culture of the generation, but the primary way trends are shaped.

But by far the biggest impact of the emergence of Millennials in the workforce is that their expectation of what enterprise IT can do for them and the company is very different from that of their older colleagues. In the eyes of Millennials, they can get sophisticated IT stuff done without the IT department—in fact, many already have. So enterprise IT departments: Prepare to win the hearts and minds of the Millennials lest they find competition for your services.

Millennials see IT as a tool to get things done. For them, however, they have a choice between using the tools of their daily lives (mobile devices, online applications, social networks) or the tools of their business lives (what we currently consider to be enterprise IT). As such, IT organizations must understand the core needs of this critical user group:

- **Physical boundaries no longer exist.** The fact that enterprise systems and data are behind a firewall are of little concern to folks who are used to Cloud and SaaS-based systems, mobile applications, and virtualization writ large. Location agnosticism is a must for future enterprise IT systems. This need is echoed in the Global Cubicle Supertrend.

- **Mobile as a first-class participant.** The days of treating mobile apps as a redheaded stepchild of the enterprise IT landscape are over. There are far more reasons to make enterprise capabilities available inherently on mobile apps than not. Especially when your users spend more time on mobile systems than they do on the ones the enterprise IT department creates.
- **The need for immediacy.** The "now" generation wants instant access to data and functionality. And they want it in a consistent manner regardless of the device they use or where they are.
- **The era of function over form is over.** The market has already proven that functionally equivalent (or even functionally poorer) applications with superior user experiences prevail over functionally superior, but user-experience-poor applications. Sound familiar? Well it should—most enterprise IT applications have utterly appalling user interfaces that are only modest improvements from the 1970s green screen era. Web-based applications are 1990s holdovers. It's time to rethink the enterprise app.

How can enterprise IT address these needs? Fortunately, both the technology and know-how exist to solve these problems. As is often the case, the solution is most often design and architecture-centric and less so technology centric. If someone sells you a Millennial Integration App, you should run *quickly* in the other direction. Instead, you should adjust your IT development and operations practices to meet the previous needs:

- **Provide immediate gratification.** Provisioning of IT capability has to be as immediate and flexible as possible. Data and functionality must be readily available regardless of device or location. The enterprise IT organization must realize that it is in competition for the hearts and minds of business users.
- **Design for location and device agnosticism.** Design for consistency of experience and action regardless of location and device. This principle emphasizes loosely coupled Services and SOA design principles. Designing for loose coupling significantly complicates testing, security, privacy, and governance—all aspects of the Agile Architecture challenge.
- **Create a compelling user experience.** User experience is no longer a luxury. You are competing with online, social, and mobile experiences. There is increasingly a fuzzy line between business and consumer IT. So, start learning from Apple, Amazon, Google, and Facebook.

A tall order, true, but there shouldn't be anything new here for enterprise IT departments that are already looking ahead to the next generation of applications and value creation for the enterprise. After all, the impact of Millennials entering the workforce becomes a crisis point only if organizations turn a blind eye to the different experiences, needs, and contributions of this age group. Millennials already know that they have sophisticated, highly usable, and instant IT capabilities available at their fingertips and online, so why should they be bothered when the comparatively slower and less-sophisticated enterprise IT department can't get their needs met? A smart IT department will realize that internal as well as external market forces impact the scope of what they need to get done.

The days of enterprise IT departments having sole control of the pace and scope of IT innovation in the organization are long gone. IT managers who ignore the changing internal dynamics of the workforce will face a crisis point when the new generation takes increasingly more senior management positions. Those managers who see the emergence of this savvy audience as a good excuse to increase the pace of innovation will not only save their own jobs, but continue to make the enterprise IT department a champion and engine for innovation in the enterprise.

CHAPTER 7

The Democratization of Enterprise IT

We expect this book to have a broader audience than your average techie book: business people as well as techies, architects and implementers, denizens of enterprise IT departments as well as people who work at smaller organizations, start-ups, or technology firms. The Agile Architecture Revolution will impact all of us, after all. But if you haven't worked in, or consulted for, an enterprise IT department, you have no idea how, well, *otherworldly* they are.

By otherworldly, we mean that they have big-company ways of thinking, talking, working, and making decisions—even though they are responsible for, and work with, technology every day. But if you look at the rest of the technology marketplace—consumer tech, small/midsize business tech, technology in academia, as well as Web-based (oops, we mean *Cloud*-based) companies, you gain a very different perspective on technology than the "enterprisey" view of big-organization IT.

Here are some examples. How much do you expect to pay for a piece of software? Nothing at all maybe? Okay, 99 cents? Ten bucks? Maybe you want some business software, so maybe $500? What about *tens of millions* of dollars or more? In enterprises, price tags with more than six zeroes at the end are commonplace.

Fine, let's say you bought that software, and now it's time to install it. How many files do you get from the vendor to execute the install process, and how long does it take? From an app store, one installer file and maybe a couple minutes at most. On your computer, maybe a bit longer. What about enterprise software? That package you just bought might come in over 10,000 separate files and require *months* to install. (Okay, months is a worst case, but you get my point.)

Next, you need to get that software to actually *work*. Wait, doesn't installing it mean that when you're done, you can use it? Not in the enterprise. Installing is only the first step. Integration, configuration, training, change management, data cleansing, and numerous other steps need to take place before we can do anything useful with that software.

Finally, it's time to use the software, so take a look at its user interface. Attractive, friendly, intuitive, self-explanatory, and dynamic, right? To be fair, these criteria set a high bar for even the slickest consumer software, but enterprise software's user interfaces are generally 20 years behind. Yes, some enterprise software packages have nice interfaces, but those are few and far between, compared to the number of kludgy, awkward interfaces most of today's enterprise apps exhibit.

You get the picture. The question, however, is *what are we going to do about it*? Something's got to give—*and it's the enterprise IT department.* The old way of doing things is simply too expensive and too inflexible to survive. But change isn't easy, of course. If you're in enterprise IT, ZapThink 2020 Crisis Points are in your future—if not your present!

Demise of the Enterprise IT Department

In our deep conversations with CIOs and other IT decision makers, we find that there's broad agreement on the multitude of forces conspiring to change every aspect of the way the enterprise does IT. Yet at the same time, everybody's in denial that these changes will happen to *them.* For us as outsiders, it certainly looks like many enterprise IT decision makers acknowledge that the world is changing, but deny that they are part of that same world. Of course, such executives simply have their head in the sand. If change is to occur, it will happen to the vast majority of enterprises, not the minority.

This realization drives the crisis points of the ZapThink 2020 Vision. However, we aren't advocating that organizations should adopt any of the crisis points. Rather we are observing that these crises are coming whether or not companies are ready for them. In particular, we believe that companies will reach a crisis point as they seek to outsource IT. However, we aren't advocating that companies outsource all their IT efforts. Rather, we are observing that siren call of offloading IT assets in the form of Cloud Computing, and outsourcing is a significant trend that is leading to a crisis point. And without a strong rudder to navigate this crisis point, many companies will indeed be dashed on the rocks.

Admit it—there is broad-based fear and uncertainty across your organization when talking about outsourcing IT functions. Part of the fear comes from the fact that many people confuse outsourcing with offshoring. *Outsourcing* is the purchasing of a service from an outside vendor to replace the performance of the task within the organization's internal operations. *Offshoring*, on the other hand, is the movement of labor from a region of high cost (such as the United States) to one of comparatively lower cost (such as India). People fear the latter because it means subcontracting existing work to other people, thus displacing jobs at home. However, the former has been going on for hundreds of years. Indeed, many companies exist solely because they are completing tasks that their customers would rather not undertake themselves.

SOA and outsourcing have long gone hand in hand, for the simple reason that SOA requires organizations to think about their resources, processes, and capabilities in ways that are loosely coupled from the specifics of their implementation, location, and consumption. Indeed, the more companies implement SOA, the more they can outsource processes that are not strategic or competitive for the organization. Furthermore, the more companies outsource their functions, the more they are motivated to implement SOA to facilitate the consumption of the outsourced capabilities. So it should come as no surprise that the combination of SOA and a challenging economic environment has motivated many companies to consider outsourcing as a legitimate strategy for their IT organizations, regardless of whether they move to offshoring.

But it's a mistake to assume the collapse of the enterprise IT department is due entirely to outsourcing the functions of IT to third parties. Outsourcing is a part of the story, but so is Cloud Computing. In much the same way that third-party firms can offload parts of IT in the outsourcing model, Cloud Computing offers the ability to offload other aspects of the IT department. Cloud Computing provides both technological and economic benefits for distributing and offloading resources, functions, processes, and even data onto location-independent infrastructures.

Though many enterprises are currently pursuing a private model for Cloud Computing, there are far too many economic benefits of the public model to ignore. As a result, we are increasingly seeing hybrid Cloud approaches, where organizations keep certain mission-critical features behind the firewall on the corporate premises while they shift the rest to lower-cost, more agile, and less costly third-party locations. The net result of this shift is continued erosion of the scope of responsibility for internal IT organizations.

The Demise of Enterprise IT Crisis Point emerges from the fact that companies will rush into this vision of outsourced IT without first thinking through the dramatic impact that this transition will have throughout their organization. For such organizations, the value of the ZapThink 2020 Vision is that it pulls together multiple trends and delineates the interrelationships among them. One of the trends most closely related to the demise of the IT organization is the increased formality and dependence on governance, as organizations pull together the business side of governance (GRC, or governance, risk, and compliance), with the technology side of governance (IT governance, and to an increasing extent, SOA governance). Over time, CIOs become CGOs (Chief Governance Officers), as their focus shifts away from technology.

As the enterprise owns fewer and fewer of the organization's IT assets, the role and responsibility of enterprise IT practitioners will be less about the mechanics of getting systems to work, integrating them with each other, and operating them, and more about the management of the one resource that remains constant: information. After all, IT is *information technology*, not *computer* or *systems technology*.

With this perspective, it's essential to view the shift to outsourcing and Cloud Computing holistically with all the other changes happening in the enterprise IT environment. For example, the move to democratization of technology means that non-IT practitioners will be utilizing and creating IT capabilities and assets without the control of the IT organization. How will IT practitioners manage the sole enterprise IT asset (information) given that they cannot manage the systems in which that asset flows? As organizations realize the Global Cubicle vision of IT, how will enterprise IT practitioners and architects enable distributed information without losing GRC visibility? As systems become increasingly interconnected despite their increasingly distributed nature, how can enterprise IT practitioners make sure the systems as a whole continue to provide value and avoid chaotic disruptions despite the fact that the organization doesn't own or operate them? As organizations move to more iterative, agile forms of Complex Systems Engineering (CSE) where new capabilities emerge from compositions of existing ones, how will movements to Cloud Computing and outsourcing help or hurt those efforts?

If you can successfully tackle these questions with a coherent, holistic strategy, then you have defused the risk inherent to movement to outsourcing and/or Cloud Computing. On the other hand, if you rush into Cloud Computing and outsourcing strategies without thinking through all the issues, you'll be sunk before you know it.

The Agile Architecture Approach to IT Project Management

One of the most challenging aspects of Agile Architecture is that rather than address a discrete problem or set of problems in the enterprise, it attempts to address a range of interconnected and perplexing issues that have long troubled IT. To be specific, long-term issues of integration in environments of continued heterogeneity; application development in the face of continuous change; governance, management, and quality in complex environments; increasing reuse and reducing redundancy across multiple IT initiatives; and organizational and methodological techniques that favor iteration over monolithic, waterfall-style approaches to development all fall within the realm of Agile Architecture.

Although none of these challenges are new, and in fact, many architects have a number of tools, techniques, and approaches at their disposal to address those issues, Agile Architecture attempts to address them in a holistic manner, providing a consistent approach to use in the face of continued business and technological change. One of the biggest impacts of this holistic approach to IT management is that discrete IT project management is rapidly going by the wayside. This trend doesn't necessarily signal the death of IT project management, but it does suggest that evolving approaches to architecture require changes not just in the technology and application development approach, but also changes in the way in which we manage the organization's overall evolution.

As a case in point, like IT, human resources (HR) and finance are two other assets of the business. Companies have long realized that it made no sense to let each function of the business manage its own finances and human resources separately. Why should each Line of Business (LOB) do its own hiring, benefits administration, and office allocation instead of centralizing those capabilities for the purpose of efficiency and optimization? So, too, with finance—why should each role in the business manage its own cash flow, investment, and company-level reporting instead of centralizing them for the benefit of the company as a whole?

The requirement here is not only for centralization, but also for *separation of responsibilities*. The HR and finance organizations are not in charge of figuring out how the enterprise should utilize the human and financial resources. They are simply in charge of managing them for the benefit of the company. It is up to each individual LOB to determine how to use the people and money available to it.

So, too, with IT. The IT organization must move away from building applications on behalf of the business to providing *Services* that the LOBs can use. Say goodbye to discrete IT project management and hello to IT portfolio management. The core concept of *IT portfolio management* is that the IT organization manages a set of continually changing resources such that when a new requirement comes along, it doesn't automatically spawn off a new development project. Rather, the IT organization leverages its growing catalog of IT Services to meet the ongoing needs of the business. Any requirement that the existing catalog doesn't fulfill will require either reconfiguration of existing assets, modification of existing assets, or new asset creation, in that priority order.

You may be scratching your head right now and wondering, "Aren't we already doing this?" Or perhaps you are saying, "I don't get how this is different from discrete IT project management." If you are wondering that, then you haven't yet experienced IT portfolio management, because IT portfolio management requires, in most cases, a fundamental change to the lines of IT control and budgeting. To attempt IT portfolio management in an environment where the funds are allocated to individual projects is a recipe for disaster.

Indeed, changing the method of IT funding is one of the fundamental requirements for a move to a portfolio-centric style of IT management. In an environment where any new business requirement might require changes throughout the organization, it makes no sense to feed IT on a per-project basis. Rather, in an environment of constant change, the IT organization requires an ongoing, steady budget that provides for continual changes via an iterative model. Each iteration will introduce new assets, versioned assets, and configurations of assets to meet the current set of business requirements. The IT organization then seeks to optimize its portfolio by minimizing the time between iterations, the amount of changes they need in each iteration, the total number of assets under management, and increasing the visibility the rest of the business has of the IT assets under management.

Basically, all businesses must manage four resources in order to maintain success: money, people, technology, and supplies. Such resources are assets, and the organization reflects either the management of these assets or growing the customer base to use or contribute to these assets. IT is no different from finance or human resources. Just as the business doesn't give HR or finance discrete budgets for specific business requirements, so, too, will it realize that it needs to treat IT the same way.

Crisis Point: The Enterprise Application Crash

Today, in spite of a full decade of vendors paying lip service to the benefits of Agile Architecture approaches like SOA, customers are more than unhappy with enterprise software. They're pissed. And they're not going to take it anymore. After all, most enterprise app vendors promised to rework their software to take advantage of SOA best practices. "We're entering a new era of standards compliance, loose coupling, and open software!" the vendors crowed. "We've drunk the SOA Kool-Aid!"

Not likely. Rearchitecting an enterprise software package along SOA lines is straightforward in theory, of course. Modularize the core functionality, expose it as loosely coupled, governed Services, and incorporate those Services into a metadata-driven composite application framework that enables customers to support flexible business processes with compositions of Services, whether from the software package or elsewhere. Deliver prebuilt compositions to the customer, empowering them to manage and modify the compositions to support changing business processes as necessary.

This SOA-enabled product story is the vision behind products from most well-known enterprise app vendors, and virtually every one of them has espoused some version of this loosely coupled, metadata-driven story for their own software packages. Sounds good, right? But here's the rub: If any of these big vendors were actually getting it right, then we wouldn't be seeing the high levels of dissatisfaction that are driving CIOs over the edge. Why, then, have all the vendors dropped the ball in such spectacular fashion?

It would be easy to say that reworking enterprise software along SOA lines is too difficult or expensive, or perhaps some vendors say they're making progress, but the real answer is that vendors haven't reworked their products to be truly agile *because they don't have to*. As long as customers keep paying them, then why change?

The incumbent vendors have a good thing going, after all: *customer lock-in*. Once an enterprise installs one of these massive packages, it's enormously expensive and risky for the customer to switch to another. Furthermore, you have to keep paying maintenance. The more lock-in a vendor is able to achieve, the better their bottom line. For these vendors, the *real* SOA story—that is, offering truly loosely coupled, composable Services, is actually more of a threat than an advantage. They pay lip service to SOA, but when push comes to shove, the last thing they want to do is modularize and loosely couple their offerings to support flexible processes.

These vendors, however, are making a huge mistake. They are confusing customer lock-in for customer loyalty. Customers only put up with vendors because they have to, but they're not happy. As soon as a viable alternative comes along, they're gone. Customers aren't loyal to their enterprise software vendors; they just don't have any choice.

The illusion of customer loyalty has caused the big vendors to become complacent. They believe they've successfully co-opted the SOA trend, making it one more excuse to buy more software. And now, of course, they're doing the same thing with Cloud Computing. So, is this battle over, with the victory to the incumbent vendors? Not so fast.

There is change in the air in today's enterprise IT shops. SOA is a part of the story, yes, but it doesn't go by the name SOA. This change consists of a broad range of shifts, from the move to Cloud Computing to how software innovation is shifting to consumer technologies to the way collaboration is breaking down barriers to global communication. This change will take a few years to play out, but it will put large software vendors out of business and fundamentally reshape the nature of enterprise IT. How organizations leverage technology at the most fundamental level is undergoing a sea change.

Here, then, are some of the IT challenges that are driving the Enterprise Application Crash Crisis Point:

- **High cost of ownership.** SOA and Cloud can lower the cost of integration over time, but cost savings is an Agile Architecture benefit that is secondary to business agility. The open source software movement is also driven by cost of ownership issues, but many organizations have struggled to show substantial cost savings with open source approaches. SaaS also has a cost of ownership driver, but perhaps the most disruptive trend today that owes its motivation to cost savings drivers is the move to consumer-centric, mobile applications in the enterprise, bypassing established IT purchasing infrastructure altogether.

- **Difficult upgrades.** Being able to upgrade software to meet changing business needs is an agility benefit, and as a result, organizations that have implemented SOA and that have purchased SOA-centric applications have an easier time upgrading. Leveraging Cloud-based enterprise applications, however, may not ease the upgrade process if the enterprise doesn't leverage those applications in a loosely coupled way.

- **Poor cross-functional processes.** Wasn't middleware supposed to address this problem? Set up complex interconnected webs of integration software, and voilà! Seamless cross-functional process automation! In our dreams. Today's software is not up to this task, because the challenges are more organizational than technological. The key to addressing such human/technology issues is via Agile Architecture approaches that center on governance rather than integration.

- **Apps don't deliver on business requirements.** Traditional IT thinking follows the waterfall methodology for software development that assumes requirements are stable, well understood, and properly communicated. Unfortunately, business requirements are typically dynamic, unclear, and difficult to communicate. Agile methodologies help to address these issues, but Agile approaches don't help much with traditional enterprise software approaches. The shift toward collaborative, Service-oriented, Cloud-based, governed applications is an inherently more agile approach that can finally deliver on the promise of the Agile movement, even for enterprise application functionality.

- **Inflexibility that limits business process change.** Providing flexibility for automating dynamic business processes is the primary motivation for SOA, to be sure, but there's more to this story, because automation isn't the only capability the business requires. After all, most business processes have human input, and the more collaborative a process is, the less automation the business wants. Here again, Agile Architecture thinking comes into play: how best to provide flexibility that supports collaborative business process change? The answer involves an architected web of governed human-technology and human-human interactions. Technology plays a role, but a very different role than traditional enterprise applications do.

It is important to note that the common theme is *transformation*. There are many enablers of this transformation, including SOA, CSE, governance, collaboration, and Cloud Computing—no one of these enablers is the whole story. But make no mistake, there's a revolution under way in how enterprises leverage technology. This sea change will shutter large IT shops, sink unsinkable incumbent vendors, redefine the role of the CIO, and turn the practice of EA upside down. In 10 or 20 years, the whole notion of enterprise IT will be unrecognizable from where it is today. And nothing we or the vendors can do will stop this transformation.

Change in the enterprise app market, in fact, has already been taking place. The last few years have seen significant consolidation in the marketplace for enterprise software. Whereas a decade or so ago there were a few dozen large and established providers of different sorts of enterprise software packages, there are now just a handful of large providers, with a smattering more for industry-specific niches. We can thank aggressive mergers and acquisitions combined with downward IT spending pressure for this reality.

As a result of this consolidation, many large enterprise software packages such as Enterprise Resource Planning (ERP), Customer Relationship Management (CRM), and Supply Chain Management (SCM) offerings have been eliminated, are in the process of being phased out, or are getting merged with other solutions—and, of course, they're all "moving to the Cloud." The result is that many companies must either reconsider or discard the purchase rationalization they used to justify spending millions of dollars on proprietary enterprise software solutions and millions more on customizing those solutions.

Furthermore, by virtue of their weight, significance in the enterprise environment, and astounding complexity, enterprise software solutions are much slower to adopt and adapt to new technologies that continuously change the face of IT. You get one IT user experience when you are at home and use the Web, personal computing, and mobile devices and applications, and a profoundly poorer experience when you are at work. It's as if the applications you use at work are a full decade behind the innovations that are now commonplace in the consumer environment. We can thank expensive, cumbersome, and tightly coupled customization, integration, and development for this lack of innovation in enterprise software.

Even the concept of enterprise software itself is a fallacy. No company can purchase and implement an enterprise software solution "out of the box." Not only does a company need to spend significant money customizing and integrating their enterprise software solutions, but they often spend more money on custom applications that tie into and depend on the software. What might seem to be a discrete enterprise software application is really a tangled mass of single-vendor-provided functionality, tightly coupled customizations and integrations with this functionality, and custom code tied into this motley mess. In fact, when we ask people to tell us about their EA, they often point to the gnarly mess of enterprise software they purchased, customized, and maintain. That's not EA. That's an ugly baby only a mother could love.

Yet, companies constantly complain about their utter dependence on a handful of applications for their daily operations. Imagine what would happen at any large business if you were to shut down their ERP, CRM, or SCM solutions. Business would grind to a halt. Whereas some people would point to the absolute necessity of enterprise software solutions as a result, we would instead insist on how remarkably insane it is for companies to have such a single point of failure.

Such dependence on a single product or single vendor for the entirety of their operations is absolutely ludicrous in an IT environment where companies simply do not have to have such dependencies. The more you depend on one thing for your success, the less you are able to control your future. Innovation itself hangs in the balance when a company becomes so dependent on another company's ability to innovate.

The emergence of Services at a range of disparate levels combined with evolutions in location and platform-independent, on-demand, and variable provisioning that Cloud Computing offers, and rich technologies to facilitate simple and rapid Service composition, will change the way companies conceive of, build, and manage applications. Instead of an application as something that IT shops buy, customize, and integrate, the application itself is the instantaneous snapshot of how the various Services are composed together to meet user needs. From this perspective, *enterprise software is not what you buy, but what you do with what you have*.

One outcome of this perspective on enterprise software is that companies can shift their spending from enterprise software licenses and maintenance (which eats up a significant chunk of IT budgets) to Service development, consumption, and composition. This difference is part of the paradigm shift that constitutes the Agile Architecture Revolution. We've had first-hand experience with new companies that have started and grown operations to multiple millions of dollars without buying a penny of enterprise software. Likewise, we've seen billion-dollar companies dump existing enterprise software investments or start divisions and operations in new countries without extending their existing enterprise software licenses. When you ask these people to show you their enterprise software, they'll simply point at their collection of Services, Cloud-based applications, and composition infrastructure.

Some people might insist that Cloud-based applications, and in particular, SaaS applications, are simply monolithic enterprise software applications deployed in someone else's infrastructure. Though that might have been the case for the Salesforce.com of the past (circa 2000), it is no longer the case. Whole ecosystems of loosely coupled Service offerings have evolved in the past decade to value-add these environments, which look more like catalogs of Service capabilities and less like monolithic applications. Want to build a Web site and capture lead data? No problem—just get the right Service from Salesforce or whatever SaaS provider you prefer and compose it using Web Services or REST or your standards-based approach of choice. And you didn't incur thousands or millions of dollars to do that.

Another trend pointing to the stalling of enterprise software growth is the emergence of open source alternatives. Companies now are flocking to no-license and no-maintenance fee solutions that provide 80 percent of the required functionality of commercial suites. Though some people might point to the cost of support for these offerings, we point out the factor of difference in support and license/maintenance costs and also that at the very least, you know what you're paying for.

It's hard to justify millions of dollars of license fees when you're using 10 percent or less of a product's capabilities. But adding more to this open source value proposition is that others are building capabilities on top of those solutions and giving those solutions away as well. The very nature of open source enables creation of capabilities that further enhance the value proposition of the suite. At some point, a given open source solution reaches a tipping point where the volume of new additions far outweighs what any commercial offering can provide. Simply put, when a community supports an open source effort, the result can out-innovate any commercial solution.

There's more to this story. Beyond open source, commercial, and SaaS offerings, companies have a credible choice in building their own enterprise software application. There are now a lot of pieces and parts available that are free or inexpensive, that companies can assemble into not only workable, but scalable offerings that can compete with many commercial offerings. In much the same way that companies leveraged Microsoft's Visual Basic to build applications using the thousands of free or cheap widgets and controls that legions of developers created, so, too, are we seeing a movement to free or cheap Service widgets that can enable remarkably complex and robust applications.

As a consequence, it's not clear where commercial enterprise software applications go from here. Surely, we don't see companies tearing out their all-too-integrated solutions any time soon, but likewise, we don't see much expansion in enterprise software sales either. In some ways, enterprise software has become every bit the legacy they sought to replace in mainframe applications, which still exists in abundance in the enterprise. Smart enterprise software vendors realize that they have to get out of the application business altogether and focus on selling composable widgets. These firms, however, also want to run the "train and the tracks," which means that the only way you can use those widgets is if you run them on their infrastructure.

In many ways, this idea of enterprise software-as-a-platform is really just a shell game. Instead of spending millions on a specific application, you're instead spending millions on an infrastructure that comes with some preconfigured widgets. The question is, is the proprietary run-time infrastructure you are getting with those widgets worth the cost? Have you lost some measure of loose coupling in exchange for a single throat to choke?

Much of the enterprise software market is heading in direct collision course with middleware vendors who never wanted to enter the application market in the first place. As enterprise software vendors start seeing their run-time platform as the defensible position, they will start conflicting with EA strategies that seek to remove single-vendor dependence. We see this trend as an area of tension over the next few years. Do you want to be in control of your infrastructure and have choice, or do you want to hand over control of your infrastructure to a single vendor, who might be one merger or business misstep away from irrelevance or nonexistence?

The last thing IT shops should do is invest more in technology conceived of in the 1970s, matured in the 1990s, and incrementally made worse since then. The reliance on single-vendor mammoth enterprise software packages is not helping, but rather hurting the movement to Agile Architecture. Now is the time for companies to pull up the stakes and reconsider their huge enterprise software investments in favor of the sort of Enterprise Architecture that cares little about buying things *en masse* and customizing those solutions, but more about building, composing, and reusing what you need iteratively to respond to continual change.

Replacing Enterprise Software: Easier Said than Done

Replacing old technology with new, of course, is not unfamiliar to enterprise IT, at least when it comes to the desktop and laptop computers in the organization. Placing such tech on a three- or four-year replacement cycle is a well-established best practice. As a result, the processes inherent in this cycle are well understood, and the vendors are only too happy to support such efforts among their enterprise customers.

Enterprise software, however, is another story altogether. Purchase an enterprise application, middleware package, or other infrastructure software, and the moment you install it, it becomes instant legacy. The vendors are only too happy to support this approach, of course, as they make most of their money on the maintenance—so the longer you have to pay, the better. But even the vendors eventually weary of maintaining old software, letting it fall out of support. Customers now face a tough decision: Keep unsupported software around and risk new security holes and incompatibilities with newer products, or go through the difficult, expensive process of replacement.

SOA was supposed to address this problem, and it has, to some extent. But though abstracting the interfaces of legacy software can lower the cost and risk of application modernization somewhat, such initiatives are still extraordinarily high risk, expensive, and time consuming. Cloud Computing takes us further in the direction of replaceability, as the Cloud abstracts the underlying infrastructure and platform that supports application software. To be sure, much of today's software isn't Cloud friendly, in the sense that it won't run in Cloud environments without substantial rework. But the mere fact that the Cloud is here and it works is driving innovation. The more Cloud friendly an app is, the more replaceable it is, whether the vendors want it to be or not.

Now, replacing a mobile phone with a newer model is quite a bit simpler than replacing an ERP system, even with the Cloud—but the differences are simply a matter of degree. Your phone contains your address book, your apps, and all their configurations. Fortunately, the mobile phone vendors try to make it easy to transition those elements to a new phone (which is admittedly easier if you don't change brands). What would it take for your ERP system to have a corresponding upgradability?

Abstracted Service interfaces are essential, but they're only the starting point. Those interfaces must support deep interoperability as well. Even more important, however, is a high level of modularization—what we call *next-generation modularization*, part of the Democratization of Technology Supertrend in our ZapThink 2020 Vision. Vendors achieve next-generation modularization when they are able to deliver modular elements for flexible assembly and deployment—and replacement.

If you are currently involved in an application modernization or consolidation initiative, ask yourself these two questions: How replaceable is our legacy app? And how replaceable is the app we're now considering to replace it? If your new choice isn't far more replaceable than the legacy you're retiring, then all you're doing is perpetuating inflexibility by supplanting old legacy with new legacy. On the other hand, including replaceability in your requirements for any new software will lower your long-term total cost of ownership. You'll also be doing your part to push the vendors to offer next-generation modular software.

Perhaps the bigger question, however, is, *Is there a future for enterprise software at all?* Software has been low tech for so long that we're all used to it that way. After all, software production is still a craft-based enterprise, with experienced practitioners turning out custom software in small teams. Just as when cobblers produced shoes and seamstresses fashioned clothing, today's software is either entirely custom or appallingly ill fitting. Custom software is enormously expensive, often requiring teams of developers, and only meets the particular needs of the moment. Meanwhile, commercial off-the-shelf (COTS) software is rarely flexible enough to meet all the needs of its users, requiring users to work within the constraints of the software, rather than the other way around. In any case, regardless of whether it's custom or COTS, today's software is of appallingly low quality.

ZapThink predicts the end of craft software, as standards mature and vendors learn how to build high-tech software. As the industry matures and becomes high tech, software will no longer be judged on how well it can meet today's requirements, but rather how flexibly it can meet tomorrow's challenges. If vendors become able to deliver software that can truly meet as-yet-undefined business requirements, then enterprises will demand such software.

Of course, the responsibility for IT innovation and architecture is where it should be the most—in the hands of the enterprise. As enterprises find an increasingly less diverse set of vendors to work with, a more economically challenging environment, and the need to innovate and manage increased complexity at an ever-increasing pace, companies will have to look inward. The solution to their IT problems is under their own control. As the vendors fight among each other for dwindling business, you should avoid those battles by focusing on developing architectural strategies that enable agility and innovation without depending on a single vendor. This is the only rational and cost-effective strategy in an increasingly unpredictable world.

PART THREE
Implementing Agile Architecture

Communication among humans is a distributed hypermedia system, where the mind's intellect, voice + gestures, eyes + ears, and imagination are all components.

—Roy Fielding

CHAPTER 8

Deep Interoperability: Getting REST Right (Finally!)

One of the more fascinating aspects of the Information Revolution is that it's only been about 60 years or so that people have been programming computers—and that means that most of us of a certain age remember the bulk of the history of computing personally. We can remember long before the Internet—we know you youngsters out there would find that hard to believe—back to when programming was something *real* men (and precious few women) did with tools like paper strips and punch cards. Ah, those were the days!

What made computers so exciting back then wasn't that they were digital (although the notion that you could do anything with zeroes and ones was remarkable in its own right). What made them so fascinating was that they were *programmable*. We had machines at our disposal that would do anything we told them to, limited only by our imagination, or so it seemed. We could apply these computers to any task, where that application was the program we wrote for the machine.

The word *application* came to mean the *computer program*, which was how we instructed the computer to apply itself to solve whatever problem we were trying to solve. The program ran on one computer, and the computer did nothing else while it was running a program. Eventually we had time-sharing, which gave us the illusion that the computer could run many programs at once, but in reality, it was just really good at getting multiple programs to take turns.

The program itself, of course, consisted of a sequence of commands. The computer's processor read one command, did what it said, and then moved to the next command, and so on. We call this type of programming *imperative programming:* imperative in the sense that we're commanding the computer to do something, and telling it in what order to execute those commands.

Today we have networks and Clouds and throngs of computer scientists who spend their careers inventing newfangled ways of programming computers, but imperative programming still provides the broader context of what it means to program a computer—in essence, forming the existing paradigm. Implementing Agile Architecture, however, means understanding new paradigms for computing. But our starting point is imperative programming: one person, one computer, one program.

Programmable Interfaces: The Never-Ending Story

Today, of course, we have all those fun toys like networks and Clouds and the like. Programs no longer run on single computers. And with networks we have *distributed computing*, where we get computers to talk to each other. And to do that, we need *APIs*.

The core notion of an *application programming interface* (API) is that you want one application to be *programmable* by something external to it, in the sense that you have an imperative control flow that goes from *here* to *there* and back to *here*.

The problem with such imperative programming in any distributed environment, of course, is that there is no end of problems that can arise between *here* and *there*. Network issues, incompatibilities, timing and sequence issues, the list goes on and on, leading computer scientists to the notion of *functional* programming. In the functional world, functions (which also go by the name *procedures*) encapsulate the software at the remote location, forming black boxes with fixed inputs and outputs. Any local piece of software, therefore, can call a remote procedure and get the desired response, without having to worry about whether multiple calls to that procedure might interfere with each other or lead to other nasty surprises that a purely imperative approach might exhibit.

We often call functional programming in a distributed environment *Remote Procedure Call* (RPC) programming. There are a number of challenges with RPC programming, however:

1. Typically, we don't simply want to send data to the remote procedure, we actually want to *execute* software remotely. But what if the software *here* and *there* are in different languages, or have other incompatibilities?
2. Somehow we have to take care of the network. We need to open sockets, send packets, deal with errors, and so forth. The last thing we want to do is write code to take care of all these plumbing issues every time we want to call a remote procedure.
3. What if we want to update the remote procedure? How do we keep its existing consumers from breaking?

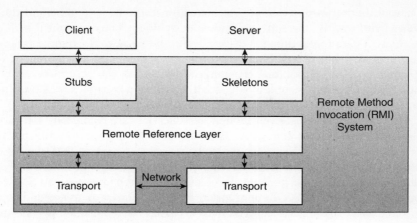

Figure 8.1   Java Remote Method Invocation (RMI)

Solving these challenges was one of the motivations for the Java programming language. Java's virtual machine (VM) architecture supports Java *Remote Method Invocation* (RMI), an approach to RPC programming that addresses problems 1 and 2 in the previous list. Basically, the way RMI works is by abstracting the network communication infrastructure with a Remote Reference Layer, as shown in Figure 8.1. RMI then packages up bits of server code (skeletons), and ships them over the network so that client stubs can access them as though they were local to the client.

In other words, we're abstracting remote software as though it were local via the portability model of Java—the write once, run anywhere mantra that differentiated Java in the marketplace, until Microsoft .NET caught up with .NET Remoting, which works basically the same way.

There are two basic issues with RMI. First is the fact it depends on *write once, run anywhere*, which any Java developer will tell you is really *write once, debug everywhere*: RMI is very particular about the particular version of Java at each endpoint. But the more significant issue is that it doesn't address problem 3. In other words, RMI is a *tightly coupled* approach. If you change the software on the server, you typically have to change the software on the client accordingly. As a result, it doesn't deal well with *change*. The challenge, therefore, with functional/RPC programming is how to deal with *tight coupling*. Even though functional programming is essentially the same thing as RPC, it is also considered to be a type of *declarative* programming.

Declarative programming has always been the ugly duckling of the programming language world, because with a declarative approach, you don't specify the control flow. Instead, you describe the desired behavior you want the software to exhibit. And somehow, via some kind of behind-the-scenes hand waving, the software miraculously does what you want it to.

Functional programming is declarative in the sense that a remote procedure acts as a black box. Specify the operations, inputs, and outputs (its *signature*, in API-speak), and the inner workings of the procedure aren't your problem. That is, unless you don't understand what it's supposed to do for you, or, heaven forbid, its behavior *changes*.

Enter Web Services. Even though Web Services are technically software interfaces, they aren't the same as APIs, at least not in the functional programming sense. What makes Web Services special is that they are *contracted* interfaces. The Web Services Description Language (WSDL) file (along with certain associated metadata files) specifies the interface, so a Service consumer need only select the appropriate contract in order to understand how to bind to (access) the Service. If you want to change the Service, simply change the contract.

Early versions of Web Services, however, still followed the RPC style. In essence, the original view of Web Services was eXtensible Markup Language (XML)-based interfaces to objects. In fact, SOAP, the XML-based message transport standard for Web Services, originally stood for *Simple Object Access Protocol*, because accessing objects was what Web Services were all about. The problem with RPC-style Web Services, however, was the same problem that RPC programming had all along: tight coupling. If you changed a Web Service, you had to change the consumers accordingly. Furthermore, RPC-style interactions were always *synchronous*—that is, request/reply.

In the early days of Web Services, the limitations of RPC didn't seem to be too great an issue, because the idea was that consumers would fetch new versions of the contract every time they invoked a Service, and furthermore, the Web Services standards team envisioned Service consumers "shopping" for Services and selecting them dynamically based on whatever business logic dictated. Although this *dynamic discovery* of Web Services appeared to be a powerful feature, it soon became clear that it was generally quite impractical. Not only would fetching contracts on every Service invocation introduce enormous overhead, but it turned out that very few people really wanted to dynamically discover Web Services after all. What they really wanted was a way to implement loosely coupled integration.

So the brilliant minds on the various Web Services standards committees put their heads together and came up with the *document style*. A document-style Web Service expected a document from a consumer, and/or returned a document to the consumer (where *and/or* indicates that they now supported asynchronous behaviors like publish/subscribe and fire & forget). WSDL still specified the interface, only now we allowed for XML schemas to specify the message interchange formats.

One of the most challenging aspects of SOA is understanding the benefits of document-style Service interactions over the contrasting RPC style. On first glance, this difference in styles between Services (Web Services in particular) appears to be a technical detail, but in fact, the difference underscores the fundamental architectural principles of SOA. In fact, understanding the true implications of the document style and its relationships both to Service independence as well as building for change goes to the heart of what it means to do SOA properly.

The primary advantage that document-style Web Services had over RPC style (in addition to allowing for asynchronous message exchange patterns) was that document-style Services allowed for many changes to Services that wouldn't break existing consumers. It's possible to add operations to a Service, add parameters to an operation, add wild cards to the schemas, and a few other changes. If an existing consumer doesn't understand the new addition, it simply ignores the change—something that RPC-style Services didn't allow.

To this day, most SOA deployments leverage document-style Web Services for just these reasons. However (you knew a *however* was coming, didn't you?), document-style Web Services still had issues that limited loose coupling: in particular, the operations themselves. Even with document-style Services, the developer (or architect) must specify the operations for the Web Service in the WSDL file. Essentially, all Web Services operations are custom, and though you can make certain changes to them, other changes (like removing an operation) would break existing consumers. Furthermore, vendors dealt with Web Service operations in different ways, leading to no end of confusion and hair-pulling. You'll be glad to know we won't go into the gory details, but suffice it to say that if you've managed to successfully implement Web Services, especially as part of an SOA deployment, then some of your biggest headaches likely involved Web Service operations.

Before we discuss how to solve the issues with Service operations, however, it's important to understand how the document style works, and how it contrasts with the RPC style—if only because Web Services are so prevalent in today's SOA deployments. For the purposes of this section we'll work through a specific example. In our example the architect must design a Create Employee Service that basically creates an employee record in the organization's human resources database. To illustrate the need to build this Service for change, we'll delineate three use cases, where the first illustrates today's requirement, the second is the requirement three months from now, and the third is the business requirement six months down the road. Let's start with the first two:

- **Use case 1 (Today's use case).** We ask the Create Employee Service to create an employee record, and it creates an empty employee record

with a unique ID and returns the ID number. We'll populate the
information in the employee record with a call to a separate Service.

- **Use case 2 (The use case in three months).** We send the Create
Employee Service a document that contains much of the information
we want to track about the employee, and it populates a new employee
record with that information and returns the unique ID number for that
employee.

Furthermore, each of the two use cases meets the needs, say, of separate
Lines of Business (LOBs), so the Create Employee Service must continue to
meet the needs of each LOB, even as the new use cases come our way.
Remember, for this Service to be loosely coupled, changing its capabilities
mustn't break existing consumers of this Service.

Next, let's begin with use case 1 and take the RPC-style approach to
implementing this Service, where, for example, we decide to build an Employee
Information Service with four required operations: `create()`, `read()`,
`update()`, and `delete()`. In other words, we're not creating a Create
Employee Service at all. Instead, we're actually implementing an Employee
Information Service, and calling the `createEmployee()` operation on that
Service, where that operation takes no parameters and returns the unique
employee ID. So far so good—this RPC-style approach offers the desired
functionality behind use case 1 and furthermore offers other operations as well.

The problem arises, however, when we try to add use case 2 to the mix.
In order to support the new parameters for the Service, we must rework the
contract for the Service, and thus we must also update the consumers as well,
or they will be sending an invalid request to the Service. Furthermore, if we
were to change which information a consumer sends to the Service, we'd need
to change the contract and the consumers yet again.

To maintain loosely coupled Services, therefore, let's implement use
case 1 following the *document style* instead. In this situation, we build a
Create Employee Service after all, and it accepts an XML document as
input, where the entire document is itself considered to be the input of
the single `CreateEmployee` operation that represents the entire behavior
of the Service. Simply receiving the document is sufficient to create the
employee record; the header of that document may contain other information like security-related content, but its body need contain no parameters
or other information.

Now when the time comes to implement use case 2, we simply add the newly
required functionality to the Service in order to accept input documents with
information in their bodies. If a request comes along with customer information
in it, we can update the customer record. If that information is missing, then we
simply follow the implementation of use case 1. Furthermore, if we change the

customer information we're accepting over time, then the Service can continue to support the newly added functionality without adversely impacting any consumers or requiring any changes to its contract. In other words, building document-style Services is essential for loose coupling.

It's important to note, however, that not all Web Services have one operation that represents the entire behavior of the Service. A Service might have many operations, dozens or hundreds, in fact. Each operation specifies a particular behavior for how the Service will handle incoming XML documents and produce corresponding results. However, at this point we're posed with a challenge. Do we define a single WSDL document that specifies a `Customer` Service, with multiple operations for creating, modifying, and deleting records, or do we create multiple Services, each purpose-built for a specific operation but accepting different XML documents to handle different use cases?

This question gets to the heart of the matter in discussing the difference between RPC style and document style approaches to Web Services. In the RPC style, Services are treated as if they were objects with methods, requiring a SOAP call to address a specific operation with a specific method call to evoke a response. The XML message in this instance looks like a call to a method, with parameters and functions. For example, we might call the `getCustomerName` operation on the `Customer` Service and pass an XML document that looks like `<getName><id type='integer'>1234</id></getName>`. Thus, the RPC style requires that Service consumers know not only the specific operation they wish to call, but also its method and type. As a result, RPC is a tightly coupled approach in which any change to the operation or method requires significant change to the Service consumers.

The document style offers a greater degree of loose coupling than the RPC style, because any changes to the methods or operations might have very little impact on Service consumers. In addition, the XML body of a document-style Web Services interaction contains the actual business message—the valuable stuff, whereas in the RPC approach, the XML typically just describes the methods and parameters of the method call.

REST to the Rescue

The main problem with Web Services is that they aren't as loosely coupled as they should be, because the document style inherits RPC-like characteristics in the form of Web Service operations. Yes, sending documents in and out of a Service sounds declarative, to be sure, especially when we represent Service contracts as metadata. But we simply haven't gone far enough.

This point in the story is when we finally get to Representational State Transfer (REST). Done properly, REST offers a *fully* declarative approach to distributed computing that doesn't have the RPC baggage of Web Services. Sounds great, right? One problem: that dreaded phrase *done properly*.

The problem is, the topic of REST is a minefield: It seems that most people don't understand it, even when they write authoritatively on the subject. And the true authoritative source, Dr. Roy Fielding, speaks in the precise yet obscure prose of an academic, often sowing as much confusion as he does clarity. Yet the answers lie in Fielding's explanations, even though studying them feels a bit like sitting at the feet of the Buddha, hoping for enlightenment.

Let's begin with Wikipedia, a source Fielding bemoans as being a poor substitute for truth—an opinion our editors wholeheartedly agree with. Be that as it may, it's an expedient starting point for our discussion, because so many people refer to the Wikipedia definition of REST as the authoritative definition. Wikipedia defines REST as "*a style of software architecture for distributed hypermedia systems such as the World Wide Web.*" We always thought this definition was rather silly: after all, how many distributed hypermedia systems can you think of *other* than the Web? But as it turns out, the notion of a distributed hypermedia application is central to REST—and a key part of the Agile Architecture story as well.

But we're getting ahead of ourselves. Let's start at the beginning: REST is an architectural style. An *architectural style* is essentially a set of constraints on the overall architectural approach. SOA is a style of Enterprise Architecture, in fact—although the constraints on EA that SOA imposes are rather flexible. Not so with REST. In the case of REST, the style consists of four constraints. You must comply with all four to be doing REST. If you miss one, what you're doing might be *REST-like*, but it isn't REST.

The reason REST is so cut and dried is because one person—Dr. Roy Fielding—invented REST, so essentially, he is the final authority on what REST is and is not. True, it's useful to have a single authority, unlike SOA, where it seems that everybody makes up their own definition of what SOA is and is not. But on the downside, Roy Fielding apparently has better things to do than spend all his time clearing up confusion about REST.

Fielding was one of the creators of the Hypertext Transfer Protocol (HTTP), making him one of the progenitors of the Web itself. In order to write his doctoral dissertation in 2000, he looked at the Web, and saw that it was *good*. Of course, by 2000, the Web was already immense, having grown well beyond the expectations of Fielding and the other folks who came up with its underlying standards and mechanisms. Fielding didn't sit down and say, hey, let's come up with a new architectural style, call it REST, and then see if the Web complies with it. In fact, just the opposite: he looked at the Web and asked if it were possible to distill the architectural principles that made the Web what it had become. The result was REST.

If REST is an architectural style for building distributed hypermedia applications, we must answer two core questions: first, what constitutes a

REST application, and second, where is the architecture and where is its implementation? Of course, Fielding's precise definition of REST differs from the Wikipedia simplification. According to Fielding, "the Representational State Transfer (REST) style is an abstraction of the architectural elements within a distributed hypermedia system." And therein lies the key to REST: REST is an *abstraction*.

Of course, abstractions are nothing new—they are a basic tool of any architect. But most people don't grok just how abstract REST is. For example, do you think that REST is HTTP-specific? No, it's not. It deals with abstracted hypertext protocols, of which HTTP is the most familiar. Does REST call for uniform interfaces consisting of GET, POST, PUT, and DELETE operations? No again. Those are examples of uniform interface operations, but REST itself doesn't specify them, other than an abstracted GET operation. And of course, resources are abstractions of server capabilities or entities, not the capabilities or entities themselves, whereas representations are abstractions of media type instances, not the instances themselves. Even the terms "client" and "server" are abstractions: a REST client may actually run on a physical server, and a REST server may serve as a client. In fact, there's nothing client/server about REST.

So when Wikipedia uses the phrase "a style of software architecture for distributed hypermedia systems such as the World Wide Web," it's pointing out that REST applies constraints to abstracted distributed hypermedia systems, of which the Web is only the most familiar example.

Confused yet? You're not alone. Architects look at the level of abstraction behind REST and wonder, "How can this mess be useful?" while developers look at it and think, "Okay whatever, let's build a RESTful API and go from there." At that point, the architects take off their architect hats and dive into the technical details alongside the coders. The result? A lot of noise and confusion, ostensible RESTful APIs that are not really RESTful at all, and the mistaken belief that you can comply with some of the REST architectural constraints but not all of them, and still be doing some kind of REST.

And that brings us to the most important question about REST: What is a RESTful application anyway? A RESTful application is a *distributed hypermedia application*, of course—something you apply a distributed hypermedia system to in order to accomplish some goal. Easy to say, but deceptively difficult to understand, until you realize that REST is *all about* distributed hypermedia applications. They're the point of REST. If you think you're "doing" REST without the goal of building a distributed hypermedia application, you're missing the point of REST entirely.

Unfortunately, most people who are trying to do REST, simply put, are missing the point of REST entirely!

It's as though we're trying to build a brick building, so we hire an architect who comes up with plans for a brick building. We look at the plans and we don't really understand them, but we know we want to build with bricks, so we spend all our time figuring out the best way to mix mortar. Once we've come up with really good mortar, we convince ourselves we know how to build the building, even though we still don't understand the plan.

That's the state of REST today. People look at REST's four architectural constraints, and say, "I don't understand the fourth one—hypermedia as the engine of application state (HATEOAS). But I think I can figure out the bits about resources and representations." What they're failing to realize is the hypermedia bit is the *point* of what they're doing, just as actually building the building according to plan is the point of the mortar.

One way of looking at this design a building vs. mix the mortar situation is to define different levels of REST maturity, where supporting HATEOAS is the most mature level. Leonard Richardson (author of the book *RESTful Web Services*) first posited this position, and today we call it the *Richardson Maturity Model* (RMM).

As shown in Figure 8.2, RMM calls for four maturity levels:

- **Level 0: The Swamp of Plain Old XML (POX).** Not REST at all, simply using POST following an RPC approach. Messages could be XML or any POST-compatible format, for that matter.
- **Level 1: Resources.** Essentially follows an object approach. Rather than calling some remote function and passing it our arguments, we call a method on a particular resource, which in turn provides arguments for

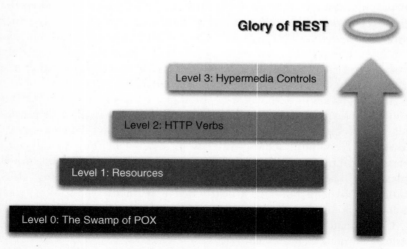

Figure 8.2   The Richardson Maturity Model
Source: Martin Fowler; www.martinfowler.com/articles/richardsonMaturityModel.html. Used with permission.

the other information we want to pass it. We're simply tunneling through HTTP.

- **Level 2 HTTP Verbs.** We use REST's uniform interface, but we're not thinking in terms of hyperlinks.
- **Level 3 Hypermedia controls.** Now we're finally using HATEOAS. The way we know what we can do next is by following hyperlinks in representations from previous requests. All we need is a starting point (which we call a bookmark, naturally), and we go from there.

The Richardson Maturity Model has essentially institutionalized the mortar-first approach to REST, suggesting that HATEOAS is at the highest level of maturity, and it's perfectly fine to start at the lower levels and work your way up. In other words, it's fine to start construction once you have good mortar; you'll figure out the plan eventually. Clearly, that's no way to build a house!

So, what is it about HATEOAS that's so difficult? State engines? Computer Science 101, Hypermedia? Not really that confusing, either. After all, *hypertext* is just a document with links in it to other documents, and by generalizing hypertext to the term *hypermedia*, we're simply allowing for media types other than HTML documents and the like. After all, a video or sound file could have a link in it, right? So, where's the confusion?

The confusion lies in the second letter A—*application*. As in *distributed hypermedia application*. The point of REST, remember? The architectural starting point for any implementation that REST constraints are appropriate for is the design of the hypermedia application that meets the given business requirements. If you look at the business requirements, and your expertise as an architect tells you that a distributed hypermedia application isn't the right thing to build, then *don't use REST*. On the other hand, a distributed hypermedia application might be just the ticket. The next question you should ask is, how dynamic should this application be? In other words, what agility does the business require? Put the analysis that provides the answer to that question in your Agility Model. Then let the Agility Model—not the Richardson Maturity Model—guide your design.

To illustrate the agility levels for distributed hypermedia applications that should frame your Agility Model, let's work through some concrete examples. As you go through these levels, compare them to the Richardson model.

- **Level 1: Static hypermedia application, consisting of a set of static Web pages containing nothing but HTML, interconnected by links.** Not particularly agile. Is it REST? Yes, but in a very simplistic way. Does it meet your requirements? Perhaps, but probably not.

- **Level 2: Hypermedia application consisting of static Web pages that contain HTML and client-side JavaScript (no funky Ajax or the like).** Pages link to each other, and the links may be dynamic, based on client-side logic in the JavaScript.
- **Level 3: Hypermedia application consisting of dynamic Web pages built on the fly on the Web server, using php or Java Server Pages or whatever server scripting environment floats your boat.** Pages link to each other, but the links may be dynamic, based on server-side logic.
- **Level 4: Hypermedia application consisting of a set of dynamic representations that conform to a variety of media types (HTML documents, XML documents, images, video, you name it), where those representations have links to other representations, and furthermore, the links may be dynamic, based on client-side or server-side logic or both, as appropriate.** Now you're getting the idea of what a distributed hypermedia application is supposed to look like.

Once you have determined the agility requirements for your application, *now* you may think about how best to implement its components—the hyperlinked representations. Answering that question finally leads you to a consideration of the resources that generate those representations. But you don't start with the resources; you start with the hypermedia application. You *finish* with the resources.

Keep in mind, however, that the examples in the agility levels are just that—*examples*— particular implementation decisions that may be appropriate for a given situation. The architecture, however, is the overall, best practice–driven approach for beginning with the business challenge and working through the levels of abstraction to come up with a working implementation at the end. As an architectural style, REST is simply a set of constraints on the architecture: one way of doing things that makes it easier to solve certain problems. The architect must decide whether REST or any other style is appropriate for the problem at hand, but if you choose REST, then you *must* begin with the distributed hypermedia application you wish to build.

It's no wonder, then, that the World Wide Web itself follows REST. The question for us is, can we bottle up whatever makes the Web the Web and apply it to distributed applications in general? The answer: *absolutely*, as long as those applications are distributed hypermedia applications. If you don't want to build such an app, then don't use REST. But if you want to build an app that is massively horizontally scalable (like the Web), enormously resilient (like the Web), has no central point of control (like the Web), and is always growing and changing (like the Web), then REST is how to do it.

Dogmatic vs. Iconoclastic REST

As an architectural style, therefore, REST consists of a set of constraints. REST also introduces some new vocabulary. Before we get to the constraints themselves, let's make sure to define our terms:

- **Resource.** An entity or capability on a network. More precisely, a resource is an *abstraction* of an entity or capability you wish to expose. A resource is anything you can give a URI to (see the next bullet). Common resources include static or dynamic Web pages, documents, images, or videos, as well as programs or scripts that can generate such files. Procedure calls or Web Services can also be resources.
- **Uniform Resource Identifier (URI).** A string that identifies a resource over a network (typically the Internet). URIs come in two flavors: either URLs or URNs. Uniform Resource Locators (URLs) are the more familiar; for example, http://www.zapthink.com. The URL identifies the resource and specifies the means of acting on or obtaining the representation (i.e., the http:// bit at the beginning). Uniform Resource Names (URNs), on the other hand, identify resources by name in a particular namespace (identifier system), but don't specify their location or how to access the resource. For example, the URN of our last book, *Service Orient or Be Doomed!*, is urn:isbn:0-471-76858-8. The identifier system here is the International Standard Book Number (ISBN).
- **Representation.** The data (and corresponding metadata) that provide a concrete manifestation of a resource. In other words, what the resource sends to the client. Resources typically have multiple representations that often conform to standard Internet media types (formerly called Multipurpose Internet Mail Extensions, or MIME types— but because they're much more useful than specifying e-mail attachments, we now call them Internet media types.) Examples of Internet media types: text/HTML, text/plain, application/XML, application/JSON, image/SVG+XML, and so on. Representations can be documents of any of these types.
- **Hypermedia.** A style of building systems for accessing information via a network of multimedia nodes connected by hyperlinks—for example, the World Wide Web.
- **Client and Server.** The REST context abstracts these terms. A server is an abstraction of a system that provides resources, and a client is an abstraction of a system that obtains representations from resources on a server. But one computer might serve both roles at once, and we're not trying to indicate that REST follows a client/server architecture.

REST also calls for *uniform interfaces*. In other words, instead of the custom operations in the Web Services world, with REST, clients interact with resources via a fixed set of verbs:

- **GET** – Query the current state of the resource.
- **POST** – Create or initialize a resource.
- **PUT** – Update a resource.
- **DELETE** – Delete a resource.

Technically speaking, the HTTP protocol defines these four verbs, and REST can work with other protocols that specify different verbs. But for most practical purposes (and for the purposes of this book), we'll stick with these four verbs.

Now that we've got the basic definitions of REST out of the way, we can finally list the four architectural constraints that constitute the REST style:

1. **Separation of resource from representation.** Remember, resources are *abstractions* of capabilities on a server. The means for maintaining state of resources (what we call the *resource state*) should be invisible to users of resource, and furthermore, resource providers must hide limitations of underlying media and technology from users. For example, a php script (or JSP script or what have you) on a server would be a resource, and the Web page (HTML file) it generates is a representation. These two files are very different, and the php script should be hidden from users.

2. **Manipulation of resources by representations.** A representation of a resource (including its metadata) can provide sufficient information to modify or delete the resource on the server, provided the client has permission, and furthermore, the information the resource provides to the user in the representation is the *only* way for the user to interact with the resource. For example, the only way to submit POST data to a resource from a Web page would be to submit a form on the Web page.

3. **Self-descriptive messages.** Each message (the message being the same as the representation) includes enough information to describe how to process the message. For example, an Internet media type may specify which parser to invoke. Responses also explicitly indicate their cacheability.

4. **Hypermedia as the engine of application state.** The client interacts with applications entirely through hypermedia. Representations reflect the current state of such hypermedia applications (what we call the *application state*) through hyperlinks, where hyperlinks contain opaque references to persistent resource state on the server.

The first three constraints are relatively straightforward, but if you find the fourth one confusing, you're not alone. Bear with us—it will take a few sections to fully explain it. Naturally, that fourth constraint is the most important—for REST, as well as for Agile Architecture in general.

Do you need to follow all four constraints? Of course not. Remember, we recommend an iconoclastic approach to architecture: Apply only those rules that help you solve the business problems you're facing. If any or all of the REST constraints don't help you, then by all means, don't use them. But—and it's an important *but*—if you want to do REST, you must follow all four constraints, simply because that's what it means to do REST. But never do REST because it's REST, only do it because it solves the problems at hand.

REST vs. Web Services

With REST, a server exposes a resource using a URI. The idea with REST is to change some state of a *resource*, rather than calling some procedure on a remote system, as traditional RPC methods of distributed computing mandate. To illustrate this point, REST might call for a resource type `Customer` which might have hundreds of exposed URIs. For example, http://mysite/customers/insurance/johndoe might refer to John Doe's customer record in an insurance application. To modify information in that record, the user would POST or PUT an XML file into that URI and then GET that information back in a subsequent call to the URI. Instead of making a call to a function called `getcustomer` and passing it a `customerID`, make a call to a resource called `customerID` and throw some XML at it.

From a REST perspective, we don't really care about the architecture of the underlying solution. We can leverage REST for n-tier applications or client/server solutions just as easily as SOA-centric approaches. Indeed, any application can be RESTful if it exposes capabilities through a GET request via HTTP.

In SOA, however, a Service does not necessarily map to a resource, but rather to a set of operations or a composite business process. Indeed, a Service maps more closely to the concepts of capabilities and processes more so than the resources that those capabilities and processes act on. In this regard, a Service may be exposed as a resource, and a resource might expose a Service, but there's no a priori equivalence between Services and resources.

The real contrast, therefore, is between REST styles of Service implementation and Web Services styles that have an operation-specific perspective. Keep in mind that Web Services don't represent an architectural approach, but rather a set of standards for how we define Services (WSDL), communicate with Services (SOAP), discover their availability (Universal Description,

Discovery, and Integration, UDDI), and perform other value-added security, reliability, composition, and management tasks.

In the Web Services world, when a WSDL file specifies a document-style interface, then the constraints on the input and output messages fall into one or more schema definitions, instead of the SOAP message structure itself. As far as SOAP is concerned, the body of the SOAP message contains a payload consisting of whatever document you like. The advantage of the document style over the tightly coupled remote procedure call (RPC) style is it allows for flexible versioning of Services: Many changes to a Service do not force a new contract version.

However, as the last section explained, the operations of a Service still cause issues, even when it's a document-style interface. We can't seem to get away from Web Services' tightly coupled RPC heritage. And furthermore, XML schemas are strongly typed, which introduces a further undesirable level of tight coupling.

To resolve such issues, REST moves the operations out of any formal contract, instead relying on the GET, POST, PUT, and DELETE operations. Even so, there's no requirement in REST that resources are necessarily documents. True, URLs that point to documents are a common and familiar pattern, but URLs could as easily point to abstracted method calls as well.

The REST approach, therefore, contrasts starkly with RPC, where an object called `Customer` would have a multitude of operations for creating, deleting, and modifying records, with multiple, discrete instances of objects each referring to a different customer. Fundamentally, therefore, REST is more like the document style, which also contrasts with the RPC style by requiring only that Service consumers know the operations they wish to call.

The fundamental difference, therefore, between REST and document-style Web Services is how the Service consumer knows what to expect out of the Service. Web Services have contracts, defined in WSDL. Because Web Services focus on the Service, rather than on the resource, the consumer has clear visibility into the behavior of the various operations of the Service, whereas in REST's resource-oriented perspective, we have visibility into the resources, but the behavior is implicit, because there is no single place we can look for a contract that governs the behavior of each URI-identified resource.

The evolution of SOAP highlights the change in thinking that eventually led to the RESTful approach. SOAP originally stood for the *Simple Object Access Protocol* when the vision for the standard was to provide, yes, a simple way to access objects—in other words, an RPC approach. Later, the World Wide Web Consortium (W3C) rechristened SOAP as just "SOAP"—no longer an acronym. SOAP is nothing more than the standardized, XML-based method for interacting with a third-party Service, now via the document style. Simple in concept, but in practice, there are many ways to utilize SOAP. SOAP still allows for RPC-style interactions. Furthermore, how do you identify end-points? And what about naming operations and methods? Clearly SOAP on its own leaves too much to interpretation.

WSDL is supposed to answer some of these questions. But writing and reading WSDL is a cumbersome affair. Data type matching can be a pain. Versioning is a bear. Minor server-side changes often result in different WSDL files and thus different Service interfaces, and on the client side, XML schema descriptions of the Service are often similarly tied to a particular version of the SOAP endpoint, and can thus break all too easily.

One of the primary reasons to use REST over Web Services is *simplicity*. As most advocates of REST will tell you, REST is simpler to use and understand than Web Services. Development with REST is easier and quicker than building WSDL files and getting SOAP to work—the reason why many of the most-used Web APIs are at least ostensibly RESTful. You can easily test HTTP-based REST requests with a simple browser call. REST can also be more efficient as a protocol because it doesn't require a SOAP envelope for every call, and REST can also leverage JSON as a data representation format instead of the more verbose, strongly typed, and complex XML.

But even more than simplicity, REST offers what we might call *architectural elegance*. The basic operation and scalability of the Web has proven the underlying premise of the fundamental REST approach. HTTP operations are standardized, widely accepted, well understood, and operate consistently. There's no need to communicate company-specific SOAP actions or methods—the basic GET, POST, PUT, and DELETE operations are standardized across all Service calls.

Even more appealing is the fact that the vendors have not polluted REST with their own interests. The primary driver for Web Services adoption has been the vendors. Say what you might about the standard's applicability outside a vendor environment, one would be very hard pressed to utilize Web Services in any robust way without first choosing a vendor platform. And once you've chosen that platform, you've essentially committed to a specific Web Services implementation approach, forcing third parties and others to comply with the quirks of your particular platform.

Not so with REST. Not only does the simplicity of the approach eschew vendor meddling, it actually negates much of the value that vendor offerings provide. Indeed, it's much easier (and not to mention lower cost) to utilize open source offerings in RESTful SOA approaches than more expensive and cumbersome vendor offerings. Furthermore, you can leverage existing technologies that have already proven themselves in high-scale, high-performance environments.

Can REST Fix Web Services?

REST introduces the notion of a uniform interface, which promises to address the tight coupling issues that Web Services operations have left us. But REST is about hypermedia applications, not uniform interfaces. The question remains, therefore, whether REST will help us improve Web Services–based SOA.

Building abstracted interfaces that enabled organizations to deal better with change is what SOA was all about, of course. Unfortunately, the tools we had at our disposal—namely, Web Services—didn't go far enough. Yes, we moved from RPC-style Web Services to document style, and that improved our loose coupling substantially. But even document-style Web Services still had operations, a holdover from the bad old functional programming days.

Enter REST. In spite of the advantages of document-style interfaces over RPC and declarative approaches over programmatic, people still aren't getting it. Not only are techies missing the point of REST, even when they build supposedly RESTful APIs, they're failing to follow the REST constraints.

For example, many of these ostensible RESTful APIs don't provide self-descriptive messages. With REST, every message from a resource should contain all the metadata necessary for any client to understand what it can do with representations of that resource. In the RPC days, procedural responses may have contained only data with no metadata. With Web Service interactions, Service responses contained some metadata in the form of the SOAP envelope, header, and the tagging structure in the body. But even with Web Services, the WSDL contract and policy metadata are external to the Service. You don't expect to get the contract when you query a Service.

With a RESTful interaction, on the other hand, contract metadata may be returned in particular representations, whether they be media type metadata, schemas, or even less structured metadata. And of course, representations also include hyperlinks, which also provide contract metadata to the client.

Separation of resources from representations is another essential REST constraint—one that developers also frequently violate. If there are any instructions to the resource in a request other than one of the four operations of the uniform interface, then you are violating this constraint. For example, if your request is instructing a resource to update a record, you're not being RESTful. It's up to the *resource* to determine whether a POST or PUT should update a record, not the representation.

Finally, hypermedia as the engine of application state—the dreaded HATEOAS—is perhaps the most overlooked of the REST constraints, even though it's the most important. The big picture of HATEOAS are the hypermedia applications that we're trying to build, but even at the API level, HATEOAS is critical, in conjunction with the self-descriptive message constraint. In any truly RESTful interaction, the resource returns a representation that contains all necessary metadata, *including hyperlinks that instruct the client what it can do next*. Likewise, a RESTful client has no idea what a resource can do for it unless it follows such links.

What so many techies lose sight of is the fact that REST isn't supposed to make the Web more like system integration; *it's meant to make system integration more like the Web*. When you click a link in a Web page, you expect to go to another Web page, or perhaps a video or sound file or some other media representation. REST takes that simple interaction and abstracts it. Now you have an abstracted client (instead of a browser) supporting a request of a resource (the Web server capability; for example, the php script that generated the response) on an abstracted server (the Web server) that returns a representation (the resulting media file or Web page) as per the uniform interface (what the link you clicked was supposed to do). These abstractions let us apply simple Web behavior to all manner of system-to-system interactions. But never, ever lose sight of the fact that you want simple Web behavior from your application.

I'm sure many readers who made it this far are muttering to themselves that their RESTful APIs are truly RESTful. Well, maybe, but probably not, and here's proof. Let's take a popular, supposedly RESTful API as an example: the Yahoo! Maps PlaceFinder Geocoding API, which you can find at http://developer.yahoo.com/geo/placefinder/. Yahoo! PlaceFinder is a geocoding Service that helps developers make their applications' location aware by converting street addresses or place names into geographic coordinates, and vice versa.

If you go to the documentation page for this API, you'll notice a "BASE URI," which it expresses as http://where.yahooapis.com/geocode?[parameters]. There are two problems with this expression. First, it's not a hyperlink (it just looks like one). Second, the URL has the question mark in it, requiring the user to know which parameters might be valid.

Let's say instead we turn this expression into a true hyperlink, leaving off the parameters because we don't know what they are: http://where.yahooapis.com/geocode. Go ahead, type that link into a browser, I dare ya. Sure enough, you get an error message. True, it's XML formatted, but the error message is missing something absolutely essential: a *hyperlink*.

In fact, Yahoo! made several serious mistakes: First, the base URI isn't a hyperlink, violating HATEOAS. Second, the metadata that tell you how to use the interface are separate from the interface, rather than returned in the response from hyperlinking to the base URI, violating the self-descriptive messages constraint. Third, the URI requires parameters as part of the search query (the characters after the question mark), violating the separation of resource and representation. And finally, the error response it *did* return didn't include a hyperlink, once again violating HATEOAS. Bottom line: There's really very little that's RESTful about this API.

Though it may be amusing to pick on Yahoo!, it's important to point out that they aren't alone. In fact, they're typical. It's quite rare, in fact, for a supposed RESTful interface to be truly Web-friendly. After all, most techies don't expect Web friendliness from APIs. APIs are, well, *programming* interfaces, whereas the Web consists of *user* interfaces. But in the REST world, programming interfaces are simply abstracted user interfaces. In other words, truly RESTful APIs aren't really like the APIs we know and love, and have been working with for years. They're fundamentally different.

We know this idea is deeply iconoclastic. However, the point of this section isn't to scold everybody for doing REST wrong. The point is to help you think differently about what it means to program in a distributed environment. The point to the programmable Web isn't to make the Web more programmable, *it's to make software more Web-like*. If we can finally free ourselves from the last vestiges of imperative, RPC-style programming, even going so far as to steer clear of functional programming, and move to a fully declarative, document-centric paradigm, only then will we be able to achieve the resilience and power of the Web when we tackle system integration challenges.

This Agile Architecture mind shift is at the core of REST. When Roy Fielding wrote his dissertation, he didn't come up with REST and then build the Web following its constraints. On the contrary: He deeply understood what made the Web itself so special, and he sought to express that specialness as an architectural style. True, tackling system integration following true RESTful principles is difficult. But remember, building the Web was easy. Take Transmission Control Protocol/Internet Protocol (TCP/IP), add a few simple standard protocols, code an HTML rendering app we called a browser, and the Web more or less took it from there. Almost 20 years later, the Web is unimaginably immense, and yet it still works just fine, thank you very much. Is it too much to ask for all of our IT systems to behave the same way?

Does REST Provide Deep Interoperability?

How can REST help us along the Deep Interoperability Supertrend: the move toward software products that truly interoperate, even over time as standards and products mature and requirements evolve? Of course, the Web Services standards don't even guarantee *interoperability*, let alone Deep Interoperability. Many vendors pick up on this point in their discussions about supporting REST. They offer a few different angles, but the common thread is that, hey, we support REST, so we have Deep Interoperability out of the box! So buy our gear, forget the Web Services standards, and your interoperability issues will be a thing of the past!

Not so fast. Such a perspective misses the entire point to Deep Interoperability. For two products to be deeply interoperable, they should be able to interoperate *even if their primary interface protocols are incompatible*. A REST-based software product would have to be able to interoperate with another product that didn't support REST by negotiating some other set of protocols that both products did support.

But this "least common denominator" negotiation model is still not the whole Deep Interoperability story. Even if all interfaces were REST interfaces, we still wouldn't have Deep Interoperability. If REST alone guaranteed Deep Interoperability, then there could be no such thing as a bad link. Bad links on Web pages are ubiquitous, of course. Put a perfectly good link in a Web page that connects to a valid resource. Wait a few years. Click the link again. Chances are, the original resource was deleted or moved or had its name changed. 404 not found.

OK, all you RESTafarians out there, how do we solve this problem? What can we do when we create a link to prevent it from ever going bad? How do we keep existing links from going bad? And what do we do about all the bad links that are already out there? The answers to these questions are all part of the Deep Interoperability Supertrend.

RMM describes this solution as *hypermedia controls*. Essentially, start from your bookmark and follow links to representations that contain additional information and further hyperlinks. But instead of simply supporting human users clicking links in browsers, support software-based agents as well. How does one piece of software learn how to interact with another? Again, simply by following hyperlinks. Of course, a piece of software is unlikely to request an HTML page, as HTML is for human consumption. Instead, it might request an XML or JSON file, or any other Internet media type it can understand.

Hypermedia controls and Internet media types don't solve all our tight coupling problems, of course, because we have yet to deal with semantic content. If our client agent can't *understand the meaning* of a representation, it may still not know what to do next. But REST—and in particular, HATEOAS—take us further toward Agile Architecture than any other approach available today.

One important point is that the modem negotiation example is only a part of the story, because in that case, you already have the two modems, and the initiating one can find the other one. But Deep Interoperability also requires discoverability and location independence. You can't interoperate with a piece of software you can't find.

But we still don't have the whole story yet, because we must still deal with the problem of *change*. What if we were able to interoperate at one point in time, but then one of our endpoints changed. How do we ensure continued interoperability? The traditional answer is to put something in the middle:

either a broker in a middleware-centric model or a registry or other discovery agency that can resolve abstract endpoint references in a lightweight model (either REST or SOA). The problem with such intermediary-based approaches, however, is that they relieve the vendors from the need to build products with Deep Interoperability built in. Instead, they simply offer one more excuse to sell middleware.

Deep Interoperability is a peer-to-peer model, in that we're requiring two products to be deeply interoperable with each other. But peer-to-peer Deep Interoperability is just the price of admission. If we have two products that are deeply interoperating, and we add a third product to the mix, it should be able to negotiate with the other two, not just to establish the three pairwise relationships, but to form the most efficient way for all three products to work together. Add a fourth product, then a fifth, and so on, and the same process should take place.

The end result will be IT environments of arbitrary size and complexity supporting Deep Interoperability across the entire architecture. Add a product, remove a product, or change a product, and the entire ecosystem adjusts accordingly. And if you're wondering whether this ecosystem-level adjustment is an *emergent property* of our system of systems, you've hit the nail on the head.

Where Is the SOA in REST-Based SOA?

If HATEOAS moves us closer to Deep Interoperability, and Deep Interoperability is core to Agile Architecture, then we should be able to tell a RESTful Agile Architecture story. What do we mean, though, by REST-based SOA? Though many architects believe that as an architectural style, REST is simpler and more straightforward that Web Services-based SOA, there is continued confusion over the principles of REST and how best to implement them. Everybody seems to get the basics—operate on resources at URIs with the four HTTP-centric operations GET, POST, PUT, and DELETE—but most people seem to miss the subtleties. Combine that confusion with the fact that you can do REST without SOA, and the specifics of REST-based SOA are even more elusive, as we must pare down the essentials of both REST and SOA to understand the true nature of the combined approach. How, therefore, should we handle Service abstractions, contracts, and compositions—arguably, the essence of SOA—in a REST-based SOA world?

At the center of the SOA approach is the notion of a Service abstraction. REST resources are abstractions as well, but resources are abstractions of capabilities or entities on the server, which is not quite the same thing as a Service abstraction. In SOA, the Service abstraction supports Business Services, which represent flexible, business-centric capabilities. A Business Service may abstract multiple Service interfaces, where routing and transformation operations on intermediaries present a loosely coupled façade.

Most RESTafarians, however, don't think at this level. They are thinking of clients (e.g., browsers) accessing resources at URIs that return representations. A representation is an HTML page, an XML file, a video, and so on. The business context is lost in a sea of URI formats and Internet media types.

What RESTafarians often overlook is that the intermediary pattern is actually one of the core architectural constraints of REST. URIs need not point *directly* to resources; it is perfectly okay for an intermediary to resolve the URI into a physical endpoint. After all, that's what DNS servers do!

From the SOA perspective, we can rely on the intermediary to execute routing rules and transformations as necessary to support the business abstraction. Furthermore, we can establish and enforce the policy (as a part of our SOA governance framework) that the *only* allowed way to access resources is via endpoints on an intermediary. From the REST perspective, think DNS server on steroids: Instead of simply resolving URLs to IP addresses, resolve any formal URI structure to physical resource endpoints by following a rich set of transformation and routing metadata.

At the technical level, a Service is a contracted interface or an abstraction of contracted interfaces. Web Services have contracts that comply with WSDL, but there's no equivalent of WSDL for REST resources. True, resources have uniform interfaces that the four HTTP operations define, but simply knowing you can GET a resource or POST to a resource doesn't tell you anything about what that resource is supposed to do. Accessing a resource does give you a representation of that resource, however. Representations can comply with standard Internet media types, but even the media type specification is insufficient to qualify as a contract.

Sun Microsystems tried to promote the Web Application Description Language (WADL) as a RESTafarian alternative to WSDL, but work on WADL has largely petered out now that Sun is part of Oracle. The point to WADL was more to stub out REST resources in Java than to provide an implementation-neutral contract language, in any case.

Where, then, is the contract? Let's look at a simple REST example: the simplest, of course, being the Web itself. Let's say you are filling in a form on a Web page and then hit submit. Where is the contract?

The form method is POST, and the POST data are the information that you filled into the form. The resource is identified by the form action URL. So far, so good. Have you found the contract yet?

In this example, the contract is the *Web form itself*. The form specifies and constrains the POST data you may input, and specifies the form action, which is a hyperlink to the next resource. You browsed to the page with the Web form by following an earlier link or loading a URL for a resource that returned that Web page as a representation of that resource.

Remember, a REST application is a set of resources that return representations that link to other resources—in other words, *hypermedia*. One resource returns one or more representations (Web pages, XML files, etc.) that contain links to other resources, and it is those hyperlinks (and their associated metadata) that specify the application behavior.

Although a Web page with a form is the simplest and most common example of how to contract POST data, we can generalize that form however we like, depending on what type of client we want to support. For machine-to-machine interactions, for example (that is, when the client is not simply a browser), the first resource may return an XML representation that provides a contracted interface to the client for POSTing to the linked resource. How your resource builds that representation is up to you.

In Web Services-based SOA, we store the contract metadata in a centralized registry/repository. In REST-based SOA, each resource is responsible for returning contract metadata either for itself or for any resource it hyperlinks to. As a result, we may not be able to obtain contracts for resources we're not (yet) able to access, but on the other hand, we can code our resources to dynamically generate contracts if we wish. In REST-based SOA, therefore, contract changes can be automated, where in Web Services-based SOA, contract change is a complex, manual process that requires rigorous governance.

The third core characteristic of SOA we look for is the ability to compose Services into applications. Such compositions might be orchestrations, when they have a predefined flow, or choreographies, when the order of steps in the composition is not determined ahead of time.

A REST application, of course, is an example of a composition of resources. From the SOA perspective, furthermore, a REST application is a *workflow*—that is, a composition with human steps. We can also consider such compositions to be choreographies, because the order of steps depends on which links the user clicks. Users may click links in a different order every time they work their way through the application.

The question still remains, how do we create *automated* orchestrations in the REST world? The answer is simpler than it looks. In REST, *everything* can be a resource. Therefore, orchestrations can be resources as well. An orchestration resource might return a Business Process Execution Language (BPEL) representation or a Business Process Modeling and Notation (BPMN) representation or perhaps a simplified representation of an orchestration that doesn't have the baggage of either BPEL or BPMN. If anything, establishing a *predefined* orchestration is simpler than a hypermedia composition, because the orchestration logic is static, whereas with a hypermedia composition, the underlying resource logic may change the composition logic on the fly. Just because we don't have to fix our application state transitions ahead of time doesn't mean we're not allowed to.

Here are some key pointers to achieving REST-based SOA:

- Make sure your Services are properly abstracted, loosely coupled, composable, and contracted.
- Every RESTful Service should have an unambiguous and unique URI to locate the Service on the network, resolved on an intermediary.
- Use the URI as a means to locate as well as taxonomically define the Service in relation to other Services.
- Use well-established actions (such as POST, GET, PUT, and DELETE for HTTP) for interacting with Services.
- Lessen the dependence on proprietary middleware to coordinate Service interaction and shift to common Web infrastructure to handle SOA infrastructure needs.

REST-Based SOA: An Iconoclastic Approach

We're proud to be iconoclasts. After all, building Agile Architectures requires critical appraisal—and frequent dismissal—of traditionally held beliefs. We know this role places us among the heretics who dare challenge established dogma.

In fact, the whole notion of agility has long suffered this battle between iconoclasm and dogmatism. We're once more jumping into this iconoclasm-masquerading-as-dogma fray with our explanation of how to implement SOA following REST principles, and how such an approach introduces important simplifications and efficiencies as compared to a Web Services-based approach.

Get out the torches and pitchforks! We're at it again! Not only are we flying in the face of established SOA dogma, we're taking on REST dogma as well! Never mind that the original vision for the REST movement was inherently iconoclastic. In fact, it's no wonder that RESTafarians use religious metaphors in their discussions (although Rastafarianism is a far cry indeed from the Catholic metaphors we're leveraging in this section).

To quote our beloved Agile Manifesto, we want to favor responding to change over following a plan—even if that plan is how SOA or even REST is supposed to be done. The goal is stuff that actually addresses the business problem, not some adherence to official dogma (another Agile principle, in case you didn't notice). Therefore, it came as no surprise to us when an organization contacted us and let us know that they are taking the REST-based SOA approach, and that it *actually works*.

The organization in question is the U.S. Coast Guard (USCG) with their SPEAR (*Semper Paratus*: Enterprise Architecture Realization) initiative. The

SPEAR approach to SOA centers on document-centric, event-driven, loosely coupled, asynchronous, message-based business Services. Now, there's nothing particularly iconoclastic about event-driven SOA, but their story doesn't end there. Another central characteristic of their SOA approach is their document-centricity.

Although it's true that document-style interfaces are the norm for Web Services, the USCG takes the notion to a new level. For SPEAR, the document *is* the interface. It has meaning both for human and machine consumption. It's self-describing and removes the need for defining a specific, formal contract. Instead, the USCG provides a basic header/body document structure. The header contains elements like requester, type, ID, timestamps, and status (request, response, publication or error, for example). The body contains different parts depending on the type of Service. Request/response Services, for example, include elements like request, response, publication, and exception. As a result, SPEAR's Service contracts (if you even decide to call them that) consist of a simple document structure and core REST operations—nothing more.

For example, take a straightforward request/response Service that executes a simple database query. The Service simply populates the response field in the request document and returns the entire document to the requester. As a result, the document still contains the timestamped request. The ESB can now publish the document or put it on a queue, and the document itself acts as its own cache.

This approach to state is a simple example of HATEOAS. With HATEOAS, documents and the hyperlinks they contain represent all the application state information a distributed environment requires. Want to know the next step in a process? Simply follow the appropriate link.

In the case of SPEAR, the USCG has established an internal standard URI representation: domain://provider:context/resource (for example, service:// uscg.mda.vesselCrew:test/sla). The domain represents a taxonomy of resource types, including system://, organization://, geography://, and service://. The provider component represents the address to the provider of the resource. The context (squeezed in where ports go in a URL), represents the business context like: `test`, `:dev`, `:stage`, and so forth.

The ESB then resolves URIs to the physical endpoint references, acting as a routing engine that delivers the business Service abstraction. Any hyperlink to such a URI, therefore, points to a document that contains all the state information the system requires, and furthermore, the architecture offers late binding to Services as a key feature. There is no build time mapping to any particular resource. Instead of using strongly typed schemas, they rely on dynamic, loose typing in the documents. Such an approach is decidedly not Web Services friendly.

Also iconoclastic is how the SPEAR approach maintains application state. SPEAR includes state information in the message, because, of course, the message is the document. As a result, they are taking a fully Service-oriented, RESTful approach to maintaining state. They are able to do so in spite of leveraging an ESB, because they selected an atypical ESB product that maintains state in a fully message-centric manner, instead of spawning threads to keep track of state as in other vendors' ESBs.

SPEAR also follows a fully asynchronous model. In spite of broadly held belief to the contrary, SOA has always allowed for asynchronous as well as synchronous Service exchange patterns. In the SPEAR architecture, the listener acts as the handler, retaining messages at their last stop. The senders simply fire and forget. Messages are sent to the bus, not the destination, allowing for dynamic routing of messages as well as publish/subscribe. In this way the ESB routes, filters, and enforces policy via the URIs themselves.

Publish/subscribe is a broadcast push exchange pattern: Many consumers can subscribe to the same topic, and the ESB pushes messages to subscribers as appropriate. Even when a single consumer queries a resource, the ESB follows a push pattern, putting documents onto a queue for the consumer to pick up. As a result, SPEAR can support different consumer behaviors, depending on the use case. If the consumer is accessing Services via unreliable network connections, or simply requires low message volumes and can tolerate some latency, then the consumer can simply poll the Service. In other cases, when latency is an issue or when there are higher message volumes, the ESB can perform a true push to the consumer via a Java Message Service (JMS) interface.

Okay, hold on just one minute. JMS? I thought we were talking about REST, you know, over HTTP. How can JMS fit into this picture?

Yes, the USCG is being iconoclastic once again. The ESB is abstracting the endpoint, while at the same time providing a push-based messaging infrastructure. If the consumer wants the resource to push a real-time stream of large messages to it, then the URI should resolve to a JMS endpoint. If not, or if the consumer doesn't support JMS (typically when it's running over HTTP), then the resource will resolve to an HTTP endpoint.

So, is the USCG implementing "pure" SOA or "pure" REST? Those questions don't deserve the dignity of a response, because the whole notion of a "pure" architectural approach is inherently dogmatic. What the USCG has done is implement an architecture that *actually works for them*—that is, it delivers loosely coupled, abstracted business Services with the flexibility and performance they require. And remember, *actually working* trumps following a predetermined set of best practices every time—especially when those best practices don't actually solve the problems at hand.

There are two important morals here. First, REST-based SOA is alive and well, and offers straightforward solutions to many of the knottier problems that Web Services–based SOA has suffered from. But even more importantly, the success the USCG has achieved shows that any architectural approach is nothing more than a loose collection of best practices. It's up to the architect to know which best practices are best for solving their particular problems. Avoid a dogmatic approach, and select the right tool for the job, even if that brands you as an iconoclast.

CHAPTER 9

Finally, Let's Move to the Cloud

I n our role as architecture iconoclast, when we see a growing hype bubble, we love being the ones to pop it. We relished dispelling the confusion over the *SOA is dead* meme, and now it's time to let a little air out of the latest gas bag: *Cloud Computing*.

Don't get us wrong—Cloud Computing is essential to the Agile Architecture Revolution, but that doesn't mitigate the fact that the hype around this trend is still ahead of the reality. So, let's begin with the reality. What is Cloud Computing, anyway?

The most widely adopted definition of Cloud Computing is the one the National Institute for Standards and Technology (NIST), an agency of the U.S. Department of Commerce, put together. NIST's formal definition of Cloud Computing is already well known—*a model for enabling ubiquitous, convenient, on-demand network access to a shared pool of configurable computing resources (e.g., networks, servers, storage, applications, and services) that can be rapidly provisioned and released with minimal management effort or service provider interaction*. Note that the word *resource* in the previous definition is different from—but often related to—a RESTful (Representational State Transfer) resource. Similarly, the word *service* is different from—but likewise often related to—the word Service in the SOA context.

NIST also hammered out now-commonly held definitions of four basic Cloud deployment models, three Cloud service models, as well as essential and common characteristics of Cloud Computing, as Figure 9.1 illustrates.

Cloud deployment models include:

- **Public Cloud.** Cloud environments available to the general public. Simply pull out a credit card, sign up, and provision your Cloud instances. Logically, *Public Cloud Providers* are the purveyors of Public Clouds.
- **Private Cloud.** Cloud environments that a single organization builds for internal use. Sometimes the organization outsources the hosting of the Cloud environment, leading to a *Hosted Private Cloud*.

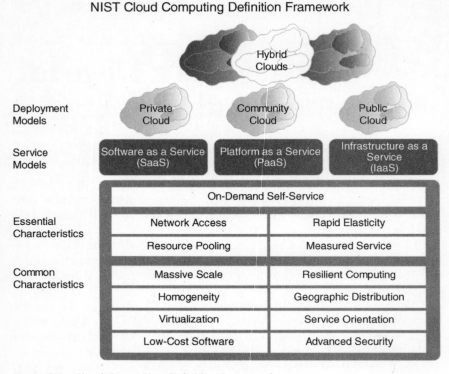

Figure 9.1   Cloud Computing Definition Framework
Source: NIST.

- **Community Cloud.** Like a Public Cloud, except that a Community Cloud is only available to a closed set of organizations, like a group of trading partners or a set of government agencies.
- **Hybrid Cloud.** Any combination of the above, as well as combinations of the above with on-premise (non-Cloud) capabilities.

Cloud service models include:

- **Infrastructure-as-a-Service (IaaS).** Offering virtualized physical infrastructure (servers, storage, and networks, typically) via a hosted provider model.
- **Platform-as-a-Service (PaaS).** Offering development, test, and/or deployment platforms via a hosted provider model.
- **Software-as-a-Service (SaaS).** Offering application functionality via a hosted provider model.

Finally, let's define the essential Cloud characteristics:

- **On-demand self-service.** Cloud providers offer dynamically provisioned capacity, and users provision their own resources.
- **Broad network access.** Cloud capabilities are available over the network, accessed through standard mechanisms. The network in question is almost always the Internet, although it could be a private network. *Virtual Private Networks* (VPNs), which are private networks that run on the Internet, are also increasingly common.
- **Resource pooling.** Resources are shared across Cloud consumers, often unbeknownst to them, via a *multitenancy* approach (more on multitenancy a bit later). Resources include storage, processing, memory, network bandwidth, and virtual machines, and the Cloud provider dynamically assigns separate physical and virtual resources on demand. As a result, from the consumer's perspective, Cloud resources are *location independent*.
- **Rapid elasticity.** Resources can be provisioned rapidly in real time in an automated fashion, and just as rapidly deprovisioned. As a result, Clouds can quickly scale out and can be released to scale back in as quickly as necessary. Rapid elasticity provides the illusion of *infinite capacity*: Resources appear to be unlimited and can be purchased in any quantity. Rapid elasticity is the most important Cloud characteristic.
- **Measured service.** Cloud providers automatically monitor, measure, and report on Cloud usage, so that they can bill (or charge back) Cloud consumers for the resources they use. Measured service also enables Cloud providers to automatically optimize resources.

Now that you have the basics, let's pop the hype bubble that is Cloud computing, and then piece together the reality, following Agile Architecture principles. You'll never look at a Cloud the same way again.

Déjà Vu All Over Again

Does this situation ring a bell? Key industry deep thinkers work out a new approach for organizing IT resources to better meet the needs of the business, but before they can work out the details, vendors turn the approach into a bandwagon and jump right on. Confused enterprise buyers are left scratching their heads, as what the vendors are selling ends up bearing only a superficial resemblance to the approach the experts are touting.

It should sound familiar—not only did the same thing happen with SOA, it happened with enterprise application integration (EAI), the Internet, Client/Server, and virtually every other architectural innovation to hit the world of IT since the earliest mainframes. What gives? Well, the key word in the previous sentence, of course, is *architecture*; that is, best practices for organizing and using technology, where *buying more* is only occasionally such a practice. Architecture is something you do, not something to buy, but the vendors, naturally, want you to think about stuff to buy!

Now it's Cloud Computing's turn. The broad benefits of Cloud Computing are so promising that the bandwagon is already chock-full of hungry vendors. "IT resources available only when needed! Pay as you go! Outsource your IT infrastructure! If Amazon.com can make it work, so can we!" Okay, enough of the noise. Let's take a closer look.

The first challenge Cloud Computing faces, of course, is that no one can agree on what it is. Ask various people and they'll often respond with a definition of something else, like SaaS, utility computing, virtualization, on-demand computing, hosted data centers, application service providers, and even the World Wide Web itself. The problem is that all of these trends have been around for a while, and there are products and solutions already on the market in each of these categories. Now along comes Cloud Computing, and the vendors of the various existing approaches now have a new label to slap on something they've been trying to sell for a while now, with limited success. And you know they've had only limited success because if their existing solution was a big hit then they wouldn't be so excited to call it something else!

Even for organizations that understand Cloud Computing, the most significant roadblock is the fact that Cloud Computing requires a level of architectural maturity that few organizations have managed to achieve. Many organizations have struggled with SOA, and run the risk of thinking Cloud Computing will solve problems that SOA attempts were unable to solve, whereas others think they're doing SOA, but are really not, and as a result, may never truly understand the connection between Agile Architecture and Cloud Computing.

The secret to realizing the Cloud Computing vision doesn't depend on buying software, and certainly doesn't rely on believing in hype. No, it depends first and foremost on *architecture*. We won't be able to achieve the benefits of Cloud Computing unless we understand the best practices for implementing and using technology resources, and furthermore, we must also have the organizational discipline to follow those best practices. In fact, as the gear we can buy improves, the more important knowing how to use it properly becomes. If Cloud Computing becomes a shortcut for bypassing architecture then it's doomed to fail.

Countering Vendor Spin with Architecture

Have you been to a Cloud Computing conference lately? Maybe you've read an article or blog post on the topic. Perhaps you've joined a Cloud-related webinar. Regardless, there is one common thread you're likely to find across most Cloud Computing information sources: They are *vendor driven*.

It's not just the vendors who spin their wheels on the topic of Cloud Computing. On the enterprise side, the focus is on the business benefits of the Cloud: the pay-as-you-go model combined with rapid, dynamic provisioning that responds to unpredictable fluctuation in demand for computing resources. Such consumption-based concerns lead to high-level discussions of Cloud Computing—"PowerPoint architectures" that fail to lead to workable Cloud-based solutions.

The result is that CIOs and other IT executives are on board with the promise of Cloud Computing, but find themselves lost in the complexities of deployment in a Cloud environment. This confusion prompts them to call their favored vendor, who is only too happy to sell them the vendor-centric model for Cloud Computing that's all the rage in the vendor-heavy conferences and blog posts.

Now, we're not saying the vendors aren't getting anything right. Purchasing a vendor-centric Cloud offering may very well meet your needs at the right price, and if so, then go for it. What we're finding, however, is a broad understanding among many CIOs that over the years, vendors have oversold and underdelivered on low-cost, fast, agile offerings. The move to the Cloud is meant to address those issues, so the last people you'd want to go to in order to deliver better, faster, cheaper are the very same vendors who gave you poorer, slower, and more expensive the last time around. Why trust them to get it right this time?

The missing link between the business benefits that Cloud Computing promises and the products on the market, of course, is *architecture*. Try this experiment: Google the phrase "Cloud architecture" and see what you get. What you'll find, other than our articles, of course, is information on how to architect a Cloud environment—in other words, how to *build* a Cloud, not how to *leverage* one. There's plenty of information on the former, but very little on the latter.

From the enterprise perspective, however, leveraging Clouds as part of the broader enterprise IT context is at the core of getting value from them. What is a best practice–based approach to leveraging Cloud-based resources in the context of the existing IT environment to address changing business needs? The answer to that question is the Cloud Architecture that is the missing link for organizations struggling to piece together a vendor-neutral Cloud strategy.

Unfortunately, part of the problem is that we don't have a good term for this critical part of the enterprise IT architecture story. Enterprise Cloud Architecture? Cloud Consumption Architecture? Enterprise Architecture (EA) for the Cloud? The vendors and Cloud providers have already co-opted the phrase "Cloud Architecture" to refer to how to build Clouds, and as a result, today's Cloud Architecture conversations involve either discussions of Cloud infrastructure or, at best, the pros and cons of public, private, and hybrid Clouds.

But even if you know how to build the Cloud deployment and service models that best suit your needs, how do you actually make use of the Cloud in the enterprise context? And furthermore, how can you be sure you selected the right type of Cloud in the first place? The vendors, of course, will recommend the type that requires selling (or renting) you the most gear. But is that what you really want?

Here's an example of what we're talking about. Let's say you have an existing legacy application that is still providing value, but there are new requirements for this aging on-premise app that include both new functionality as well as a new requirement to support unpredictable spikes in user demand. And of course, you're on a tight budget, so you want to avoid overprovisioning any new on-premise infrastructure to meet the spiky traffic demand requirement. As a result, Cloud Computing is now on the table.

There is a lot more for your architects to consider than whether or not to move to the Cloud, or what type of Cloud is appropriate. They have to consider how to deal with the existing legacy app. They have three basic options:

- Option 1: Leave the existing app where it is, but extend it by adding new capabilities in the Cloud.
- Option 2: Migrate the existing app to the Cloud, eventually retiring the existing app altogether.
- Option 3: Expose the existing app as loosely coupled Services, and compose them with Cloud-based Services that are either already available to you or that you've built or purchased for this purpose.

You should recognize option 3 as an SOA-based approach. However, it's important to note that option 3 isn't necessarily the best option, regardless of whether you have an SOA initiative in place or not. In fact, your architects must consider many different questions in order to make the appropriate decision; for example:

- What are the business process requirements that are driving this change? If there is a strong process requirement then the SOA approach may be warranted, but if the underlying requirement is more data-centric, then options 1 or 2 might be more efficient.

- What are the characteristics of the legacy app? How well does it lend itself to modularization and Service enablement?
- How important are elasticity and horizontal scalability to you? Or more precisely, where do you require elasticity and horizontal scalability, and where do traditional on-premise architectures suffice? It's likely not cost-effective to spend a lot of money moving a legacy app to the Cloud if your elasticity and scalability requirements are minimal.
- What part of the new app is likely to experience the traffic spikes?
- What is the reuse potential for the planned Cloud-based capabilities?
- For the Cloud-based portion, should we consider public, private, or hybrid?
- There is also a trade-off between elasticity and data consistency. We'll cover this point a bit later in this section.

There will be a number of other considerations, but the previous list provides a flavor of the sorts of considerations that should be part of your Cloud Architecture.

We identified option 3 as being the most clearly representative of a SOA approach, but trying to distinguish between SOA and non-SOA is a pointless endeavor. Rather, SOA best practices are fast becoming a part of the fabric of Agile Architecture, even when we no longer identify some particular approach as being specifically Service-oriented.

So in fact, all three options are best placed in the context of Agile Architecture. That is, if your organization has already gone through the rigors of SOA, establishing a governance framework and a business Services abstraction layer, then Cloud consumption naturally follows from the best practices you have already been following. Is what you're doing still SOA? It doesn't matter. What matters is that you're solving the problems of the business in the best way available, even when the vendors are trying to sell you a bill of goods. That focus was the key to Agile Architecture success, and it's the key to Cloud Computing success as well.

Interlude: Neutralizing the Cloud Threat

A Secret Meeting Somewhere in California, 2008

"This meeting will come to order," Larry Baldman, the CEO of International Micro OraTib (IMO) said. "We have a threat to deal with."

"Indeed we do," chimed in Twitter Offin, the CMO. "There's a new trend on the horizon, called Cloud Computing. If we don't watch out, it'll put us out of business."

"How's that?" asked Lowly Wonk, a product manager on Twitter's team.

"The basic idea of Cloud Computing is that large organizations won't have to buy software or hardware anymore," Larry said. "Instead, they will simply access it as needed from a Cloud provider."

"Yes, that could be a problem," Bill Geekazoid, the chief product architect said. "If our customers can rent what they need, then why would they buy it from us? After all, we've been overcharging for what amounts to repackaged spaghetti code for years."

"I don't understand," Lowly said. "What is Cloud Computing, anyway?"

"Well, here is where it gets interesting," Larry responded. "In reality, Cloud Computing is a myth—or it's a myth that it's anything new, anyway. It's really just old wine in new bottles."

"What do you mean?" Lowly said.

"Allow me, Larry," Bill said. "Cloud Computing is a combination of economic and technical trends that have been going on for years. It's a confusing mishmash of Software-as-a-Service, virtualization, utility comput-ing, on-demand computing, application service providers, and the World Wide Web itself."

"The Web itself?" Lowly was incredulous.

"Yes," Twitter said. "Some of these new Cloud startups are saying things like they have capabilities delivered over the Internet via standard protocols." Bill snickered. "In other words, their stuff runs on the Web."

"But we've been doing that for over 15 years!" Lowly was getting increasingly confused.

"That's right, Lowly," Larry said. "But it's still a threat. Reality is irrelevant, you know; it's all about perception. So, team, what are we going to do to get our butts out of the fire on this one?"

"I got an idea, boss," Twitter said. "Let's turn lemons into lemonade."

"I'm listening," Larry said.

"Well, everybody's heard of Amazon's early Cloud efforts, right?" Twitter explained. "Publicly available, multitenant Cloud environments, where they offer capabilities to a large number of customers, which gives Amazon enormous economies of scale."

"Right, Twitter," Bill said. "It's those economies of scale that will eat us for lunch. They can simply offer software and infrastructure at a vastly lower price point than we could ever dream of."

"Precisely," Twitter said. "So, how about we convince customers they have to build their *own* Clouds?"

"Their own Clouds?" Lowly was lost. "But, isn't that just saying that they have their own data centers running virtualization software?"

"Absolutely, but we don't tell them that," Twitter explained. "Perception is reality in marketing, as Larry said. We use the mystique of Cloud Computing to convince our customers they need to build Cloud environments for themselves. We call them 'Private Clouds.' That way they need to buy all the gear from us to set those Private Clouds up."

"Cha-ching!" Larry smiled. "I like it! But how are we going to convince our customers they need their own Private Clouds?"

"Well, that's where marketing comes in," Twitter said. "We emphasize all the risks of Public Clouds, and convince them they get the benefits of a Public Cloud without the risks if they build their own Private Clouds."

"I still don't get it," Lowly said. "Isn't the whole point to a Public Cloud the on-demand, dynamic provisioning? I mean, by spreading out infra-structure resources over so many customers, a Public Cloud provider can deal with large spikes in demand in a cost-effective way. But with a Private Cloud, won't they need to buy a bunch of equipment that will sit idle most of the time, on the off chance they need to scale up suddenly to handle a spike in demand?"

"That's why I like the plan so much, Lowly!" Bill said. "When a customer buys gear from us that they don't need, it makes our shareholders happy! Hell, if our customers only bought stuff they needed and actually *used*, our profit numbers would be in the toilet."

Lowly laughed. "Okay, I get it! This is a crazy business, you know!"

Bill's eyes lit up. "Hey, I have another idea," Bill said.

"Let's hear it, Bill," Twitter prompted.

"What if we set up a Cloud of our own, and put all of our old middleware in it. We set it up so that customers could essentially rent our middleware in the Cloud."

"How does that help solve the problem, Bill?" Larry asked.

"Well, here's the point: They already own our middleware, right? And they're stuck with it, so we have a never-ending stream of maintenance revenue anyway. But now we can rent it to them *at the same time*. Get it? We sell it and rent it to the same customers!"

Larry sat back in his chair, as a big grin came over his face. "Perfect! They rent middleware from us that they'll end up connecting to the middleware they already bought from us. The good old 'middleware for your middleware' story that we used to neutralize the SOA threat a couple years ago, only with a Cloud twist. So what should we call that?"

"Let's call it 'Platform-as-a-Service,'" Twitter said. "Can you imagine? Customers thought they were saving money by moving to the Cloud, but in reality they're paying us three times instead of once!"

Everybody had a great laugh. "Boy, this was a great meeting," Larry said. "We pulled our butts out of the fire for sure. Okay, let's gear up the marketing engine. Focus on Private Clouds and Platform-as-a-Service. I'll give the CEOs at our top accounts a call. It looks like IMO is in the Cloud business, people!"

Why Cloud Computing Scares the Platform Vendors

All right, we've had our fun. But seriously, excessive vendor focus on Private Clouds and PaaS are skewing the Cloud marketplace. Just as platform vendors sought to co-opt the SOA story to sell more middleware, leading to customer disillusionment and the *SOA is dead* meme, the battle today in the enterprise middleware marketplace is over PaaS offerings. PaaS is essentially the delivery of a computing platform and/or solution stack as a service. "We make our money on traditional systems integration," say the platform vendors, "so let's move traditional systems integration to the Cloud!" If there's an opportunity to sell new stuff to their existing enterprise client base, what's not for a platform vendor to love?

The reality, as so often happens, is far more complex. The platform vendors are running scared. They were caught by surprise by the SOA debacle, and now they see the same writing on the Cloud Computing wall. Just as their customers started figuring out that SOA success didn't depend on buying new software after all, but rather was a better way to organize existing IT assets, now Cloud Computing may replace the need to own those assets altogether. Imagine a world where enterprises no longer purchase software at all! Why bother, when they can rent it on the Cloud, pay as they go, and never have to worry about maintaining or upgrading the big packages that have kept the vendors' stock prices up for so long?

So, how are the platform vendors dealing with this threat? Basically, by trying to turn lemons into lemonade. There are two primary ways these software companies can leverage Cloud Computing to their advantage. First, they can provide software to the Cloud providers themselves. There's definitely money to be made there, but once the dust settles, there will only be so many Cloud providers in the world, and thus that addressable market is limited.

The second opportunity for the big vendors is in PaaS. If the middleware vendors become Cloud providers themselves, where they are offering middleware for rent in the Cloud, then they will have turned the Cloud risk to their advantage. At least, that's what they are thinking. Unfortunately for these vendors, the PaaS strategy is inherently flawed, in a surprising parallel to the "middleware-first SOA" debacle of the last decade. Hopefully, enterprise practitioners who were either burned by the Enterprise Service Bus (ESB)-first SOA fiasco, or who were smart enough to dodge that bullet and tackle architecture first, will avoid this mistake this time.

Don't get us wrong: The PaaS market is exploding, and once the dust settles, we're bound to see some truly valuable offerings. But there's a huge difference between a cutting-edge PaaS start-up offering and warmed-over middleware that an old-guard vendor never originally intended for the Cloud. They can clean it up and call it PaaS, but it's still lipstick on that old pig. The challenge for the customer is in telling the difference.

Architecting beyond Cloud Computing's Horseless Carriage

PaaS, of course, is only part of the Cloud story. From the enterprise perspective, there are a number of Cloud deployment scenarios that focus more on *integration* and *modernization* of legacy, on-premise capabilities than on developing new software in the Cloud. To this end, NIST has developed a comprehensive set of Cloud deployment scenarios. In fact, NIST has followed up their formal definition with a Cloud Computing technology road map, a Cloud Computing reference architecture, a standards road map, and many other documents and specifications. As concise as the NIST definition of Cloud Computing is, it only marks the beginning of the work NIST is doing to formalize and standardize the full breadth of Cloud Computing approaches, both within the U.S. Government as well as for the world at large.

We've reviewed NIST's documents in the context of Agile Architecture, however, and we've identified a missing link. Of course, looking at something and trying to identify what's missing is always difficult, especially when so many contributors have already pored over the material so carefully. The trick is to break out of *horseless carriage* patterns of thinking: Instead of considering the Cloud to be little more than an outsourced, virtualized data center, put on your architect's hat and consider how Cloud Computing's unique characteristics will change how you do architecture.

We found this missing link when we reviewed the Cloud deployment scenarios in the NIST Standards Road Map document. Figure 9.2 shows their diagram illustrating the eight generic deployment scenarios that they identified:

They sort the various deployment scenarios into three categories:

1. Single Cloud
   - Scenario 1: Deployment on a single Cloud
   - Scenario 2: Manage resources on a single Cloud

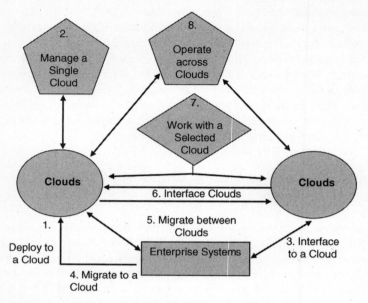

Figure 9.2   Generic Cloud Computing Deployment Scenarios
Source: NIST.

- Scenario 3: Interface enterprise systems to a single Cloud
- Scenario 4: Enterprise systems migrated or replaced on a single Cloud

2. Multiple Clouds (serially, one at a time)
- Scenario 5: Migration between Clouds
- Scenario 6: Interface across multiple Clouds
- Scenario 7: Work with a selected Cloud

3. Multiple Clouds (simultaneously, more than one at a time)
- Scenario 8: Operate across multiple Clouds

From our perspective, the most interesting of these are scenarios 1, 3, and 4, because they consider the relationships between enterprise systems and the Cloud.

NIST has divided their Cloud standards efforts into three categories: interoperability, portability, and security. Interoperability standards are the most straightforward, especially for anyone who has worked with Web Services, which of course are little more than standards-based interfaces intended to promote interoperability and loose coupling. Portability standards are more complicated, because NIST considers both application portability and data portability. In the Cloud context, application portability centers on the ability to move virtual machine (VM) instances from one Cloud to another. Data portability, however, is more difficult, because applications process different kinds of data, and those data flow throughout an entire system. For one organization, data portability might mean moving a single database from one Cloud to another, but for a different organization, the requirement might be for the portability of an entire SaaS application, along with all of its distributed data.

NIST's focus on interoperability and portability (and security, of course, which is an entire conversation in its own right) makes perfect sense in light of their focus on standards, because the standardization of these three capabilities will go a long way in furthering NIST's core mission. So it's no wonder that their three Cloud deployment scenarios that involve enterprise systems consist of deploying or migrating to a Cloud (facilitated by portability standards), or interfacing with a Cloud (facilitated by interoperability standards).

It should come as no surprise, therefore, that NIST missed another deployment scenario: building applications that leverage both on-premise and Cloud-based capabilities, where those applications rely on more than interoperability, portability, and the ubiquitous security.

Building applications that are compositions of Cloud-based and on-premise Services is a simple example, but it doesn't go far enough, because even this scenario falls into the horseless carriage trap of considering the Cloud to be nothing more than a virtualized data center. Factor *elasticity* into the equation, however, and we must consider new approaches to architecting such applications that go beyond considerations of interoperability and portability.

More than any other characteristic, elasticity distinguishes true Clouds from simple virtualized data centers. If your app requires more resources, the Cloud will provision those resources automatically, and then release them when you're done with them—until you need them again. Furthermore, those elastic resources may be among any of the different types of Cloud resources (networks, servers, storage, applications, and Services, as per the NIST definition), or any combination thereof.

As a result, when you architect your app, you don't know how many of each of these resources you will be using at any point in time, because the number can change with no warning. You must take this change into account when architecting your data, your middleware, your execution environments, your application logic, and your presentation tier—in other words, your entire distributed application.

Cloud providers do their best to hide the underlying complexity inherent in delivering elastic infrastructure. But when you're building a hybrid app—that is, one that includes Cloud-based as well as on-premise capabilities—your architects must have deeper knowledge of the underlying capabilities of the Cloud environment than Cloud providers are typically comfortable revealing. In other words, even once Cloud interoperability and portability standards mature, architects will still require additional information about the underlying capabilities of their Cloud environments that such standards won't cover.

BASE Jumping in the Cloud: Rethinking Data Consistency

Whether you're looking to integrate on-premise systems with the Cloud (NIST's scenario 3), modernize legacy systems by moving them to the Cloud (scenario 4), or building Service-oriented applications that span both on-premise and Cloud-based resources (the missing scenario we discussed in the previous section), you don't want to make the mistake of assuming that the Cloud is nothing but a pay-as-you-go server in the sky. On the contrary, you must typically *rearchitect* your existing applications to take advantage of the value propositions of the Cloud.

One of the most important architectural considerations that impact this transition to the Cloud is *data consistency*. To illustrate this point, let's say that your CIO is all fired up about moving your legacy inventory management app to the Cloud. Lower capital costs! Dynamic provisioning! Outsourced infrastructure! So you get out your shoehorn, provision some storage and virtual machine instances, and forklift the whole mess into the stratosphere. (Okay, there's more to it than that, but bear with me.)

Everything seems to work at first. But then the real test comes: the holiday season, when you do most of your online business. You breathe a sigh of relief as your Cloud provider seamlessly scales up to meet the spikes in demand. But then your boss calls, irate. Turns out customers are swamping the call center with complaints of failed transactions.

Frantically, you dive into the log files and diagnostic reports to see what the problem is. Apparently, the database has not been keeping an accurate count of your inventory—which is pretty much what an inventory management system is all about. You check the SQL, and you can't find the problem. Now you're really beginning to sweat.

You dig deeper, and you find the database is frequently in an inconsistent state. When the app processes orders, it decrements the product count. When the count for a product drops to zero, it's supposed to show customers that you've run out. But sometimes, the count is off. Not always, and not for every product. And the problem only seems to occur in the afternoons, when you normally experience your heaviest transaction volume.

The problem is that although it may appear that your database is running in a single storage partition, in reality the Cloud provider is provisioning multiple physical partitions as needed to provide elastic capacity. But when you look at the fine print in your contract with the Cloud provider, you realize they offer *eventual consistency*, not *immediate consistency*. In other words, your data may be inconsistent for short periods of time, especially when your app is experiencing peak load. It may only be a matter of seconds for the issue to resolve, but in the meantime, customers are placing orders for products that aren't available. You're charging their credit cards and all they get for their money is an error page.

From the perspective of the Cloud provider, however, nothing is broken. Eventual consistency is inherent to the nature of Cloud Computing, a principle we call the *CAP Theorem: no distributed computing system can guarantee (immediate) consistency, availability, and partition tolerance at the same time.* Essentially, the theorem states that you can get any two of these, but not all three at once.

Of these three characteristics, *partition tolerance* is the least familiar. In essence, a distributed system is partition tolerant when it will continue working even in the case of a partial network failure. In other words, bits and pieces of the system can fail or otherwise stop communicating with the other bits and pieces, and the overall system will continue to function.

With on-premise distributed computing, we're not particularly interested in partition tolerance: Transactional environments run in a single partition. If we want ACID transactionality (atomic, consistent, isolated, and durable transactions), then we should stick with a partition-intolerant approach like a two-phase commit infrastructure. In essence, ACID implies that a transaction runs in a single partition.

But in the Cloud, we require partition tolerance, because the Cloud provider is willing to allow that each physical instance cannot necessarily communicate with every other physical instance at all times, and furthermore, each physical instance may go down unpredictably. And if your underlying physical instances aren't communicating or working properly, then you have either an availability or a consistency issue. But because the Cloud is architected for high availability, consistency will necessarily suffer.

The knee-jerk reaction might be that because consistency is non-negotiable, we need to force the Cloud providers to give up partition tolerance. But in reality, that's entirely the wrong way to think about the problem. Instead, we must rethink our priorities.

As any data specialist will tell you, there are always performance vs. flexibility trade-offs in the world of data. Every generation of technology suffers from this trade-off, and the Cloud is no different. What is different about the Cloud is that we want virtualization-based elasticity—which requires partition tolerance.

If we want ACID transactionality, then we should stick with an on-premise partition-intolerant approach. But in the Cloud, ACID is the wrong priority. We need a different way of thinking about consistency and reliability. Instead of ACID, we need BASE (catchy, eh?).

BASE stands for *basic availability* (supports partial failures without leading to a total system failure), *soft state* (any change in state must be maintained through periodic refreshment), and *eventual consistency* (the data will be consistent after a set amount of time passes since an update). BASE has been around for several years and actually predates the notion of Cloud Computing; in fact, it underlies the telco world's notion of best effort reliability that applies to the mobile phone infrastructure. But today, understanding the principles of BASE is essential to understanding how to architect applications for the Cloud.

Let's put the BASE principles in simple terms:

- **Basic availability.** Stuff happens. We're using commodity hardware in the Cloud. We're expecting and planning for failure. But hey, we've got it covered.
- **Soft state.** The squeaky wheel gets the grease. If you don't keep telling me where you are or what you're doing, I'll assume you're not there anymore or you're done doing whatever it is you were doing. So if any part of the infrastructure crashes and reboots, it can bootstrap itself without any worries about it being in the wrong state.
- **Eventual consistency.** It's okay to use stale data some of the time. It'll all come clean eventually. Accountants have followed this principle since Babylonian times. It's called *closing the books*.

So, how would you deal with your inventory app following BASE best effort principles? First, assume that any product quantity is approximate. If the quantity isn't near zero you don't have much of a problem. If it is near zero, set the proper expectation with the customer. Don't charge their credit card in a synchronous fashion. Instead, let them know that their purchase has probably completed successfully. Once the dust settles, let them know if they got the item or not.

Of course, this inventory example is an oversimplification, and every situation is different. The bottom line is that you can't expect the same kind of transactionality in the Cloud as you could in a partition-intolerant, on-premise environment. If you erroneously assume that you can move your app to the Cloud without reworking how it handles transactionality, then you are in for an unpleasant surprise. On the other hand, rearchitecting your app for the Cloud will improve it overall.

Intermittently stale data? Unpredictable counts? States that expire? Your computer science profs must be rolling around in their graves. That's no way to write a computer program! Data are data, counts are counts, and states are states! How could anything work properly if we treat such basics as optional?

Welcome to the twenty-first century, folks. Bank account balances, search engine results, instant messaging buddy lists—if you think about it, all of these everyday elements of our wired lives follow BASE principles in one way or another.

And now we have Cloud Computing, where we're bundling together several different modern distributed computing trends into one neat package. But if we mistake the Cloud for being nothing more than a collection of existing trends then we're likely to fall into the horseless carriage trap, where we fail to recognize what's special about the Cloud.

Cloud Multitenancy: More than Meets the Eye

Taking an Agile Architecture approach to the Cloud requires an increased emphasis on elasticity, scalability, and data consistency, true—but we're not done yet. We also need to consider *multitenancy*, a key element of the essential resource pooling characteristic of Cloud Computing.

In particular, multitenancy is one of the most important characteristics of Public Clouds. Put multiple customers on the same physical infrastructure, sharing the same resources. Establish appropriate security measures so that they can't interfere with each other or snoop on the other's data. Presto! Cost savings, efficiency, and scalability are yours!

To be sure, multitenancy is one of the key enablers of the Public Cloud value proposition. But of course, there's more to multitenancy than meets the eye. There are actually different degrees of multitenancy, with different advantages and disadvantages, as Figure 9.3 illustrates. And as you might expect, there's plenty of vendor hype as well. As a result, understanding the various degrees of multitenancy is essential for understanding what you're paying for when you use a Public Cloud in particular, as well as when you're leveraging a Private Cloud.

The first type of multitenancy is *First-Degree Multitenancy*, which we also call the *Shared Schema Approach*. With the shared schema approach, all customers share all tiers of the SaaS application: presentation, processing tier, and the underlying database. In fact, each table of the underlying database would typically contain data for each SaaS customer. The app keeps these data separate via a customer number or other unique identifier that every table would have to contain.

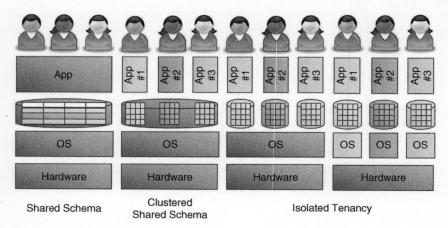

Figure 9.3 Types of Multitenancy

The advantages of the shared schema approach include:

- **Simple updates.** Because there is essentially only the single SaaS application, any application updates automatically apply to every customer at the same time. No configuration differences, no branching code.
- **Supports social capabilities, analysis, targeted marketing, and so on.** The app vendor can easily support any application capabilities that require queries across multiple customers, because all customer data are in the same tables. As a result, building any kind of cross-customer capability, like collaboration or social networking, is straightforward. It's also simple for the app vendor to analyze information across their customer base.
- **Simple to manage.** Simple to update means simple to manage, as there will only be one version in production at any time.
- **Simple integration with back-end infrastructure.** Identity management, backups, and other back-end capabilities are straightforward to implement.

The disadvantages of the shared schema approach include:

- **The vendor must architect the application for multitenancy.** Moving a single-tenant app to the Cloud won't give you first-degree multitenancy without a lot of rework.

- **Relatively vulnerable to certain attacks like SQL injection and so forth.** Because your data are in the same tables as everyone else's, any attack that exposes other rows in the tables you can access has a chance of succeeding. Make sure your SaaS provider has addressed these issues.

Requirements for scaling out a shared schema–based application:

- **Some vendors deploy duplicate stacks.** Essentially, they run identical application instances (including all tiers) for different customer segments. As long as the vendor is careful to ensure that each application instance is identical, they are still able to achieve the benefits of the shared schema approach. However, this approach does not improve the app's fault tolerance; if one stack goes down, then all customers on that stack are affected.
- **Segment the database by customer.** Instead of every customer putting their data into every table, segment or *shard* the database into multiple database instances, each supporting a different customer segment. Scale out the other tiers as well. This approach provides the greatest fault tolerance but is more difficult to manage than the duplicate stack approach.

Furthermore, with the shared schema–based approach, individual infrastructure elements (processors, storage, etc.) can take advantage of the elastic provisioning capabilities of the Cloud.

With *Second-Degree Multitenancy*, also called the *Clustered Shared Schema Approach*, the SaaS vendor intentionally segments customers onto different application instances running on separate stacks, where the instances are generally not identical to each other.

The advantages of the clustered shared schema approach:

- **More customer choice.** The vendor configures each cluster according to customer requirements, instead of the "one size fits all" limitation of the shared schema approach.
- **Allows for round-robin updates.** Instead of updating every app instance at once, the vendor can rotate their updates, which requires a smaller administration team.

The disadvantages of the clustered shared schema approach:

- **Increased maintenance complexity.** The vendor may have multiple different versions of their app in production at once, with different release cycles or the potential of branching code. As a result, management is more complicated than the shared schema approach.

- **Collaboration and analysis across clusters is problematic.** Any capability that requires data from multiple clusters requires data integration that can deal with the different application versions in each cluster.

Requirements for scaling out the clustered shared schema approach:

- **Add new clusters.** Essentially, scalability is built in, because adding new clusters is straightforward.

With the clustered shared schema approach, individual infrastructure elements (processors, storage, etc.) can take advantage of the elastic provisioning of the Cloud, as with the shared schema approach.

The third multitenancy approach is the *Isolated Tenancy Approach*, sometimes called *Megatenancy*. With the isolated tenancy approach, every customer has their own application instance, as though they were running the app on their internal infrastructure. These application instances may share an operating system, or even share nothing on the physical server but the underlying hardware, depending on how the infrastructure handles virtualization. But either way, because the applications are running in the Cloud, the customer is none the wiser—at least in theory.

The advantages of the isolated tenancy approach include:

- **Maximum customer choice.** Every customer gets the configuration they want, and the vendor can apply new releases or customizations on the schedule each customer desires.
- **Minimal rearchitecting of the original app.** If the vendor is trying to take an existing application they designed for on-premise installations and move it to the Cloud, the isolated tenancy approach requires minimal changes to the internal architecture of the app.

The disadvantages of the isolated tenancy approach include:

- **Highest management complexity.** Because every customer has a unique configuration, the vendor must manage every application instance as a separate, distinct application, because after all, that's what they are.
- **Most expensive.** Management, integration, updates, customer support, and so forth all cost more. With isolated tenancy you lose any cost savings benefits the Cloud might have provided.

- **Lack of vendor commitment.** Vendors typically offer isolated tenancy because they're rushing to offer an SaaS version of their app, and they don't have the time, money, or will to rearchitect it for the Cloud. But because it's such a hassle to support, as soon as one of the other approaches is viable, they'll want to move their customers to it. Then again, they may not wait. They may simply change their mind about supporting the app altogether, leaving customers in the lurch.

Requirements for scaling out the isolated tenancy approach:

- **Add more application instances.** In other words, add more stacks, each of which supports an application instance.

With the isolated tenancy approach, individual infrastructure elements (processors, storage, etc.) may or may not be able to take advantage of the elastic provisioning of the Cloud, depending on the architecture of the application. In other words, the isolated tenancy approach may not really be SaaS at all. It may simply be a hosted provider model masquerading as SaaS.

The moral of this multitenancy story, of course, is *caveat emptor*: Let the buyer beware. Not all SaaS offerings have the same type of multitenancy, and each approach has its advantages and disadvantages. And as with all IT decisions, do your homework to make sure your vendor isn't trying to pull the wool over your eyes.

It's also important to take these lessons to heart when you are planning a Private Cloud. You might think that because Private Clouds are inherently single tenant that you don't need to worry about multitenancy. Architecturally speaking, however, there may be advantages to a multitenant approach even in a Private Cloud, where instead of multiple customers, you consider multiple users or user types.

Taking a shared schema approach to a Private Cloud can reduce your costs relative to the other approaches, but will give you more of a "one size fits all" set of applications. Ignore the best practices of multitenancy, however, at your peril, as you may not achieve the cost savings and efficiency benefits that led you to consider a Private Cloud in the first place.

Keys to Enterprise Public Cloud

The Cloud Computing marketplace exhibits a surprising bifurcation. Public Cloud providers like Amazon.com are all the rage among small companies, start-ups, and individual developers. Enterprises, however, are largely investing in Private Clouds. Public Clouds are too risky, so the story goes, or perhaps enterprise decision makers are only willing to dip their toe in the water of the Public Cloud.

We find this trend surprising, because in many ways the Public Cloud value proposition is stronger than the Private Cloud's, even for large organizations. The perceived security issues are largely FUD (fear, uncertainty, and doubt), as Private Clouds are generally as susceptible to the same risks as Public ones (if not more so). Building out a Private Cloud requires capital expense, eliminating the pay-as-you-go benefit that Public Cloud customers enjoy. And perhaps most striking, you must purchase excess server capacity to handle unexpected loads in a Private Cloud. What's the point to having a Cloud in the first place if you can't be elastic and save money at the same time?

The enterprise challenge Public Cloud providers have is telling the proper story at the proper time. If most enterprises are at the toe-in-the-water phase, then best to give them toe-in-the-water options, like Cloud storage, Cloud-based e-mail, and self-contained Web sites running in the Cloud. Established SaaS offerings fall into this category as well. After all, if a Cloud Provider positions their value proposition to the enterprise too far ahead of where the customers are focusing, they may get a lot of smiles and nods in their meetings, but no purchase orders.

Be that as it may, many of today's enterprises are ready to move forward with more strategic Cloud initiatives. What's holding them back is a lack of solid information and expertise from the marketplace. Traditional software and hardware vendors are still the source of most of the information out there, and their advice emphasizes buying software and hardware, naturally. You can't really blame them—that's their business, after all—but from the enterprise practitioner's perspective, there is a gap in the available information and expertise that Private Cloud providers are uniquely qualified to fill.

Marketing, of course, is only one side of the story. The Public Cloud providers must base their story on real capabilities that enterprises not only need today, but will require in the near future. Perhaps not 10 years hence, but capabilities that organizations can include today in their strategic Cloud planning for the next few years. Many organizations are ready to move forward with their Cloud initiatives, and the Public Cloud providers can lead the way.

To this end, we've assembled a list of capabilities that organizations require from Public Cloud providers. It is now up to those providers to build out the requisite offerings and expertise and also tell the appropriate stories about those capabilities, so that architects who are piecing together their Cloud road maps have useful information that balances the biased vendor spin that currently characterizes the Cloud marketplace. Here are four essential Public Cloud capabilities that enterprises may require to move past the toe-in-the-water phase of Cloud to more strategic Cloud initiatives:

1. **Hybrid Cloud integration.** Phase one of an enterprise Public Cloud strategy may be to access some Cloud application or infrastructure simply via Web interfaces. Phase two, however, typically involves integration between on-premise resources and Cloud-based capabilities, typically as part of a SOA initiative (but not necessarily). Public Cloud providers must therefore support all manner of integration with a range of legacy on-premise systems. In other words, enterprise Public Cloud means some flavor of Hybrid Cloud offering.

2. **Fine-grained governance.** The Cloud Provider must be willing and able to offer whatever level of control and visibility the customer requires. For example, the customer may require that the provider locate their data in specific geographic locations, or may require detailed audit and management logging capabilities. The challenge for the Cloud Provider will be to offer such customized capabilities to customers without adversely impacting the elasticity or automated provisioning of the Cloud.

3. **Platform-level security measures.** Some enterprises will require a level of security control that exceeds what IaaS vendors typically provide, essentially requiring IaaS vendors to offer PaaS-like security controls over infrastructure elements like caches, queues, log files, and any other temporary storage mechanisms.

4. **End-to-end, continuous Hybrid Cloud testing.** Just as SOA requires continuous quality across the Service life cycle, so, too, do Hybrid Cloud solutions, whether they follow a SOA approach, a RESTful approach, or traditional tightly coupled integration. Remember, the Cloud doesn't offer a rigid reliability guarantee; instead, it provides dynamic, automated approaches for recovering from failure. Enterprises must have a comfort level that such inherent Cloud behavior won't adversely impact on-premise or end-to-end capabilities.

Public Cloud providers pride themselves on their black box approach to delivering IT capabilities. Outside the black box they offer all the wonderful benefits of a Cloud environment, including elasticity, dynamic provisioning, and automated recovery from failure. Inside the black box, well, who knows? They aren't telling.

That underlying mystery of the Public Cloud may work well in start-ups or among developer teams, but for enterprises to gain the comfort level they require from the Public Cloud, the providers must think of themselves more as partners, sharing the responsibility for ensuring the technology meets the business need, than as magicians, waving a magic wand and saying, "Presto! It's a Cloud!"

And though the hype surrounding the Cloud in the marketplace today may suggest otherwise, the fact remains that Clouds—even Public Clouds—aren't magic. We continue to make progress in offering scalable, elastic, automated solutions, but inside the box it's just servers, networks, and software. Public Cloud providers must work with their enterprise customers at whatever level is appropriate to meet their needs, even if it means opening up the black box and letting them inside.

Why Public Clouds Are More Secure than Private Clouds

Conventional wisdom would have you believe that Public Clouds are inherently insecure, and that the only way to meet your organization's stringent security requirements in the Cloud is to implement your own Private Cloud. Conventional wisdom, you say? Unfortunately, there is precious little wisdom available of any kind when it comes to Cloud Computing, let alone the conventional type!

In fact, large software and hardware vendors are largely responsible for the whole *Public Cloud is insecure* canard, introducing FUD into the marketplace. After all, building a Private Cloud means buying a lot of new gear. The last thing the big vendors want is for their customers to move to Public Clouds—unless, of course, they belong to the vendor in question. Don't be fooled. Public Clouds are typically more secure than Private Clouds, for a number of reasons. Here's why.

Why Public Clouds are more secure:

- **Public Clouds are hardened through continual hacking attempts.** Public Cloud providers are a juicy target. Hackers know how to find them, realize there's good stuff inside, and would be the envy of all their hacker pals if they were able to breach the Public Cloud's defenses. As a result, h4x0r types (that's *hacker* to you n00bs) have been hammering on Amazon Web Services, Microsoft Azure, and all the others. Thousands of them. For years now.
- **They attract the best security people available.** Public Cloud providers attract not only hackers, they attract talent. If you're a top Cloud security expert, where would you rather work: Amazon? Or some big insurance company or manufacturer or government agency? I thought so.
- **They get the latest security gear due to economies of scale.** How many Cloud data centers do the big Public Cloud providers own? And how fast are they building new ones? You don't need to know the

specifics to realize the answers are *boatloads* and *wicked fast*. And they're buying gear for them. New gear. Boatloads of it. Wicked fast.

Why Private Clouds are *less* secure:

- **Private Clouds suffer from "perimeter complacency."** It's amazing how many enterprises think that their DMZs and firewalls give them adequate security. If it's on the internal network, it must be secure! As though they completely missed the Internet. And e-mail. Not to mention viruses. What about twenty-somethings downloading malware to the corporate network through their phones? Now the enterprise wants a Private Cloud, so they can put the whole kit and caboodle on their internal network for security purposes. Good luck with that.

- **Competence of their staff is unknown.** Sure, your organization has a lot of great security people. They all know their stuff. Try this: Have a big party for them. Two hours in, take a look around the room. See that guy with the lampshade on his head? He's responsible for Private Cloud security.

- **Their penetration testing is insufficient.** How do you test to make sure your Private Cloud is secure—or any other part of your IT infrastructure, for that matter? Simple: Have your testers run a series of security tests. Or maybe hire a third party to run them for you. If all the tests pass, you're secure, right? Maybe for like a *minute*, until the hackers figure out new attacks that didn't make it onto your list of security tests. Whoops.

- **They may have older gear in use.** You spent hundreds of thousands of dollars on security hardware. Three years ago. Now you're putting the final touches on your Private Cloud. Try this: Ask your CIO for hundreds of thousands of dollars more to replace that three-year-old gear. The response? Maybe next year. Try updating the patches. I'm sure you can make do with what we have. And maybe you can—but don't expect it to compare with the brand new shiny stuff going into Public Cloud data centers every day.

So, maybe Virtual Private Clouds will come to the rescue. With a *Virtual Private Cloud* (VPC), a Public Cloud provider gives you a dedicated, secure connection (usually via a VPN) to your Public Cloud instances. In some cases, those instances are physically separated from other customers, so that your stuff can't end up on the same box as somebody else's stuff.

VPCs may actually be the most secure option available, as you have the best of both worlds. Furthermore, they may address specific regulatory or other governance issues that may prevent your organization from using a multitenant Public Cloud. If you think that neither Public nor Private sounds secure enough, then a VPC may be the way to go.

However, VPCs aren't for everyone. They may only be marginally more secure than Public Cloud, as Public Cloud providers have generally done a bang-up job securing their multitenant architectures. And keep in mind, a single-tenant VPC will typically be substantially more expensive than a regular Public Cloud equivalent. The bottom line: VPCs are more about peace of mind than actually increasing security.

So, are all Public Clouds more secure than all Private Clouds? Well, it's certainly possible that *your* Private Cloud is more secure than *some* Public Clouds out there. The true message here is that building a truly secure Private Cloud is much harder than it sounds, and the extra work necessary has largely already been taken care of by the Public Cloud providers. And it should now be obvious that Private Clouds are by no means *inherently* more secure than Public ones.

But there's a bigger lesson here. Security is all about risk mitigation, and it's simply impossible to reduce your risk to zero. There's no such thing as perfect security, which is another way of saying that perfect security is infinitely expensive. Risk mitigation involves weighing *acceptable* risks, given the nature of those risks and the cost involved in mitigating them. When you deliberate on the question of Public vs. Private Clouds, keep in mind that both approaches are inherently risky—but then again, choosing neither is also risky. Your job is to get the necessary facts in order to make the best decision you can about which risks you are willing to accept. Confuse FUD with facts at your peril.

Why You Really, Truly Don't Want a Private Cloud

Maybe you buy that Public Clouds are more secure than Private ones, maybe not. You might be thinking that if it will take time and effort for the Enterprise Public Cloud market to mature, that means that Private Clouds are inherently a better option for most large organizations. You'd be wrong. The more you focus on the business benefits of Cloud, the more likely you'll be leaning toward public over private deployment models. Furthermore, this mind shift isn't all about security risks. Once you work through the issues, you'll likely come to the same conclusion: *There's generally little or no solid business reason to build a Private Cloud.*

The best way to understand the limitations of the private deployment model is to take the business perspective. What are the business benefits behind the move to the Cloud, and how can you achieve them?

- **Cloud will shift capital expense to operational expense.** Instead of having to invest in hardware and software, you can pay as you go for what you need as an operational expense, and write it off your taxes right away. Except, of course, with Private Clouds, where you have to build out the entire data center infrastructure yourself. If anything, Private Clouds *increase* capital expenditures.
- **Cloud increases server utilization while dealing with spikes in demand.** Instead of setting up a data center full of servers that run idle most of the time on the off chance you need them to deal with the occasional Slashdot post or Justin Bieber tweet, the Cloud improves utilization while its elasticity deals with those annoying spikes. Except, of course, in Private Clouds, unless your organization is so huge that multiple divisions look to your Cloud to handle many different spikes in demand that you fervently hope arrive at different times. But what if that Kim Kardashian visit to your corporate HQ causes traffic to all your divisions to spike at once?
- **Cloud keeps infrastructure costs very low for new projects, because they don't have much traffic yet.** Again, this benefit works much better in a Public Cloud. How many such projects do you expect to have at any one time? If the number isn't in the hundreds or thousands, then Private Cloud is massive overkill for this purpose.
- **The elasticity benefit of the Cloud gives us the illusion of infinite capacity.** Infinite capacity is all fine and good, but it's an illusion. And illusions work fine until, well, until they don't. Elasticity provides the illusion of infinite capacity as long as there is always sufficient capacity to meet additional demand for Cloud resources. You'll never consume all the capacity of a Public Cloud, but your Private Cloud is another matter entirely. It's only so big. If one of your developers has the bright idea to provision a thousand virtual machine instances or a petabyte of storage for that Big Data project, and your Private Cloud doesn't have the physical capacity to do so, then bye-bye illusion.
- **We already have a significant investment in our existing data center, so converting it to a Private Cloud will save us money while enabling us to obtain the benefits of the Cloud.** In your dreams. One essential requirement for building an effective Private Cloud is rigorous homogeneity. You want all your physical servers, network equipment, virtualization technology, storage, and such to be completely identical across every rack. Look at your existing, pre-Cloud data center. Homogeneity isn't even on your radar.
- **We don't want to be in the data center business.** That's why we're moving to the Cloud. Guess what? Building a Private Cloud puts you in the data center business!

- **Whatever cost efficiencies the Public Cloud providers can achieve we can also achieve in our Private Cloud.** This argument doesn't hold water either. Not only do the leading Public Clouds—Amazon, Microsoft Azure, Rackspace, and so on—have enormous economies of scale, but they're also operating on razor-thin margins. Furthermore, if they can wring more efficiencies out of the model, they'll lower their prices. They're taking this price war approach to their margins for all the regular business school reasons: to keep smaller players from being competitive, and to push their larger competitors out of the business. It doesn't matter how big your Private Cloud is, it simply cannot compete on price.

Okay fine, you get it. Private Clouds suck, fair enough. You'll even buy our arguments that Public Clouds may actually be more secure than private ones. But you're in a regulated industry or otherwise have stringent regulatory requirements about data protection or data movement that the Public Cloud providers can't adequately address. The only way you can move to the Cloud at all is to build a Private Cloud.

Not so fast. Although it's true that regulatory compliance business drivers and limitations are becoming an increasingly important part of the Cloud story, any regulatory drawbacks to using Public Clouds are essentially temporary, as the market responds to this demand. A new class of Public Cloud provider, what is shaping up to be the *Enterprise Public Cloud Provider* marketplace, is on the rise. The players in this space are putting together offerings that include rigorous auditing, more transparent and stringent service-level agreements, and overall better visibility for corporate customers with regulatory concerns.

The incumbent Public Cloud providers aren't standing still either. For example, while Amazon built their Public Cloud (and with it, the entire industry) on a one-size-fits-all model aimed initially at developers, start-ups, and other small-to-midsize companies, they have been working on building out their enterprise offerings for a while now. Though you may not be able to get solutions from the big players that meet your regulatory needs today, you can be sure it won't take them long to figure out how to compete in even the most regulated industries. In a few years, if you look back on your decision to build a Private Cloud on the basis of regulatory compliance, you'll likely feel quite foolish, as your competitors who waited will soon have fully compliant public alternatives while you're stuck paying the bills on your Private Cloud initiative that will have become an expensive money pit.

So, should any organization build a Private Cloud? Perhaps, but only the very largest enterprises, and only when those organizations can figure out how to get most or all of their divisions to share those Private Clouds. If your enterprise is large enough to achieve economies of scale similar to the public providers, then—and only then—will a private option be a viable business alternative.

In many such cases, those large enterprise Private Clouds essentially become community Clouds, as multiple divisions of an enterprise share a single internal Cloud provider that operates much like a Public Cloud, albeit for internal use across the enterprise. This community model makes sense, for example, for many federal governments. They can achieve the cost efficiencies of Public Clouds while maintaining the control benefits of Private Clouds by supporting the Cloud initiatives across multiple agencies.

Still not convinced? Well, ask yourself why, and the answer is likely to be a question of *control*. Many executives will still be uncomfortable about Public Clouds, even when we address the security and compliance issues that currently face Public Cloud providers, simply because they don't control the Public Cloud. Our answer? Distribution of IT control is essential to the Agile Architecture Revolution. The Web doesn't have centralized control, after all, and it works just fine. The app store model for enterprise IT, the rise of bring your own device (BYOD), and the fundamentally mobility-driven architecture of the Internet of Things are all examples of the broader shift to decentralized control over IT. Fighting to maintain control is a losing proposition, and as a result, Private Clouds will be a mostly forgotten bump on the road to the Next Big Thing.

Avoiding Unexpected Cloud Economics Pitfalls

Anybody who is considering a move to the Cloud knows that the greatest economic motivation for Cloud Computing is the pay-as-you-go, pay-for-what-you-need utility computing benefit, right? Deal with spikes in demand much more cost effectively, the Public Cloud service providers gush, because we can spread the load over many customers and pass the savings from our economies of scale on to you. The utility benefit is also a central premise of Private Clouds. Build a Private Cloud for your enterprise, the vendors promise, and you can achieve the same economies of scale as Public Clouds without all that risk.

Unfortunately, what sounds too good to be true usually is. There are a number of gotchas on both the Public and Private Cloud provider sides that limit—or even prevent—organizations from obtaining a full measure of the utility benefit. Let's go back to economics class and take a closer look.

First, let's look at the utility benefit of the Cloud. Turn on the faucet; only instead of water, you get Cloud. Sounds good, but we use water very differently than we do IT resources. With water, we generally use all we need without worrying about price. We may try to economize, and perhaps we'll go through the trouble of digging a well if we need to fill our pool, but generally we don't think about the cost of each flush or load of laundry.

The Cloud is just the opposite. The techies might not be thinking in terms of cost, but the bean counters definitely are. For a CIO or purchasing manager comfortable with entering resource costs into annual budget spreadsheets, the unknown nature of the Cloud bill strikes fear into their hearts—and their wallets. Instead of focusing on lowered costs, their worry is *increased costs*, because Cloud usage is inherently unpredictable. After all, that's why landlords don't like including heating costs in the rent. If the tenants aren't responsible for keeping costs down then *pay-as-you-go* inevitably translates into *pay more*—and just how much more is a mystery until the bill arrives.

Enterprise Cloud customers in particular are beginning to push back, and as a result, Public Cloud providers must change their pricing model accordingly. Unfortunately, there aren't many alternatives to simple pay-as-you go. One increasingly popular alternative that might ease Cloud purchasers' minds is for providers to offer a tiered pricing system, with a fixed price for any consumption up to a predefined threshold, and pay-as-you-go above that. However, tiered pricing is not a panacea. Although such a pricing model is straightforward and gives organizations an increased measure of predictability, it still doesn't solve the problem of cost spikes.

If tiered pricing sounds more like paying for your mobile phone service than for utilities like water or electricity, you're right. Not only does this approach reduce perceived risks for Cloud purchasers, it's also a familiar model for the telcos, all of whom are looking to enter the Cloud market, or at the least, grow their existing Cloud offerings. As a result, we expect tiered pricing to become the norm for Public Cloud services over time, in spite of its drawbacks.

The irony with tiered Cloud pricing is that the more you require elasticity, the greater is the risk that you'll use up your allotted consumption for the month—but elasticity is the most important benefit of the Cloud. Sure, if you have steady, predictable consumption then tiered pricing is low risk, but if all you want is steady, predictable availability, then chances are keeping your resources on-premise or in a traditional hosted facility will be more cost effective than moving to the Cloud in the first place, because you're not particularly worried about spikes in demand.

To make matters worse, not everyone likes tiered pricing. Anyone who's used up their minutes or texts for the month only to be surprised by an excessive phone bill knows what I'm talking about. It seems the mobile phone providers love to play games with their pricing plans for the sole purpose of squeezing every penny out of their hapless customers. I'm sure we don't want our Cloud providers to play the same dirty tricks.

Cloud churn presents other, more subtle problems. Though it's a common watercooler pastime to demonize mobile phone companies for their under-handed pricing policies, there is a downside for the providers as well: the dreaded customer churn. Because it's relatively easy for customers to change phone providers, especially now that number portability is a reality, shifty behavior on the part of providers simply chases away customers.

Cloud churn is a very real problem for Public Cloud providers as well, as the ease of deprovisioning Cloud resources naturally eases the deprovisioning of customers. But there is an extra complication with Cloud churn that doesn't have a parallel in the mobile phone world: Cloud resources that are no longer being used but still remain allocated to customers. Depending on the provider's pricing model, the cost to the customer to maintain such resources may be minimal, but it's not always clear whether those minimal amounts sufficiently cover the providers' costs.

Furthermore, the proliferation of such idle instances may be a more significant issue for Private Cloud providers, because they typically have constrained budgets for data center buildouts. Amazon may be building new data centers as fast as they can, but your Private Cloud likely has a maximum practical size given your budget for the effort. The last thing you want is to fill it up with idle resources that various people in your organization can't be bothered to fully deprovision.

For the Public Cloud provider, the obvious solution to the problem of idle resources leftover from Cloud churn is to charge enough for those resources. Either the cost will motivate people to fully deprovision them, so the argument goes, or at the very least, they generate enough money so that keeping them around is worthwhile for the providers.

But what if we're talking about Private Clouds here? The way to charge internal customers for using Cloud resources is via *chargebacks*. And *everybody* hates chargebacks. Not only are they a bookkeeping hassle, but they also demotivate the consumption of shared resources. We went through this problem when we dealt with shared Services and SOA, and now we're sharing Cloud resources, the problem remains: The whole point to the Private Cloud is to achieve economies of scale across the enterprise, but the only way to make such economies work is if most or all divisions participate. Chargebacks, however, discourage that participation.

As it was with shared Services, the way to compensate for chargebacks is through *effective governance*: Establish and enforce Cloud consumption policies that counteract the demotivational effects of chargebacks, and come up with a way to motivate people to follow such policies. While you're at it, formulate policies governing the deprovisioning of instances that no one needs anymore. But in the Cloud, such governance is especially challenging because of the diversity of resources and their corresponding consumption scenarios: policies for provisioning virtual machines as part of IaaS are quite different from, say, provisioning development tools on PaaS. It will take organizations with Private Clouds a good bit of trial and error to get the balance right.

Another downside to the idle-resource-masquerading-as-paying-customer problem is that it makes it very difficult for financial analysts to gauge the health of a Public Cloud provider. This obfuscation can skew traditional metrics like number of customers or revenue per customer, and the distortion may be different from one provider to another. Combine the resulting confusion with the lean profit margins in today's Cloud space, as providers push their prices ever lower to encourage growth, and you have a recipe for disaster. An ostensibly healthy Cloud provider might suddenly collapse due to a foundation of underperforming customers and idle resources.

Private Clouds face a corresponding problem, as executives review the financials for the Cloud effort. We even predict a backlash against Private Clouds in the next year or two, as vendors underdeliver on their Cloud promises—not necessarily through any fault of their technology, but rather because the reality of achieving cost advantages with Private Clouds is far more difficult than the vendors' and analysts' spreadsheets might have you believe.

Rethinking Cloud Service Level Agreements

It's so easy these days to purchase Cloud-based services. Go online, click a few times, enter your credit card info, and presto! You're in the Cloud. There's no question the novelty really hasn't worn off yet. Have you ever wondered, however, what you're really paying for? Sure, you have some expectation that the service provider will provide you with some services. But what are they *promising* to give you, specifically?

Enter the *Service Level Agreement* (SLA). The SLA is part of the contract between you and your service provider. It spells out the specifics of what they're providing you as well as penalties the provider must pay in the event that they don't live up to the SLA.

Or, maybe not.

The reality is, what's actually in a Cloud SLA, or what *should be* in such an agreement, is all over the map. Ask the public IaaS providers, and they'll give you one answer. Ask SaaS or PaaS providers, and they'll tell you something different. And what about Private Clouds? SLAs take on an entirely new meaning there as well. Let's see if we can make sense of it all.

This confusion over what belongs in Cloud SLAs centers on the fact that there are very different contexts for SLAs depending on the heritage of the organization writing them:

- **The managed hosting provider context.** For service providers who had traditionally been in the hosted data center business, SLAs center on *availability*, measured in the familiar multiple-nines of uptime. Want 99.9% uptime? Pay one price. Want four nines, or five nines? Pay increasingly higher prices. If the provider drops the ball, they pay you a penalty, usually in the form of service credits. In other words, the crappier the service is, the more of it you get.
- **The software vendor context.** When you buy a piece of software, you don't get an SLA at all. Instead, you get an *end-user license agreement* (EULA). Instead of spelling out what the vendor will do for you, EULAs tell you what you are allowed to do with the software, and more importantly (to the vendor, anyway), what you're *not* allowed to do with it. And then there's all the boilerplate about no warranties or fitness for a particular purpose. When the vendor moves their software to a Cloud delivery model, thus becoming a SaaS or PaaS vendor, they typically retain the EULA context for their offering. From their perspective, SaaS is more about *software* than about *services*.
- **The enterprise operations context.** It is the responsibility of the operations (Ops) team to provide and support the IT capabilities the enterprise requires and pays for. If a business unit requires, say, a Web site with a three second or less response time, then infrastructure and solution architects specify the necessary hardware, software, and network capabilities to meet that requirement, the business cuts the check, and the Ops team keeps all that gear running as per the requirements. A different business unit may have different non-functional requirements, which might cost more or less, but in any case, would lead to a different SLA. In this case, if the Ops team drops the ball and violates an SLA, predetermined mitigation activities that are part of the governance framework kick in, but service credits are unlikely to be on the list.

For consumers of Cloud services, therefore, simply having a conversation about SLAs with your Cloud provider can lead to confusion, especially when there is a collision among these contexts. Salesforce.com provides an eye-opening case study that shows how confusing the aftermath can be when these three contexts collide. On the one hand, Salesforce is a SaaS and PaaS provider, built from the ground up to deliver software capabilities via a Cloud provider model. On the other hand, a substantial part of their business is with large enterprises that have come to expect uptime-based SLAs from their service providers.

For many years, Salesforce refused to publish SLAs of any kind, instead favoring EULA-type agreements. That is, until some well-publicized down-time back in the 2006 time frame. Large customers finally realized that their businesses depended on Salesforce, and sought to strong-arm the vendor into publishing—and sticking to—negotiated SLAs.

The word in the blogosphere was that Salesforce fought the publication of such SLAs tooth and nail, relenting only in the case of their largest customers—and then, required those SLAs to be confidential, presumably so that different customers might get different promises. And what about all those Salesforce customers who didn't have the clout to wrest an SLA from the vendor? Salesforce rolled out trust.salesforce.com, a PR effort meant to convince their customers that they could be trusted to provide good service. In other words, *trust us, we're Salesforce.com. You don't need an SLA.*

Salesforce's apparent anticustomer stance might seem quixotic, but it makes sense from the perspective of a software vendor. Why offer to provide free service credits or other bonuses when most customers will buy your stuff regardless? But from the customer perspective, people are left scratching their heads, wondering if some other customer has extracted a better SLA. If everybody is sharing the same underlying infrastructure, then why would Salesforce promise different service levels to different customers?

Private Cloud providers must also navigate their own context collisions. On the one hand, these organizations' Cloud teams are simply a part of the Ops team, responsible for keeping the lights on as they always have. But on the other hand, their internal customers are likely to be comparing Private and Public Cloud options, or at the least, comparing their internal Private Cloud with virtual Private Cloud offerings from Public Cloud providers. Remember, from the Cloud consumer's perspective, a Cloud is a Cloud. Why would you expect service credits from one provider and internal service level guarantees from another?

Of the three contexts discussed, the managed hosting provider's focus on uptime is perhaps the most familiar context for SLAs. If you're contracting with a third party for IT capabilities, then making sure those capabilities are up and running is certainly the most important nonfunctional require-ment, correct?

Not so fast. Clouds are fundamentally different from managed hosting providers in one significant respect: *Elasticity* is even more important than *reliability*. When working with the Cloud you must plan for and expect failure; it is the Cloud's ability to automatically recover from such failures that compensates for the Cloud's underlying shortcomings. How fast your Cloud can scale up, its ability to do so regardless of the demand, its ability to deprovision instances even more rapidly, and in particular its ability to recover automatically from failure, are the characteristics you're really paying for.

The surprising conclusion to this focus on elasticity over reliability is that none of the three SLA contexts are actually well-suited for the Cloud. Instead, you want your SLA to focus more on how well the Cloud deals with unexpected events, including failures, spikes in demand, and other situations that fall outside the norm. After all, these are the characteristics of the Cloud that make it a Cloud. You could say that Cloud SLAs should measure just how *Cloudy* that Cloud is: in other words, how well it lives up to the core value propositions that differentiate the Cloud from traditional hosted computing environments.

However you look at Cloud SLAs—measuring reliability, Cloudiness, or something else—never forget where the rubber hits the road: the business value the Cloud provides. Why not base Cloud SLAs on how well the Cloud meets business needs? Such a mission-focused SLA would have to focus on specific, measurable goals for the Cloud. For example, if you move your payroll app into the Cloud, your key metric might be whether you made your payroll on time.

Such mission-focused SLAs might be workable when dealing with a SaaS provider, but promise to be quite problematic with PaaS or IaaS offerings, because the mission success with those service models depends on the software running on the respective platform or infrastructure. In these situations, if something goes wrong, is it the Cloud that's violating its SLA, or is it something wrong with the software you put in the Cloud?

For system integrators and software developers who are building bespoke Cloud-based apps for their customers, this question is paramount. After all, the customer simply wants their requirements to be met. If something goes wrong, and the consultant points their finger at the Cloud provider and vice versa, the customer will only become more upset. The problem is, poorly architected apps aren't able to take advantage of the elasticity benefit of the Cloud, through no fault of the PaaS or IaaS provider.

There is an important warning here. It seems that every enterprise and government agency is looking to move many of their apps to the Cloud, and they're hiring consultants to do the heavy lifting. However, both customer and consultant are still thinking of the Cloud as a glorified managed hosting provider, responsible for maintaining uptime-based SLAs. The reality is quite different. As Cloud-based deployments mature, the line between development and operations blurs, as Cloud behavior merges with application behavior.

Are Your Software Licenses Cloud Friendly?

The rise of Cloud Computing is part of the Agile Architecture paradigm shift precisely because we won't need to hire pricey consultants or buy a lot of gear to use Clouds. In fact, enterprise software vendors are running scared. Just as they crossed off the word "Web" from their software boxes and wrote in "SOA" back in 2004, now that word has gotten the axe, and "Cloud" is the mantra of the day—a process the blogosphere has snarkily named *Cloudwashing*. We're talking specifically about the heavyweight enterprise apps here—enterprise resource planning (ERP), customer relationship management (CRM), supply chain management (SCM), and their brethren. The challenge that vendors of such dinosaur applications face is both architectural as well as economic. On the architectural side, they never envisioned the elastic, partition-tolerant nature of the Cloud when they built their now-aging monolithic products. But the economic challenges are every bit as intractable: how to shift to a pay-as-you-go SaaS model, while at the same time continuing to offer a more traditional licensing model to satisfy customers who want to install software into IaaS Clouds?

Put yourself for a moment in the shoes of an enterprise app vendor executive. You have some old software—ERP, say—and you want to move it to the Cloud, because that's what you're customers are saying they want you to do. So you come up with a two-pronged strategy: First, you'll roll out a SaaS offering, where you host the software for your customers and they pay as they go per seat per month. Second, you'll have an IaaS option, where customers can take your software and install it onto their own Cloud infrastructure, either in a Public or Private Cloud.

So far so good, but here's where things get complicated. Because your app isn't architected for multitenancy, you have a hard time building a scalable, elastic SaaS offering. But you make do, even though the result isn't nearly as elastic as it should be. You launch your SaaS version, and provide an EULA to customers who want to use it. After all, they can take it or leave it: It's SaaS, and in the SaaS world, one size fits all. If customers don't like it, they can go for option #2.

The second option requires customers to license your product as they have done in the past, only now they're installing it themselves in their IaaS Clouds. Whatever licensing scheme you currently have should do—per processor, per server, per user, or whatever combination your bean counters came up with.

But now you have another problem. One of your largest customers gives you a call and explains that they want to install your app in their dynamic IaaS environment. In other words, the number of virtual machines it will run on might vary from day to day or even hour to hour. And sometimes the number of instances will spike. How do you charge for that? As a favored customer, you need to offer them preferred pricing, but how do you calculate it?

This conundrum has no easy answer. Fundamentally, traditional software licensing schemes are antithetical to the elastic nature of the Cloud. The more customers understand and leverage the true value of the Cloud, the less friendly your dark-age licensing models will work for them. Bottom line: Traditional software licensing models, as well as any per-instance licensing model, do not work in the Cloud.

From the customer perspective, the obvious solution to this problem is to bail on commercial software altogether, and move exclusively to open source software in the Cloud. And yes, there's no question that Cloud Computing only strengthens the open source value proposition. But open source isn't right for every organization, and there will continue to be opportunities for commercial application software even as we transition to the Cloud.

Obtaining app functionality via SaaS models also addresses the licensing issue, but SaaS isn't for everyone either. Some organizations are worried about the lack of predictability inherent in pay-as-you-go pricing, whereas others require customized or bespoke solutions that aren't economical for vendors to offer via a SaaS model. Even with open source and SaaS, there will continue to be a market for commercial enterprise app software that you actually need to install, albeit into an elastic IaaS Cloud environment.

But even this notion of installing software into virtual machine instances misses the larger architectural picture. We've been implementing distributed computing for 20 years now, after all—no longer are applications *software running on a box*, but rather *software running on many boxes in multiple tiers*. Cloud takes this model to a new level, where instead of thinking about database, app server, or Web server clusters that support scalable Web apps, we can now think about elastic tiers that change dynamically as needed. Distributed computing on steroids. Even the network is no longer the computer. Now the Cloud itself is the computer.

The bottom line: Any software licensing scheme that counts the number of processors, servers, or virtual instances is fundamentally Cloud-unfriendly. In the pre-Cloud days, servers were expensive and difficult to install and configure, so we operated in the context of scarcity: Add a server, pay a lot of money. The Cloud changes this equation to one of abundance: Instances are cheap, plentiful, and easy to configure, so nothing we put on a particular instance should cost us very much or have much importance in and of itself.

As for the commercial enterprise app vendors? We feel your pain, really we do. You're being squeezed on three sides: Cloud continues to strengthen the open source value proposition, eating away at yours. The siren song of SaaS presents architectural challenges as it potentially lowers your revenues. And the Cloud is rapidly making your core license revenue model obsolete. Is it time to abandon hope?

No, at least not for all such vendors. After all, enterprise customers will continue to need the benefits of your apps. The challenge is how to approach and leverage the Cloud. Trying to fit the Cloud into your existing business is doomed to fail. The only way to survive is to rework your existing business to thrive in the Cloud.

And what about the enterprises themselves? Proper architecture was important before, but now it's absolutely essential. Building and running software in the Cloud is fundamentally different from existing operational environments. Add legacy to the mix and you have a recipe for disaster— or for a new era of IT-enabled agility, depending on whether you get the architecture right. Looking to the incumbent app vendors, however, is not likely to lower your risk, as they are more concerned with protecting their existing business models than leveraging the Cloud to build new ones.

Garbage in the Cloud

> On two occasions I have been asked,—"Pray, Mr. Babbage, if you put into the machine wrong figures, will the right answers come out?" . . . I am not able rightly to apprehend the kind of confusion of ideas that could provoke such a question.
>
> —*Charles Babbage, 1864*

The long-standing computer science principle of *garbage in, garbage out* (GIGO) is so fundamental to IT that it predates digital computing by almost a century. And yet here we are in the twenty-first century, moving to the Cloud, and Babbage's exasperated response is no truer or more on point. For not only is the Cloud a magnet for all sorts of garbage, it is also generating new garbage at a brisk clip.

In today's frantic rush to move to the Cloud, too many organizations are failing to ask *what* they should move to the Cloud. Instead, they envision the Cloud as some kind of huge, nebulous server in the sky, a perfect receptacle for whatever they have on-premise. Got e-mail? Put it in the Cloud! Got data? Put your data in the Cloud, the bigger the better! Running business processes on-premise? Move them to the Cloud!

Not so fast. Let's slow down a bit and consider the ramifications of moving too quickly—and haphazardly—to the Cloud:

- **Unclean data.** This is the obvious example; pure GIGO. If your current on-premise data are unclean, say, you have inconsistent customer demographic information, obsolete product information, or any other data quality challenge, it goes without saying that moving such information to the Cloud won't do your data, or your business, any good. Instead, think of moving your data to the Cloud as though you were moving your elderly parents to a condo. It's a wonderful excuse to finally dig through the layers of detritus so that you only move data that are clean, accurate, and valuable to the business.
- **Spaghetti code.** You may be eyeing that old custom-coded legacy app as a prime Cloud candidate. It's too slow, it doesn't scale well, and it's a bear to integrate now, so won't the Cloud automatically make it fast, scalable, and easy to integrate? Sorry to burst your bubble. If you're focusing on an IaaS approach, what you'll find is that spaghetti code is every bit as intractable in the Cloud as it is on-premise. What about PaaS? Chances are that old code won't run at all. Today's PaaS environments expect and enforce a certain level of code quality.
- **Obsolete and Cloud-unfriendly business processes.** Does this sound familiar? The business asks IT to automate a set of processes, but states unequivocally that the processes are fine the way they are. Automate them but don't change them. After all, we've been doing things the same way for years. Why change now? Yes, the business often says that, but seasoned IT veterans have long realized that the business never actually means it. When the business asks IT to touch a process, there is always at least an implied requirement to try to make it better: faster, more streamlined, better aligned with the underlying business need.

Moving business process implementations to the Cloud raises the stakes in this complex dance between business and technology, because the Cloud offers a wealth of new opportunities for improving processes. Furthermore, how users interact with Cloud-based assets is often fundamentally different from how users interact with traditional enterprise apps. Any organization that has moved from an older CRM app (or no CRM app at all) to Salesforce .com has learned this lesson first hand. But Salesforce is merely a harbinger of greater change to come. One of the main reasons Salesforce has been so successful is because they offer their clients new ways of conducting business—in other words, better processes. Any SaaS solution should build on their example.

The garbage problem doesn't end with garbage you might put in the Cloud. The Cloud also presents numerous opportunities to generate new kinds of garbage:

- **Zombie instances.** It's so easy and cheap now for anyone in your organization to spawn their own Cloud instances, including virtual machines, storage instances, and more. Furthermore, such instances are elastic: Need more of them? The Cloud is only too happy to oblige. But what happens when you're done with them? You're supposed to delete them. After all, elasticity works in both directions. All too often, however, instances that have served their purpose are left around like so much space junk. After a while, nobody remembers what they're for or if they still have something important in them. The last thing you want to do is delete an instance with valuable data or code on it. So to play it safe, you leave it around. Forever. Your Cloud provider is only too happy to keep billing you for these Zombie instances.

- **Data with no provenance.** Any *Antiques Roadshow* aficionado knows that antiques with provenance are more valuable than those without. The same goes for your data. Do you know if the data you're working with are the latest version? Do you know they haven't been tampered with? If not, then those data are worse than useless, because they may be incorrect, or even worse, keeping them around may violate any number of regulations. Here again, the elasticity of the Cloud works against you.

- **Manual or poorly abstracted configurations.** Let's say you've built a sophisticated Cloud app based on elastic VM instances. If you need more, simply provision more. But then let's say some admin somewhere in your IT shop goes into one of these instances and changes a config file in order to get an app to run on that instance. Now you have no way to update your instances without breaking your app—and if that admin didn't tell anybody about the reconfiguration, then tracking down the problem will present a time-consuming challenge.

  Simply creating a static image file to generate new VM instances— and keeping rogue admins from monkeying with them—won't solve the problem, because there is more to your app than the instances. Instead, you need a next-generation configuration management approach that automates configuration for the Cloud.

- **Cloud-unfriendly architecture choices.** Inappropriate state information is just more garbage in the Cloud. Another example would be inappropriate transactionality in the Cloud. Cloud Computing lends itself to particular ways of architecting applications, and attempting to shoehorn the wrong architectural approach into the Cloud is about as effective as Cinderella's stepsisters' efforts with the glass slipper.

How do you avoid garbage in the Cloud? Architecture is a large part of the answer, of course, but governance is equally important. Organizations should establish and enforce Cloud-centric policies as well as extending current IT governance to the Cloud. With great power comes great responsibility, and the Cloud offers enormous new power to many different roles within the IT organization. The Cloud is fraught with pitfalls. Without sufficient governance, you're bound to fall in one.

It is also important to note that Cloud garbage issues apply equally to private as well as Public Clouds. Organizations generally realize that Public Clouds present numerous governance challenges, and look to Private Clouds because they are ostensibly less risky. But such a stance offers little more than a false sense of security—one that may backfire, if organizations assume that in the absence of proper architecture and governance, a Private Cloud is the better choice. Don't wait to implement adequate Cloud governance until after you've run into these problems. Governance should be an integral part of any Cloud strategy, *before* you move to the Cloud.

Beware Fake Clouds

In spite of the title of this section, the distinction between a "real" or "fake" Cloud isn't particularly useful, because it could be argued that any subscription-based Web site is a simple example of SaaS. What really matters is the value proposition. If all you want is a pay-as-you-go subscription model for something you access over the Web, then virtually any vendor's purported SaaS offering may qualify. However, a subscription model doesn't guarantee elasticity or automated recovery from failure, two essential Cloud characteristics. If you don't care about these characteristics, then fine. But don't be fooled. A vendor may say their offering is Cloud-based, suggesting they have an elastic offering even if they don't.

It's also important to understand the different types of elasticity. Even if a vendor says their offering is elastic, you may need to dig further. They may simply be referring to the elasticity of their virtualization layer. An IaaS provider might offer you, say, a VM with a gigabyte of RAM, with the promise that if you need two gigabytes, you'll get it automatically, and only pay for it while you're using it. Yes, this is a form of elasticity, but it has limits. After all, your VM is rubbing elbows with other VMs on some physical server with physical memory somewhere, and there's only so much RAM to go around. Allotting you more might even mean borrowing it from someone else's VM.

However, you may be looking for the unlimited type of elasticity that gives Clouds the illusion of infinite capacity—in other words, the elasticity that makes Clouds *Cloudy*. For this type of elasticity, what we might call Cloud elasticity to distinguish it from the limited form in the paragraph above, the Cloud provider must be able to provision and deprovision additional instances quickly and automatically, where *instances* might refer to VMs, storage, queues, databases, or whatever resources you're interested in acquiring from the provider. IaaS vendors find this kind of horizontal elasticity relatively straightforward, because it's up to you how you're going to use your new instances. But for PaaS and SaaS vendors, Cloud elasticity can be unexpectedly problematic.

For example, take a look at the *Oracle Database Cloud*. This offering essentially takes the enterprise workhorse Oracle Database 11g and places it into a virtualized environment—what Oracle refers to as a PaaS offering in a Private Cloud. The architectural emphasis, however, is on database consolidation, not horizontal elasticity. The problem is that the Oracle Database is inherently partition intolerant, because it guarantees availability and immediate consistency. Their offering may very well meet your needs, but don't expect it to offer Cloud elasticity.

There's more to getting what you pay for in the Cloud than ensuring that the elasticity on offer meets your needs. Here are some tough questions you can ask to separate the wheat from the chaff:

- **Did the SaaS provider simply cross out the word "Web" on their marketing and replace it with "Cloud"?** Yes, this Cloudwashing might be all you require, but chances are you're looking for something more. Remember the dot-com days where mundane companies would stick the word "Web" in their marketing and automatically become dot-com players? Well, now the spinmeisters are doing it again. Accessing software with a browser over the Internet doesn't make it *Cloud*. That's what we used to call the *Web*.

- **Will moving to the Cloud really save me money?** Saving money may or may not be your reason for moving to the Cloud, but for many organizations, it's their primary business driver. However, if your capacity requirements are relatively stable—that is, elasticity isn't particularly important to you—then IaaS in particular may actually be more expensive than just leaving your apps where they are. Make sure you crunch the numbers before taking the plunge.

- **Do you like the idea of SaaS, but no existing SaaS offering is quite right, so you're thinking about hiring someone to build you a "custom" SaaS solution?** If so, you're almost certainly on the wrong track. The whole point to SaaS is that you're leaving the software development as well as hosting work to someone else who can make money from many customers, thus lowering the cost for all of them.

Paying someone to build a bespoke solution defeats the whole purpose. It's really not SaaS at all, even if you access it over the Web.

- **Does your PaaS provider's platform give you the application programming interfaces (APIs) you require?** For PaaS providers who've built their platforms from scratch to run in the Cloud, this is a silly question. Take the Facebook app platform, for example. The whole point of running your app on Facebook is to interface with the core Facebook app, so *of course* they provide the APIs you need to do so. But what if your PaaS provider took some old middleware product, say an ESB, stuck it in the Cloud, and called it PaaS? You'll be lucky if the APIs you get simply reflect the fact they're running in the Cloud at all, let alone offer you specialized capabilities unique to the environment.

- **Just how automated is a Public Cloud provider's automated provisioning and configuration?** Elasticity doesn't just require *dynamic* provisioning and deprovisioning, it requires *automated* provisioning and deprovisioning. If provisioning a VM means sending a work order to a sysadmin who'll get back to you in a few days, it's not Cloud at all. We'll cover automated provisioning in an upcoming section.

- **Similarly, are you considering investing in a Private Cloud, but your vendor can't provide fully automated configuration and provisioning tools?** If so, they're pulling the wool over your eyes. How do you expect to handle configuration and provisioning—by hiring a room full of monkeys pounding on keyboards all day? We have a phrase for a Private Cloud without automated configuration and provisioning. We call it a traditional data center.

Learning the Right Lessons from the 2011 and 2012 Amazon Crashes

Ready for more Cloud doom and gloom? In April 2011, a misconfiguration brought down several of Amazon Web Services' Availability Zones—and with them, numerous Cloud-based applications, both large and small. Public Cloud naysayers pounced, pointing to the calamity as evidence that Public Clouds weren't yet ready for prime time. And though Amazon was reasonably sure the particular problem that caused the 2011 outage wouldn't happen again, they couldn't be completely sure some other set of circumstances wouldn't lead to a similar meltdown. Sure enough, bad weather took down part of the Amazon Cloud in June 2012.

In light of this lack of certainty, should you avoid Public Clouds? Not so fast. If we place these Amazon crashes into their proper context, we are in a better position to learn the right lessons from these crises, rather than reacting out of fear to an event taken out of that context. Here, then, are some essential lessons we should take away from the crashes:

- **There is no such thing as 100 percent reliability.** In fact, there's nothing 100 percent about any of IT—no code is 100 percent bug free, no system is 100 percent crash proof, and no security is 100 percent impenetrable. Just because Amazon came up snake eyes on these throws of the dice doesn't mean that Public Clouds are any less reliable than they were before the crises. Whether investing in the stock market or building a high-availability IT infrastructure, the best way to lower risk is to diversify. You got eggs? The more baskets the better.

- **These particular crises are unlikely to happen again.** We can safely assume that Amazon has some wicked smart Cloud experts, and that they had already built a Cloud architecture that could withstand most challenges. Suffice it to say, therefore, that the latest crises had an unusual and complex set of causes. It also goes without saying that those experts are working feverishly to root out those causes, so that these specific sets of circumstances won't happen again.

- **The unknown unknowns are by definition inherently unpredictable.** Even though the particular sequences of events that led to the current crises are unlikely to happen again, the chance that other entirely unpredictable issues will arise in the future is relatively likely. But such issues might very well apply to private, hybrid, or community Clouds just as much as they might impact the Public Cloud again. In other words, bailing on Public Clouds to take refuge in the supposedly safer Private Cloud arena is an exercise in futility.

- **The most important lesson for Amazon to learn is more about visibility than reliability.** The weakest part of Amazon's Cloud offerings at the time was the lack of visibility they provided their customers. This "never mind the man behind the curtain" attitude is part of how Amazon supports the Cloud abstraction. But at the time of the crashes, it was working against them and their customers. For Amazon to build on its success, it must open the kimono a bit and provide its customers a level of management visibility into its internal infrastructure that it's been uncomfortable delivering to this point.

Abstractions hide complexity from consumers of technology, but if you do too good a job hiding the underlying complexity, then the abstraction can backfire. But that doesn't mean that abstractions are bad; rather, you need different abstractions for different audiences.

The latest crises impacted a wide swath of small Cloud-based vendors. These firms' customers simply wanted their tools to work, and were disappointed and inconvenienced when they stopped working. But the end-user customer may not have even been aware that Amazon's Cloud was behind their tool of choice. Clearly, those customers wouldn't find better visibility into the Cloud particularly useful.

No, it's the technology departments at the small vendors that require better visibility. They are the people who require management tools that enable them to gain a greater level of control over the Cloud environments they leverage in their own products. As Amazon supports such management tools, Amazon's customers will be better able to provide the seamless abstraction to the Cloud end user, who simply wants stuff to work properly.

Failure Is the Only Option

As we discussed earlier, *recovery from failure* is more important than *reliability* in the Cloud. In fact, planning for failure is nothing new. I ran a computer department for a small private school back in 1991. I remember rolling out our first Macintosh computers, the ones with one megabyte of memory and no hard drive (the hard drives were too expensive for us). I managed to get them up and running with no disk in the floppy drive, so that students could load and save their work to their own floppy.

This diskless approach was not particularly stable, however, and the computers would crash on a regular basis. As a result, my mantra was SAVE YOUR WORK! Expect your computer to crash, and plan accordingly!

School kids being school kids, however, they frequently ignored my admonition. Sure enough, periodically one would come up to me with a tear in her eye. "Mr. Bloom! I just spent all period writing my English paper and the computer crashed! Please help!" But of course, there was nothing I could do at that point.

Two decades later, the computers are bigger, faster, and cheaper, we have the Internet and all it has done for us, and today we even have the Cloud. But in some ways nothing has changed. Failure is still unpredictable, yet it is around every corner. The core best practice, *expect and plan for failure*, is still as important as it was in the floppy days.

In fact, it was the spectacular Amazon Cloud flameout of April 2011 that brought back memories of the days in the school computer lab. One of the core architectural principles of Amazon's Cloud—or any Cloud for that matter, public or private—is our old friend, *expect and plan for failure*. After all, each individual node in the Cloud, whether it be a server, hard drive, or piece of network equipment, consists of cheap commodity hardware. Each Cloud provider architects their Cloud environment so that any such piece of equipment—or even several pieces at once—can fail, and the environment should recover automatically.

In fact, fault tolerance and elasticity go hand in hand. Elasticity requires the same bootstrapping that fault tolerance calls for. Sometimes, the reason to bootstrap a box is to meet additional demand (elasticity) or to replace some other box that is having issues (fault tolerance). Essentially, when you need a new box, it boots and asks what it's supposed to do, and then it finds and installs the appropriate resources to become the piece of equipment it needs to be.

However, just because your Cloud provider architected their internal infrastructure to be elastic and fault tolerant doesn't mean that your app will automatically inherit these traits once you move it to the Cloud. When an organization wants to run an application in the Cloud, it is important to architect the application to take advantage of the elasticity and fault tolerance the Cloud provides. Moving a big chunk of legacy spaghetti code into the Cloud is asking for trouble, as is trying to migrate a tightly coupled set of objects. Where you might have been able to get away with such design antipatterns for an in-house app, the Cloud forces you to clean up your act and deploy modular, loosely coupled apps that can take advantage of the inherently elastic, fault-tolerant nature of the Cloud.

There is an important story here: The internal architecture of the Cloud is forcing organizations to rearchitect their apps, enabling them to take advantage of the Cloud, but as a welcome side effect, gives them better architected apps. But that's not the only story.

The broader story is especially ironic. The irony, of course, is that a core Cloud best practice is to expect for and plan for failure—not only within the Cloud, but of the Cloud itself. If you tell yourself that Cloud architectures are inherently fault tolerant, and therefore it's sufficient to count on a single Cloud provider, you're fooling yourself.

Architecting for the Cloud doesn't mean sticking your app into the Cloud as though it were a black box. On one hand, it means rearchitecting your app to take advantage of the Cloud, and on the other hand, it means considering each Cloud provider instance as one element in your broader Enterprise Architecture. And if you want that Enterprise Architecture to be fault tolerant, avoid any single point of failure—even if that point of failure is the Cloud itself. Bottom line: SAVE YOUR WORK. We don't want you coming up to us at the end of class because you lost your data. We won't be able to do anything about your data, but we will be able to tell you we told you so!

Cloud Configuration Management: Where the Rubber Hits the Clouds

Let's hang out for a while longer in the early 1990s. This time it's in your data center. The server you ordered finally arrives. Could be Windows, Linux, some flavor of Unix, doesn't matter. You unpack it. Boot it up. Patch the OS. Configure the OS. Install software off of CDs. Patch the software. Configure the software. Move data to the box. Test. Tweak. Test again. Finally, the box goes live.

Cut to today. You're working in the Cloud now. You provision a VM instance in the Cloud. Or three. Or maybe a few dozen. Only you're not just provisioning VMs. You also provision some dynamic storage. Maybe some Cloud-based queues. You also want some SaaS-based services.

And your software release cycles? Weekly. No, daily. How about hourly? Now what?

Clearly, it's impractical to set up your Cloud instances manually, the way we used to set up servers in the good old days. So you go through the process once and create an image file that represents your Platonic ideal of what a fully configured VM instance should look like. Now, every time you need to provision a new VM instance, simply reconstitute the image. Right?

Not so fast. There are numerous gotchas to this scenario. Every time you need to patch anything, you would need to create a new image. If different VM instances are meant to differ in any way—say, contain different application data—you would need to configure those differences manually. But most significantly, there is far more to your Cloud environment than single VM instances. What about the storage? Databases? Network configuration? What about the *architecture*?

Remember, *automated* means *not manual*, in the sense that *hands are not allowed*. You want the ability to deploy, update, and repair your entire application infrastructure using nothing but predefined, automated procedures. Ideally, you would prefer to automatically provision your entire environment from bare metal (hardware with no operating systems—or anything else—installed on them) all the way up to running business services completely from a predefined specification, including the network configuration. Furthermore, there should be no direct management of individual boxes. You want to manage the entire Cloud deployment as a single unit.

Deploying sophisticated provisioning tools, of course, is a large part of the secret. And the more sophisticated the tools, the less skilled your staff has to be. Ideally, any people familiar with a few basic commands and possessing the appropriate permissions should be able to deploy any release to any integrated development, test, or production environment. They only require minimal domain-specific knowledge. You don't need a senior sysadmin. You don't even need a systems developer. Any junior techie should be able to handle the task.

If something goes wrong, you should be able to revert to a *previously known good* state at any time. In a mature Cloud environment, it's always easier to reprovision than it is to repair. Reprovisioning could mean an automated cycle of validating and regenerating application and system configurations, or even rerunning the full provisioning cycle from the base OS up to running business applications.

In many cases, of course, the previously known good state isn't good enough, typically because there are live data in the real-time state that would be lost with this kind of rollback. As a result, such rollbacks must be handled carefully, as they really aren't rollbacks in the sense of a two-phase commit. Instead, with fully automated provisioning, the provisioning system should be able to *roll forward to a previous version*, where the provisioning tools will automatically return your applications to a functionally acceptable state, with all your data intact.

Automated provisioning depends on the *environment specification*. This spec is essentially a declarative representation of how you want to configure your entire deployment. Your provisioning tools will then essentially execute the spec, starting with bare metal and possibly stock VM images, and then they will automatically deploy, configure, and start up the entire system or the application stack (or both), with no run-time decisions or tweaking by an operator. The spec should also contain sufficient detail to direct the appropriate tools to test whether the automation is implemented correctly, and if it isn't, to take the appropriate action.

This specification can be as sophisticated as your tools and your architecture allow it to be. It may vary from release to release, and you should be able to break it down for specific tools that handle different parts of the configuration. The spec may also have conditional logic, and can also specify deployment or configuration changes over time; for example, the instruction to provision additional instances when traffic numbers cross a threshold.

You may also want to handle the automatic configuration of the application stack separately from the configuration of the system stack, as your applications may change more frequently than the systems. The goal is to make the spec sufficiently sophisticated so that the automation itself doesn't vary from release to release. It will only require updates when your requirements call for a significant architectural change.

There are fundamentally two sides to this story: the view from the perspective of the Cloud service provider (including the internal providers of Private Clouds) vs. the view from the consumer of Cloud-based resources. Clearly, Amazon, Microsoft, and the other Public Cloud providers have figured out how to automate the configuration of their Public Cloud environments. For organizations building their own Private Clouds, the challenge is to take a page out of the public service providers' playbooks on how to run a Cloud environment. Bottom line: If you don't get automated configuration management down pat, you're not running a Private Cloud at all. You simply have a traditional data center with some Cloud-like features—and furthermore, you have a data center that is more expensive to run than necessary.

If you're in a position to consume Cloud resources, regardless of the Cloud deployment model, then automated provisioning is every bit as important as it is for Cloud service providers, only now it impacts your existing IT processes and policies. As organizations adopt the Cloud, they increasingly transform the role of operations. No longer does your Ops team actually take care of servers, networks, and applications. Instead, you're automating that work, shifting the expertise required to the development team who must now create and manage the automation scripts that form the specification. Or perhaps the Ops team moves their cubicles to the dev area, working hand-in-hand with developers to handle those scripts. Either way, Cloud changes everything in the IT department.

Reworking the relationship between Dev and Ops, or DevOps, is nothing new, of course. DevOps is an emerging set of principles and practices for collaboration between the software development and IT operations staff. It has developed in response to the emerging understanding of the interdependence and importance of both the development and operations disciplines in meeting an organization's goal of rapidly producing software products and services. In other words, DevOps is an essential aspect of iterative, full–life cycle governance—an essential enabler of Agile Architecture.

Now, with the rise of Cloud Computing, DevOps is entering what might be its golden age. As Cloud provisioning specifications become more sophisticated, creating them becomes more of a development task than an operational one. Ops doesn't go away, of course, but it moves to the other side of the Cloud: supporting Cloud data centers. In other words, if you have a Private Cloud, your ops team is responsible for managing the Private Cloud infrastructure. And yes, if you use a Public Cloud, you have the luxury of outsourcing operations to your Cloud provider. Good sysadmins need not worry, of course. If anything, demand for your skills is only increasing with the move to the Cloud.

Clouds, SOA, REST, and State

Earlier in the book, we shook up preconceived notions of REST, shifting its focus from APIs to distributed hypermedia applications where it belongs.

And now we've shaken up the Cloud story as well, centering the discussion on architecture and how Cloud Computing can enable Agile Architecture—but only if you get it right. Now it's finally time to connect REST and the Cloud together.

There's a topic of central importance to REST that we haven't fully explained: the concept of state. What is *state*, anyway? *State* refers to some information about the past, such as a customer record or purchase transaction, and in general reflects the information about all the changes a system has been through up to the present. State is especially important to processes because without it, we in effect have a system with no history or record. Indeed, most of the systems that we have developed are either responsible for storing state in some form or another or acting on that state. Furthermore, companies depend on state in order to back out of transactions and situations that result in some error. In essence, without state, we can't accomplish any sort of reliable transaction, because there would be no way to undo the things we have done.

In our discussion of REST, we differentiated between application state and resource state, but that's as far as we took it. But now that we're talking about the Cloud, it's time to delve more into the topic of state. After all, REST stands for *Representational State Transfer*. Transferring application state in representations is so important, it gives REST its name. As it happens, state transfer is an essential enabler of a broad class of Cloud-based applications.

However, you might think the RESTful Cloud story has to do with RESTful APIs to the Cloud. Sure, we want to be able to access Cloud resources as well as Cloud management capabilities via RESTful interfaces. There are many such efforts, and many of them are promising, to be sure, but that's not what we're talking about here. RESTful APIs to the Cloud miss the point to REST, and don't address the core challenge of architecting for the Cloud.

We must now explain how the elasticity property of Clouds impacts how we architect applications for the Cloud, and combine those principles with the fact that REST is really for building distributed hypermedia applications. The story of RESTful Clouds, therefore, isn't about RESTful APIs to the Cloud at all, useful though they may be. Instead, the fact that the REST architectural style focuses on hypermedia applications addresses one of the knottiest challenges of architecting for the Cloud: how we deal with application state.

How we deal with state is a challenge for SOA deployments as well, because Services are inherently *stateless*. In fact, statelessness is essential to implementing loosely coupled Services. A Service, after all, exposes an interface to software that communicates by sending and/or receiving messages. There is no notion of a Service instance analogous to object instances; instead, the Service simply stays put, exchanging messages as per its contract. More specifically, because SOA involves collaborations of independent entities through Service composition, we are only dealing with passing messages and data from one Service to the next. These loosely coupled, heterogeneous, composite applications require that all Services should be stateless such that they don't impose their knowledge of a system or process unnecessarily on other parties, thus tightening their level of coupling, reducing their ability for reuse, and limiting broad applicability.

However, the primary reason for composing Services is to create applications that implement business processes, and processes must be stateful, because after all, one instance of a process may be in a different state than another. The challenge of how best to maintain this application or process state in an environment of stateless Services becomes a critical issue for architects planning and implementing SOA. Implement process state improperly, and the loose coupling benefits of stateless Services, and hence the SOA itself, are at risk.

Even in the context of SOA, therefore, we must maintain state outside of each independent Service implementation in order to achieve long-running processes, especially when they span organizational or company boundaries. In addition, there must be some representation of state as well for most security, governance, and quality processes that maintain some context across multiple Services.

The stateless Web presented the very same problem in which Web sites had to maintain some notion of a session across individual Web queries, each of which maintained no state on their own. There were basically two approaches to maintaining state on the Web: Store a cookie on the browser that maintained state across multiple interactions, or track state within the Uniform Resource Locator (URL) or POST data for every interaction between the browser and server that required maintenance of a session.

Cookies only worked to maintain state on the Web because they were a feature of HTTP, the underlying transport protocol of the Web, and every browser by definition supported HTTP, but because people can simply turn cookies off or delete them, they aren't particularly reliable. In the case of Services, however, we're allowing for arbitrary system-to-system communication, with no expectation that consumers will all be browsers or, in general, support any particular protocol. That leaves *the message itself* as the only place we can maintain state in the context of SOA.

For this reason state maintenance in the Web Services world has always been problematic. There are basically three ways to maintain state information in interactions among inherently stateless Services: Rely on the Service consumer to maintain a correlation ID (either not broadly adopted or relies on an underlying protocol like HTTP cookies); rely on the underlying execution environment (vendor dependent); or place state information into the message. Unfortunately, Web Services offer no standard way of accomplishing the latter task, requiring SOA teams to customize their SOAP headers—which is usually a deal killer.

Even so, it's possible to maintain state across multiple Service invocations by applying some sort of persistent token to each Service message. This token would represent a persistent state across multiple Service interactions, and well-behaved Services will simply pass on that token to other Services in a composition without needlessly modifying or removing it, as per the contracts that govern those Services. In this manner, individual Services remain stateless, but the messages can maintain the state that particular Service compositions require.

This message-based approach to maintaining state begs the question as to how to manage the processes that the Service compositions represent. Traditional Business Process Management (BPM) tools utilize a run-time composition engine that maintains state on behalf of all running processes. The advantage to this approach is that it provides visibility into running processes and maintains state across relevant Services.

However, this approach has some critical issues: A central process execution environment can only maintain state for Services and compositions that the server has visibility into. Once a Service request passes outside the boundaries of the system, the process tool can no longer control the process. Second, the robustness of the processes depends on the robustness of the process tool—if the tool crashes and loses state information, then there is no way to recover process instances in progress. But perhaps most significantly, a centralized process execution environment reduces loose coupling, because all Service providers and consumers must defer control over the processes to the centralized tool.

The answer to these problems is to maintain process state essentially in a Service-oriented manner. In other words, offer state management via contracted Services whose purpose is to maintain state for process instances. In essence, this approach uses messages as events that the state maintenance Services can audit, log, and later analyze to determine some given state. This approach basically considers state to be an implicit side effect of a running system rather than something that a run-time process environment must persist. This event-driven, Service-oriented approach tracks all relevant events, and a separate set of Services analyze the event stream and perform specific actions based on process requirements, policies, and Service contracts.

Basically, what we've done here is separate traditional BPM from Service-oriented BPM based on the fundamental issue of state management. One way of understanding the difference is to try the "unplug the server" thought exercise. What happens to running process instances when a centralized BPM tool goes down? Because the centralized tool controls all process logic, including state logic, bringing down the tool typically hoses all running processes, often in an unrecoverable way.

Now, what happens when a process management Service goes down? Because the messages that the Service providers and consumers are exchanging contain the persistent token that represents the process state, no process information is lost. Instead, messages to the process management Service should simply queue up, waiting for it to come back online. Once it does recover, it can continue executing the process logic where it left off, because the queued messages will tell it everything it needs to know about current process state. Recall that the U.S. Coast Guard's SPEAR architecture worked that way.

From the architects' perspective, therefore, it's essential to think about state in a Service-oriented way. Services don't maintain state unless they are specifically contracted to do so in the case when they are state management Services, and in that case, they are managing state for running processes that are external to the state management Service itself. In no instance do we have a Service manage its own state, because a Service consumer would have to know the internal state of the Service in order to determine whether to send a message to that Service. That situation would break the loose coupling and encapsulation principles of SOA.

The Secret of a RESTful Cloud

The traditional approach to maintaining application state for any distributed application, therefore, is to use some kind of stateful object on the server. A stateful object contains data that maintain the context of that application for a particular user across conversations consisting of multiple calls to a specific instance of that object. In essence, stateful objects keep track of what individual users are doing when they use an application.

A familiar example of a stateful object is the traditional shopping cart. Every shopping cart instance belongs to an individual customer. Therefore, if you had ten thousand customers shopping at the same time, you would have ten thousand shopping cart instances, which can cause problems for your application. Not only do all these carts present an obvious scalability challenge, but if you need to update a given customer's shopping cart, you must first locate the correct shopping cart instance for that customer. No other shopping cart will do.

Furthermore, remember that in the Cloud, you must plan for and expect failure. If you are dependent on a single instance of a shopping cart, and the resources that support that cart crash, then you are faced with another challenge. Hopefully you've been saving the cart's state somewhere (and of course, the state for every other cart for every other customer), so that you can reconstitute the failed cart elsewhere. Perhaps the worst that would happen would be that the customer would have to start their shopping over, but in other situations, the failure of a stateful instance can leave the customer in an inconsistent state. That's a surefire recipe for losing customers.

Stateless objects, on the other hand, don't contain any information or context between calls of that object. In other words, each such call stands alone and doesn't rely on prior calls as part of an ongoing conversation. You could call one instance of a stateless object, and then make a call on a different instance of the same object, and you wouldn't able to tell the difference.

If an object is stateless, therefore, the Cloud is free to use any instance of that object to get its work done. You no longer have to worry about contention for a single instance of an object, a situation that could lead to a variety of distributed computing challenges including race conditions (where the output is unpredictably dependent on the order that messages arrive), deadlocks (where two or more actions wait for the other to finish), and starvation (where a process can't finish because other processes deny it sufficient resources). Instead, you can simply rely on the elasticity of the Cloud to add more instances as needed.

It is an important best practice, therefore, that all application logic in the Cloud should be stateless. No object instances, no session Beans, no server cookies. If the load on your application spikes, the Cloud should respond elastically by provisioning adequate resources to meet the need. The more stateless your application is, the better able the Cloud will be to achieve this seamless elasticity.

Okay then. Elastic, stateless shopping carts are all well and good, but what about *my* shopping cart? I just put my holiday shopping in there. *Of course* it has to be stateful!

Here's where our discussion of state gets a bit murky, because we have to differentiate between the two different types of state: *application state* and *resource state*. In the case of the shopping cart, the application state consists of what happens to be in individual carts as customers work through the purchasing process, and where in the process they are at any point in time. The resource state includes information the application must access or update, including the customer mailing address, credit card information, and the actual purchase transaction. In other words, the application state is *dynamic* and specific to each client, and the resource state is *persistent* and shared across all clients.

When you deal with resource state in the Cloud, therefore, you're working at the persistence tier, where traditional approaches to scalability like database sharding and traditional approaches to reliability like replication and caching work reasonably well. There are limitations on Cloud persistence, however; don't expect to achieve two-phase commit levels of reliability, because the Cloud's inherent partition tolerance and availability prevent it from exhibiting immediate data consistency. Data within a particular Cloud instance, however, are still internally consistent.

Application state is a different matter. Treating application state as though it were resource state—writing your application state to your database every time a customer does anything with their shopping cart—limits your scalability, elasticity, and reliability. Don't go there if you can avoid it. Instead, you want *hypermedia* to be the engine of application state. In other words, your stateless application instance must give the *client* everything it needs to know in order to work its way through the purchasing process, and the client maintains the application state for the entire process. You don't need to spawn a stateful shopping cart instance on the server every time a customer hits your application, because after all, the more users you have, the more clients you have. Why not let the client do the work?

To explain how such RESTful shopping carts might work in the Cloud, we must set up two separate RESTful interactions. The first is between the application tier and the persistence tier. The application tier serves as the client in this case, requesting a representation of the customer's shopping cart instance from the resource on the persistence tier. This application tier client is stateless; the representation has all the necessary information about the customer as well as the process logic for the purchasing processes that you want the customer to follow.

The second interaction is between the customer's client and the application tier, which now serves as the server for this interaction. The customer follows links in the representations that the resources on the server return, and thus the client executes the purchasing process as per the customer's requirements. But the code on the application tier is still completely stateless; it is in charge of following in a declarative manner the instructions that the persistence tier provided.

If the application instance on the application tier crashes, the Cloud environment automatically spawns a replacement. When the customer clicks a link, that replacement knows to repopulate the customer's shopping cart representation based on the information in the GET, POST, or other operation on that link's Uniform Resource Identifier (URI), and furthermore, knows where the customer was in their purchasing process based on the information in the operation on the URI as well. In other words, the client runs the shopping cart application by enabling the customer to follow links, and those requests tell the Cloud environment everything it needs to know to meet the customer's needs, without maintaining any application state of its own. That's hypermedia as the engine of application state (HATEOAS) in action.

A great application of RESTful Cloud principles is the Amazon.com shopping cart. Try this experiment: Log into your Amazon.com eCommerce account simultaneously from two different browsers. Add an item to your cart from one browser. Reload the Amazon home page on the other: Note that the number of items in your cart went up by one. Why? Because you haven't actually begun the purchasing process yet. The shopping cart count on the Amazon home page is part of your resource state.

Next, proceed on one browser as though you were purchasing the item. In the middle of the process, change the quantity of the item you're trying to purchase from one to two. Again, reload the Amazon home page from the other browser: *This time the cart count doesn't change.* You have two items in your cart according to one browser and one item according to the other, even though you only have one shopping cart.

What's going on here? Amazon's persistence tier handed your purchase process off to a Cloud instance, and your first browser is maintaining application state for that instance. The Cloud instance can therefore be entirely stateless, which enables Amazon to maximize the elasticity of their environment. If Amazon does it that way, then so should you for any stateful application you want to move to the Cloud.

Architecting your Cloud-based app so that all Cloud-based code is stateless is essential for implementing rapid elasticity—and furthermore, such Cloud-based code may be in VM instances, in application packages running on PaaS environments, or in SaaS applications. Furthermore, HATEOAS is essential for handling application state in such a way that enables server resources to be stateless. Therefore, REST is essential for rapid elasticity in the Cloud.

It's likely, however, that many RESTafarians won't fully understand this important conclusion, because so many of them focus on RESTful interfaces—the proverbial forest for the trees. They take a developer's perspective rather than an architect's. From the architect's perspective, REST is no more or less than an architectural style for building distributed hypermedia applications. And you're not doing REST unless you follow HATEOAS.

BPM in the Cloud: Disruptive Technology

The battle over application state promises to reopen some old wounds of the SOA days to be fought over the new territory of the Cloud: BPM. The fundamental idea behind BPM software is that you need some kind of engine to coordinate interactions between actors and disparate applications into business processes. Those actors may be human or other applications themselves. To specify the process, you must create some kind of process representation the process engine can run.

Vendors loved BPM because process engines were a natural add-on to their middleware stacks. Coordinating multiple applications meant creating multiple integrations, and for that you need middleware. Lots of it. And in spite of paying lip service to cross-platform Service compositions that would implement vendor-independent processes, in large part each vendor rolled out a proprietary toolset.

We saw the world of SOA-enabled BPM quite differently. In our view, the Service-oriented way of looking at BPM was to free it from the engines and focus on Services: composing them and consuming them. But there was a catch: Services are inherently stateless. The challenge with the Service-oriented approach to BPM was how to maintain state for each process instance in an inherently stateless environment.

Although we have to award victory to the vendors in the SOA-based BPM war, the move to the Cloud offers an entirely new battleground with completely new rules. Today, of course, the vendors (and, it seems, everyone else) want to put their software in the Cloud. So it's a natural consequence that the BPM vendors would seek to move their BPM engines into the Cloud as well, perhaps as part of a PaaS provider strategy. Clearly such a move would be a good bet from the business perspective, as it's likely that many BPM customers would find value in a Cloud-based offering.

Here's where the story gets interesting. In order to achieve the elasticity benefit of the Cloud for a distributed application, it's essential for the application tier to be stateless, as we discussed in the previous section. The Cloud may need to spawn additional instances to handle the load, and any particular instance may crash. But because the Cloud is highly available and partition tolerant, such a crash mustn't hose the process that Cloud instance is supporting.

As a result, there is simply no way a traditional BPM engine can run properly in the Cloud. After all, BPM engines' raison d'être is to maintain process state, but you can't do that on a Cloud instance without sacrificing elasticity! In other words, all the work the big vendors put into building their SOA-platform-centric BPM engines must now be chucked out the door. *The Cloud and REST have changed the rules of BPM.*

The vendors, however, are far from shaking in their boots, because they aren't the ones responsible for the misinformation about REST. In fact, REST is about *Hypermedia-Oriented Architecture*. At the risk of extending an already-tired cliché, let's use the abbreviation HOA. In HOA, hypermedia are the engine of application state—the dreaded HATEOAS REST constraint. With HATEOAS, hyperlinks dynamically describe the contract between the client and the server in the form of a workflow at run-time. That's right. No process engine needed! All you need are *hyperlinks*.

The power of this idea is obvious once you think through it, because the World Wide Web itself is the prototypical example of such a run-time workflow. You can think of any sequence of clicking links and loading Web pages as a workflow, after all—where those pages may be served up by different resources on different servers anywhere in the world. No heavyweight, centralized process engine in sight.

The big vendors aren't worried now, because they don't understand the power of hypermedia. If HOA-based BPM takes off, however, then their whole middleware-in-the-Cloud approach to PaaS is doomed to fail. If they're smart, they'd better dig their trenches now. After all, they have too much invested in the old way of doing things. HOA-based BPM is potentially a disruptive technology, and they're facing the innovator's dilemma.

On the other hand, there is a substantial opportunity for the innovators— new entrants to the BPM marketplace who figure out how to build a Cloud-friendly BPM engine. Think you have what it takes? Here are some pointers to architecting a partition-tolerant, RESTful BPM application.

- **Separate the resources that build process applications from the representations of those resources.** Servers are responsible for generating self-descriptive process maps that contain all the context necessary for any actor to work through a process. After all, orchestrations can be resources as well. In other words, the persistence tier doesn't host a process engine, it hosts a model-driven resource that generates stateless process applications to run on the elastic application tier.

    The application tier acts as the client for such process representations, and as a server that supports the clients of the process. Keep the application tier stateless by serving application state metadata in representations to the clients of the process. In other words, the application tier processes interactions with clients statelessly. As a result, any application tier instance is interchangeable with any other. If one crashes, you can bootstrap a replacement without affecting processes in progress. This interchangeability is the secret to maintaining elasticity and fault tolerance.

- **Separate user interface representations from application state representations.** If a client has the state representation, it should be able to fetch the appropriate UI representation from any application tier instance. As a result, the state representations are portable from one client to another. You could begin a process on a laptop and transfer it to a mobile phone, for example, and continue where you left off.

- **Use a lightweight, distributed queuing mechanism to address client uptime issues.** If a client (typically a browser) crashes in the middle of a process, you want to be able to relaunch the client and pick up where you left off. But if the client has the only copy of the application state, you have a problem. Instead, allow the client to fetch a cached copy from a queue.
- **For processes that require heavy interactions among multiple actors, follow a peer-to-peer model.** Most processes that involve multiple actors call for infrequent interactions between those actors; for example, processes with approval steps. For such processes, support those interactions via the resource state in the persistence tier. However, when you require heavy interactions among actors (imagine a chat window, for example), enable the actors to share a single application instance that initiates a peer-to-peer interaction.
- **Maintain integrity via checksums.** Conventional wisdom states that you don't want to let the client have too much control, or a bad actor could do real damage. To prevent such mischief, ensure that any invalid request from the client triggers an error response on the application tier. As a result, the worst a hacker can do is screw up their own session. Serves them right!

Not much to it, is there? It's surprising no vendor has stepped up to the plate to build a fully partition-tolerant, RESTful, BPM app. But then again, it's not the technical complexity that's the problem—it's the paradigm shift in thinking about the nature of stateful applications in today's Cloud-ready world. That shift is what makes Cloud-friendly BPM a disruptive technology, and a representative part of the paradigm shift to Agile Architecture.

An obvious question at this point would be whether we are recommending *RESTful BPM*. Unfortunately, using that terminology would have introduced unfortunate confusion, because that phrase has already been co-opted by vendors who use it to mean *traditional BPM engines with RESTful APIs*. But that's the old way of thinking. We're proposing a different way of thinking about BPM applications altogether.

Although you can think of a hypermedia application as a glorified Web site, it's actually more than that: it's a *run-time workflow*. The idea of RESTful applications as run-time workflows is both simple and deeply powerful, as it entirely changes the way we might look at BPM tools. Traditional BPM tools are heavyweight, integration-centric tools that typically rely on layers of infrastructure. Even lightweight BPM tools still rely on centralized state engines. With REST, however, hypermedia become the engine of application state, freeing us from relying on centralized state engines, instead allowing us to take full advantage of Cloud elasticity, as well as the inherent simplicity of REST.

Cloud-Oriented Architecture and the Internet of Things

We're almost done discussing the Cloud elements of the Agile Architecture paradigm shift, but there's one more piece of the puzzle to put in place. Quick quiz for all you Cloud aficionados out there: What's *missing* from the NIST definition of Cloud Computing? Give up? What's missing are *data centers*. Sure, today's Clouds consist of resources in data centers, running one way or another on racks full of physical servers. But there's nothing in the definition of Cloud that specifies anything about the physical location of Cloud resources.

Look at the NIST definition again. If you've seen this definition before, you may notice a new word that NIST presumably added after their now-seminal definition entered the blogosphere: *ubiquitous*. We don't know what fevered discussion led to the late inclusion of this word, but its addition is telling. After all, it doesn't matter how many data centers you have, they will never be ubiquitous. But NIST in their wisdom never intended the resources in the definition of Cloud to be limited to data centers, or for the list of Cloud resources to be exhaustive, for that matter. We could add, say, mobile phones, automobiles, factory equipment, and the proverbial fridge to the list, and as long as we have the convenient, on-demand network access as well as the automated provisioning, then this entire *Internet of Things* is *part of* the Cloud.

This globally ubiquitous interpretation of Cloud Computing should be especially exciting to architects, because it falls to them to understand all the technology resources at the disposal of the organization and how to address business challenges with such resources. From ZapThink's perspective, the Internet of Things provides a grand stage for our ZapThink 2020 Vision to play out. There are fundamental differences, after all, between data centers and the Internet of Things, which means that fundamental Cloud architecture principles must also transform to support this new reality. This transformation promises to be truly disruptive—a true paradigm shift as we figure out what it means to implement the part of Agile Architecture we like to call Cloud-Oriented Architecture.

Because Cloud-Oriented Architecture (COA, natch) extends past the data center to the ubiquitous resources of the Internet of Things, we must expand our definition of *resource* beyond the list in the NIST definition of Cloud Computing. The obvious place to go for such a definition is the REST architectural style, which defines a resource as "an entity or capability on a network." Note that resources in "traditional" (i.e., data center–based) Clouds are a subset of this broader definition of resource. In RESTful terms, Web pages, php scripts, and ASP/JSP pages, for example, can all be resources. We wouldn't normally lump such resources in with servers, storage, networks, and the other Cloud resources we typically talk about. But in COA, where we free the Cloud from the data center, *anything* we can give a URI to can be a resource. And of course, with IPv6 we have plenty of IP addresses to go around, where anything might have one—and if a thing has an IP address, it can have one (or more) URIs.

So far, so good, but beware a pitfall in our path: *Resource-Oriented Architecture* (ROA). ROA takes certain elements of REST and recasts traditional integration by leveraging RESTful APIs. ROA has its place to be sure, as it resolves some of the knottier problems of Web Services-based SOA, but ROA is decidedly *not* COA. In fact, they are at opposite ends of a philosophical spectrum that underscores the paradigm shift inherent in moving to the Cloud.

In fact, COA is really more about HOA than ROA. The point to assigning URIs to resources, after all, is to build distributed hypermedia applications. This is where you need to make a conceptual leap: Though the traditional notion of a hypermedia app is a glorified Web site, with COA, applications consist of hyperlinked resources of any type, from mobile apps to traffic signals.

We've been networking traffic signals for decades, so what's really new here? The answer: *control*. Traditional distributed applications have centralized control, whereas distributed hypermedia apps do not. In fact, this distribution of control is what we mean by the prefix "hyper," and is what makes the Web what it is today. Remember the green screen menu-based interfaces from the 1960s and 1970s? You clicked on a menu item to load a different screen. But those links weren't *hyperlinks*, because they couldn't take you to a screen (or page) on a different system. The secret of hypertext (now hypermedia) is that it enables the Web to be *worldwide*, with no central point of control.

Fast forward to the present, and today's world of distributed computing has a schizophrenic nature: the world of enterprise IT with its inherently centralized control, and the world of the Web—horizontally scalable, partition tolerant, and lacking a single point of control. And now we have the Cloud, and COA bringing the two together. We're bringing enterprise IT into the twenty-first century, kicking and screaming. We managed to survive the rise of the Web itself, as IT managers begrudgingly provided Internet access to employees' desktops. Now with the ubiquitous penetration of mobile technology (there's the U word again!), those managers are once again struggling to maintain control, lest the enterprise rank and file download some app or other malware that brings the organization to its knees.

This situation is only going to get worse—or better, depending on your point of view. Mobile devices are only going to get more powerful. The Internet of Things will continue to grow past our smartphones as Cloud resources penetrate every aspect of our daily lives. The cybersecurity implications are profound, let alone the day-to-day issues of governance. Enterprises who don't rise to the challenge and revamp their thinking about how technology contributes to the operations of the business are sticking their heads in the sand. Yes indeed, we have a revolution on our hands.

Today's question, therefore, is whether the market—that is, *you*—are ready for COA. Are you ready to free the Cloud from the data center? Are you ready to give up centralized security in favor of a lightweight, federated approach? Are you ready to discard the API-centric ROA in favor of the truly RESTful HOA? Perhaps. But such changes in thinking take time.

So, we're eschewing ROA in favor of HOA, and we pointed out that WOA was little more than Web-oriented SOA. Now we're adding COA to the mix. So, COA, HOA, SOA—how many "OAs" do we need anyway? The answer: however many it takes to achieve the agility meta-requirement of Agile Architecture. Remember, Agile Architecture is inherently iconoclastic. Follow only those practices that address the business problem: the right tool for the job. COA, HOA, and SOA are nothing but sets of tools in your tool belt. Getting Agile Architecture right means knowing which tools to use when.

Location Independence: The Buckaroo Banzai Effect

Clearly, if our discussion moves beyond SOA to COA and HOA, it's clear that SOA is not the end state. In fact, an increasing number of people are asking us what comes after SOA. If SOA is one step in the evolution of distributed computing, the reasoning goes, then something is bound to be next in line. Furthermore, just as SOA built on Web architectures, client/server, and the rest of what are now today's legacy technologies, so too will this Next Big Thing (for want of a name) build on, rather than replace SOA. In other words, where does Agile Architecture take us?

Well-meaning pundits, analysts, bloggers, and others have sought to name this Next Big Thing—SOA 2.0, Web 3.0, and so on, not to mention the admittedly repetitious COA and HOA—but simply naming a concept before anybody really knows what that concept represents is sheer folly, and inevitably a lightning rod for derision. This book, therefore, will do no such thing. Instead, we'll seek to identify the elements of the Next Big Thing that we can find in today's trends, and identify one of many Supertrends— location independence—that may lead us to understand this business transformation attractor.

The problem with discussing the Next Big Thing, of course, is that no one term does it justice. SOA is a critical part of this story, but it's only a part. A key part of SOA's notion of a business abstraction is location independence: The business doesn't care what server, network, or data center the implementation underlying a Service runs on. All they care is that the Service works as advertised.

Saying, however, that successful SOA boils down to successful abstraction of technology is a subtle oxymoron, because if you've successfully abstracted your tools, you no longer care what those tools consist of, or where they're located. The point to abstracting the interfaces between people and their tools is basically because people don't care about their tools; they care about what they want to use those tools for. Whether I'm at work or at home, having a conversation, creating something new, or providing value to someone, I don't want to be concerned with the tools. Tools are always—always!—a means to an end. Fundamentally, that's what we mean by the word *tool*.

To understand the Next Big Thing, therefore, we need to pick up the thread of abstracting our tools beyond SOA, where it's not only the location of the tool, but the tool itself that disappears behind the abstraction. In the big picture, the technology fades from view behind the abstraction. All people see are location-independent capabilities and information. Everything else lives in the Cloud.

When we say "the Cloud," however, we're still not naming the Next Big Thing. After all, when we use such terms, they come with the baggage of immature abstractions. When we say the Cloud, we think of Cloud Computing, an approach to abstracting specific IT infrastructure resources. In other words, Cloud Computing is still more about computing than about the Cloud itself at this point in time.

Location independence is nothing new for the World Wide Web, of course. URLs abstract the IP addresses of physical devices, and in turn, URIs abstract the location component of URLs. Now we can load any Web page we want without any care about where the box serving that page is physically located. Nevertheless, the Web abstraction is only part of the way toward the Next Big Thing, because it doesn't abstract the tools. When we say the Web, we think browsers and HTTP, instead of thinking of a technology and protocol-independent abstraction.

Touting the Web as the golden path to the Next Big Thing, however, quickly leads us astray. To be sure, there's a big hullabaloo over Web-Oriented Architecture (WOA), and the REST approach that underlies it, and an ongoing thread about the virtues of WOA vs. SOA. However, the entire WOA vs. SOA debate is missing the point—or in reality, missing several points. In fact, WOA is really Web-oriented SOA, essentially at a lower, tool-specific level of abstraction. Furthermore, the WOA vs. SOA debate often devolves into a religious battle over protocols, as though architects really cared about whether REST or SOAP-based Web Services sucked less.

Oddly enough, this devolution into a religious spat has offered us a convenient misdirection, as though it were a magic trick designed to keep the eye away from what was really going on. The real story, in fact, centers on the core notion of location independence. From the SOA perspective, location independence is a property of the business abstraction, where from the REST perspective, it's an inherent property of URIs (and in fact, is what distinguishes URIs from their location-dependent cousins, URLs). But there's a third context for location independence, and understanding this third perspective goes to the heart of the matter: the context of mobile presence.

By mobile, what immediately comes to mind? A cell phone, naturally. But of course, I could have meant a laptop, iPad, or perhaps a GPS device or even a GPS-enabled piece of equipment. If we think architecturally, we can abstract the device itself, and we end up with the notion of mobile presence, which is in essence the abstracted notion of location: Am I available? What am I doing? Where am I going? And though we may think today about presence in the context of people, presence can apply equally well to technology capabilities or information—in other words, to Services.

There is a subtle but critically important point here: Location independent doesn't mean location unaware; on the contrary, mobile presence is location aware. Rather, it means location *agnostic*. What we're really looking for are Services that are available whenever, wherever we are, independent of what kind of technology we happen to be using at the time. To understand the Next Big Thing, therefore, you need to merge the concepts of SOA, the Web, and mobile presence in order to flesh out the Cloud.

Unfortunately, we're really not ready yet to achieve such über-convergence. Today, the notion of mobile presence lies squarely in the telco world, as various service providers flesh out the relationship between standards like the Session Initiation Protocol (SIP) and mobile presence. And as with SOA, Cloud Computing, and the Web, proponents of mobile presence are looking at the trees and missing the forest by focusing on the mobile devices and the device-centric products that the telcos can sell their customers. Only when we can abstract the tools themselves in a location-independent way will the Next Big Thing come into focus, and we'll finally be able to live the words of Buckaroo Banzai: "No matter where you go, there you are!"

So, add SOA to Cloud Computing to Web 2.0 to mobile presence, and what do you get? Maybe you get the computer on the Enterprise from *Star Trek*, where all anyone had to do was utter the word "computer," and it responded, no matter where they were. Or maybe we'll see Google acquire a telco—not for the telco's traditional business, but to complete Google's vision of the Cloud. Or maybe we'll see communication sessions (what we used to call "phone calls") span not only a variety of devices, but move seamlessly from one device to another. Imagine a conversation with an audio component as well as an instant message component, carried seamlessly as you move from your work environment, to a mobile environment as you drive home, and then to your home environment, without having to dial back in.

One feature of the Next Big Thing that does come through clearly is that the focus is on people and their interactions, much more so than on the technology that enables those interactions. We're so used to the technology being in our face that we lose sight of the fact that we techies are the only people who appreciate such a state of affairs, but that most people would be perfectly happy if the technology faded from view.

It's also clear that the lines between companies and consumers are blurring, as businesses finally figure out how to communicate with their customers, and the collaboration capabilities that are so key to Web 2.0 empower individuals and the communities they belong to. The Next Big Thing isn't a Cloud in the sense of abstracted data centers full of technology; it's a Cloud of people, communicating, creating, and conducting business, where the technology is hidden in the mist.

Postscript: The Cloud Is the Computer

First there was software development. Write a bunch of code and run it on a computer—"the computer is the computer."

Then there was systems development. Write a bunch of code and put it on a bunch of computers, and have them serve up bits of it to many more computers—"the network is the computer."

Now we're at the dawn of Cloud development: Create sophisticated Cloud provisioning/deployment/management specifications, and run those in the Cloud. We're not talking IaaS, PaaS, or SaaS here. Even those oh-so-2011 Cloud service models are only elements of the spec, for automated provisioning tools to provision and configure dynamically.

Yes, *the Cloud itself* becomes the computer.

CHAPTER 10

Can We Do Agile Enterprise Architecture?

There are certain characteristics that differentiate formal professions from other careers. Physicians and lawyers must obtain certification, typically from a government-run or government-sponsored certification body. These professions have standards of practice and codes of conduct that Congress or other legislatures (or their global equivalents) pass into law. If a professional violates such practices or codes, they are guilty of malpractice, opening them up to lawsuits and potential loss of license. As a result, such professionals must purchase malpractice insurance to address the resulting liabilities.

In essence, what distinguishes a profession from other careers is the governmental regulation that protects customers from incompetents and charlatans. Enterprise Architecture (EA), of course, has no such regulations. So, are we calling for governmental regulation of the EA profession? Not so fast.

The problem is that we are nowhere near ready to involve legislation in the EA profession. There would need to be broad agreement among EA practitioners as to what constituted proper, professional EA. Today, however, EAs cannot even agree on what EA *is*, let along how best to conduct the practice of EA.

It's as though we were asking what it would take to become a cardiologist, but nobody in the medical profession had made it past pre-med anatomy. Everybody is still arguing over what to call the various parts of the architecture, while discussions of how best to go about architecture are still quite broad and vague.

What about the various EA frameworks and methodologies on the market today, from the Zachman Framework to The Open Group Architecture Framework (TOGAF) Architecture Development Method (ADM)? The creators of these tools will be the first to tell you that they lack sufficient detail and formality to provide the rigor required for professional licensure.

In fact, The Open Group is the first to admit that the ADM is necessarily generic, and they call on architects to extend and customize it for particular purposes.

If the medical professions took this approach, you'd never want to see a physician again. After all, patients would die if medical specialties were "necessarily generic," and called on physicians to "extend and customize" the formal methodologies that their profession calls for. Certainly, physicians must have the experience and courage to interpret the rules of their profession in the context of the needs of the patient. But the flexibility we expect from our medical professionals is a far cry from the inherent ambiguity and generality in the ADM or any other EA methodologies on the market.

You might argue that today's enterprises are too varied and too heterogeneous for any such methodology to provide specific, verifiable guidelines for EA best practice. But that perspective doesn't hold water either. After all, the human body is arguably more varied and heterogeneous than any large organization. The problem may simply be inadequate motivation. Whereas human life is at stake in the case of the physician, what is at stake in the case of EA? The viability of the enterprise?

Perhaps, but probably not. Indeed, if poor EA clearly correlated to business failure, then the marketplace would be louder in its demands for a formal EA profession. Business failure is too high a bar to set. Instead, poor or absent EA typically leads to disorganized organizations struggling under the burdens of bureaucracy, politics, and management inefficiency. Which enterprises have such afflictions? *All of them.*

Time for another metaphor: It's as though we're in the Middle Ages. If you have a headache, head to your barber for some bloodletting. No scientific method, no real idea of how the body actually works, nothing but a bit of impromptu trial and error that gives our poor barber a hint that sometimes bloodletting helps with headaches. Without the underlying science, the formalized experimentation that leads to reasoned conclusions about cause and effect in Complex Systems, there's no good reason to believe today's EAs can achieve any greater level of professionalism than the medieval barber.

If you consider yourself an Enterprise Architect, please excuse this line of reasoning. We don't mean to insult the numerous EAs out there who endeavor to help their organizations deal with the change and complexity that all enterprises face. You're doing the best you can with the tools you have. It's not your fault your tools are still too primitive to establish EA as a formal profession. But look on the bright side: At least you don't have to purchase malpractice insurance!

On the other hand, the challenges facing the EA profession present enormous opportunities, both for enterprises themselves as well as for the software vendors and consultants that are in business to help their enterprise customer base. If any large organization is able to improve on their formal EA practices to the extent that they *actually solve* internal bureaucracy, politics, and inefficiency issues, they will be able to rise above their competition and achieve strategic value. Instead, the fact that all large organizations are in the same boat has led to complacency: Why bother trying to solve such intractable problems if everybody has the same issues?

From the perspective of the vendors and consultants, there is a substantial prize that will go to the first service provider who can formalize EA best practices and provide the necessary tools for executing on those processes. Today's EA tool marketplace is still serving the bloodletting barbers.

Of course, this need in the marketplace is the reason why we wrote this book. Our vision for Agile Architecture is essentially to actualize the promises of EA—promises that we have in large part failed to deliver on. Unfortunately, this book cannot provide a recipe for Agile Architecture—not because we don't know how to do it (although many questions obviously still remain), but rather because architectural approaches that have recipes are inherently not Agile. Instead, if we can challenge your assumptions and preconceptions and help you think about Agile Architecture properly, we've done our job.

Frameworks and Methodologies and Styles, Oh My!

Architects love arguing, so here's a question sure to elicit consternation: Is the Department of Defense Architecture Framework (DoDAF) relevant to SOA? One perspective is that as an EA framework, DoDAF is at a higher level than SOA, and doesn't have any SOA-specific content; another perspective is that the Department of Defense (DoD) strongly supports DoDAF and SOA, and thus interested parties both within the DoD as well as at defense contractors would be quite interested in learning how architects might apply DoDAF to SOA. Okay, take your position, and start arguing!

The moral of this story, of course, is that both perspectives are correct. The argument, however, brings up some interesting questions that apply to EA frameworks in general: How do such frameworks apply to Agile Architecture (if at all), and more importantly, how should you use an EA framework to support your Agile Architecture efforts in order to increase your chances of success with your Agile Architecture initiatives?

We've challenged EAs to step up to the plate and come out swinging at their organization's SOA projects for years. Even today, now that SOA is a mainstream style of EA, many EAs still think that SOA and EA are separate, mostly unrelated initiatives—to their organization's detriment. The sad truth is that for many practitioners, the connection between EA and SOA is tenuous at best. You'd think that because SOA enables organizations to better organize IT resources to better meet changing business needs—the essence of Agile Architecture, after all—that EAs would be fully supportive of their organization's SOA efforts. Unfortunately, for many seasoned EAs, the tools and approaches they've been using for years have little or no connection to the artifacts that are the SOA architect's stock in trade.

To understand the EA's point of view, a good starting point is the EA Framework. An architecture framework is a *tool for assisting in the acceptance, production, use, and maintenance of architectures*, according to TOGAF documentation. The architectures that definition refers to may be different types, including business architecture, data architecture, application architecture, technology architecture, and so on. When the architecture framework is an *Enterprise Architecture* framework, then, it provides tools for any or all of these narrower architectures, depending on the broader needs of the enterprise as a whole.

SOA, on the other hand, is a *style* of Enterprise Architecture. In other words, SOA best practices are a subset of all EA best practices, but don't fall neatly into a narrower type of architecture. Herein lies much of the confusion: An EA framework provides tools for various architectural activities independent of whether those activities fall into the category of SOA best practice, even when an organization is implementing SOA. Furthermore, as an EA style, SOA best practices fall under each of the narrower architecture definitions. For example:

- Business architecture: Best practices for applying SOA to the organization's governance framework.
- Data architecture: Best practices for specifying and maintaining the Data Services Layer.
- Application architecture: Best practices for abstracting legacy application capabilities as Business Services.
- Technology architecture: Best practices for designing and deploying the intermediary pattern.

The tools an EA framework provides are largely orthogonal to such style-specific best practices. In other words, the EA framework might provide data architecture tools that architects might see fit to use to put together their Data Services Layer, but then again, they might use those same tools for tackling data architecture in a non-SOA way as well. Furthermore, the EA framework will let such architects have it either way.

On first glance, the natural conclusion might be that EA frameworks are too high level to be of much use for SOA projects—and by extension, any Agile Architecture project. Though that perspective might be true of some frameworks, it doesn't necessarily follow for all of them. Rather, the tools that make up the framework apply to different architectural styles by design, and as a result, leave many of the specifics up to the architects to work out for themselves.

Perhaps the greatest issue with many EA frameworks is that they are not sufficiently *prescriptive*—that is, they provide tools but they don't tell you how you should use them. The processes the architecture team must follow to successfully create and implement an architecture are more of a *methodology* than a framework per se. You can think of a methodology as a recipe, or more precisely, many recipes that an organization can follow to achieve specific results. Methodologies are familiar from the software development world, where techniques such as the Rational Unified Process, the Spiral Methodology, or Agile methodologies like Extreme Programming or Scrum are now quite mature. Such methodologies are explicitly prescriptive: They tell various members of the software development team what they should do in particular situations.

Architecture as a practice, however, doesn't lend itself to a methodological approach. There is no recipe for good architecture. It would be great if there were an "Agile Architecture wizard"—you know, click, click, click, and voila! You have an Agile Architecture! But that will never happen, because there is no such recipe. The actual steps you must take to design and implement Agile Architecture properly vary too widely from one organization to the next, because such steps depend on the specific business problems, the existing technology environment, as well as cultural and political issues within the enterprise.

Just because there are no wizard-like recipes for how to do Agile Architecture styles like SOA, or any architecture style for that matter, that doesn't mean that it's impossible to come up with an effective architectural methodology. After all, architecture consists of best practices, so a resource that delineates such best practices in sufficient detail might be considered a methodology. The problem, however, is that architecture best practices aren't absolute, but, rather, dependent on the problem at hand—what we call the right tool for the job.

This point brings us back to the discussion of EA frameworks. The fact that architecture consists of problem-dependent best practices is inherent to what it means to do architecture, and all useful EA frameworks reflect this fundamental point. Remember, an EA framework is a set of tools, and as with any complex task, the tools themselves don't complete the task; rather, *people that know how to use the tools do*. A methodology may be a set of recipes, but no cookbook transforms you into a cook. Furthermore, Agile Architecture cuts across frameworks and methodologies to provide specific techniques—the ingredients in the recipe, if you will. Successful architecture depends on all of these: tools, recipes, ingredients, and most of all, skilled architects who have the knowledge, experience, and common sense to put them all together.

The Beginning of the End for Enterprise Architecture Frameworks

So, just how useful are EA frameworks like the Zachman Framework, anyway? And given that other popular EA frameworks, including TOGAF and DoDAF, descend from the Zachman Framework, just how useful are the entire crop of EA frameworks? Maybe we need to rethink what kinds of tools we really need to help us with Agile Architecture. In fact, the Fall of EA Frameworks is another crisis point in the ZapThink 2020 Vision.

The Zachman Framework is admittedly a useful way of organizing concepts that are relevant to the enterprise. Fundamentally, the Zachman Framework is an *ontology* rather than a *methodology*. That is, it helps you organize concepts without telling you what to do with those concepts. Although this ontology, or organization of concepts, does serve an important role, we also point out that it has limitations as well.

The focus on defining terms and organizing concepts to the exclusion of actually taking actions that will solve business problems is at the core of the Frameworks Crisis Point. Too many architects find themselves immersed in such framework-related tasks, including creating models, developing standards, and communicating various concepts to other people in the organization. Eventually, CIOs will come to realize that the money they are spending on EA could be better spent elsewhere.

Zachman's entire approach to EA reinforces the unfortunate belief that ontologies are central to the practice of EA. They are important, to be sure, but they are nothing more than a starting point. If we spend a year discussing EA we might spend the first day defining our terms, and the rest of the year figuring out how best to actually do EA. Zachman, however, is still focused on the first day.

The Framework itself has taken on a kind of cult status in the world of IT. Architects still worship at the altar of Zachman as though he had a special kind of wisdom that only he was able to impart. In reality, however, the entire framework approach to EA is largely obsolete. In fact, the sorts of changes Zachman has made to the Framework are indicative of this lack of progress in the approach. He recently hired a team of linguists to improve the Framework. These experts in language and communication recommended the removal of all adjectives from the Framework. Now, instead of *logical system model* there is a *system logic* row, and instead of *physical system model* the row below now has the label *technology physics*. Perhaps the terms *logical* and *physical* were confusing, but so is the phrase *technology physics*. So, let's get all the architects together and have a lovely argument over which is better, *physical technology model* or *technology physics*—meanwhile, our enterprise continues to struggle with cost overruns, regulatory compliance challenges, and marketplace pressures. Arguing about terminology is just so much easier!

If ontologies don't give us effective Enterprise Architectures, then maybe we need a methodology as well. TOGAF, in fact, fleshes out the ADM, but the ADM is little more than a methodology for creating an Enterprise Architecture—in other words, an ontology. The end result of following the ADM is still an organization of concepts, rather than an approach for architecting an organization that will actually help the organization solve its problems.

Perhaps the missing piece to today's EA is an *effective* methodology, a recipe of sorts that lays out everything an enterprise must do in order to achieve its goals. However, even if you were able to write down such a recipe, step-by-step instructions for everyone in your entire enterprise to follow, and even if you were able to convince everyone to follow those instructions—both implausibly Herculean tasks in and of themselves—you would still have the problem of *change*.

Long before everybody has had the chance to learn and follow their parts in this gigantic play you've written for them, the needs of the organization will have changed. Change, after all, is constant and never ending, so no recipe will ever be suitable, because you always need to know what you want to make before following a recipe. Imagine following a recipe for a chocolate cake only to learn halfway through the process that you want a blueberry pie instead. How would you write a recipe to accommodate such a change, without it simply being a recipe for disaster?

The ZapThink 2020 Vision illustrates how to address the Frameworks Crisis Point. We place this crisis point squarely in the Complex Systems Engineering Supertrend, because the only approach that makes sense is to treat the enterprise as a Complex System. Let's rework the changing recipe example into a Complex System example—what we call a meta-methodology.

Let's say that instead of a chocolate cake, you want to build an oak tree. The recipe for oak trees is in the DNA in acorns, so you plant an acorn. But this recipe is quite different from the cake recipe; the DNA doesn't specify ingredients or steps for assembling the tree. Instead, the DNA provides general rules for how to create the trunk, roots, branches, and leaves, and also gives the tree a way to deal with forces in its environment, like how to deal with too little water, or how to maximize the sunshine hitting its leaves. But there are no "branch goes here" or "leaf goes there" instructions that would characterize the DNA instructions as a methodology.

The challenge for the EA, by analogy, is in helping to create a set of rules or policies that encourage desirable behavior for the enterprise while discouraging undesirable behavior. The architect must then place these policies into a framework that coordinates them across the organization. If this approach sounds like governance, you're right. But governance alone doesn't address the broader problem of how to architect an enterprise for change.

We can find the answer to this question in our DNA example as well. Nobody sat down and deliberately coded the pattern of amino acids in the oak tree's chromosomes; rather, millions of years of natural selection did that. The Enterprise Architect must take a page out of nature's playbook and establish a governance framework essentially based on the principle of natural selection: Of all the rules and policies that an organization might enact, keep the ones that move the organization toward its goals and retire the ones that don't. Over time, the inherently dynamic governance framework will be optimally suited to support the strategic goals of the organization.

How to Buy an Agile Architecture

In spite of many vendors' sales pitches, Agile Architecture, just like any architecture, is something you *do*, not something you *buy*. Expecting to get architecture by buying software is about as likely as learning to play Mozart by buying a piano. Be that as it may, however, many organizations are struggling today with their Agile Architecture initiatives, and as a result, are looking for outside help to move them along their Agile Architecture road maps. Some enterprises are turning to vendors for help, others are turning to consulting firms, and many find the best Agile Architecture assistance comes from those providers who offer a combination of products and professional services. Regardless of which kind of firm you look to for help with your Agile Architecture initiatives, though, at some point you must select that firm—and that typically means putting together a Request for Proposal (RFP) and circulating it to prospective providers.

Putting together RFPs for Agile Architecture initiatives, however, is fraught with peril. What precisely do you want the third party to do for you? Regardless of whether you're shopping for software, professional services, or some combination, chances are you're looking at Agile Architecture in the first place to provide a greater level of agility from your IT environment. Yet, the traditional approach to writing an RFP is to specify a particular set of requirements. How, then, should you craft an RFP for Agile Architecture that adequately details your organization's true requirements for agility, in such a way that you're able to compare the responses you're likely to get and make the right selection?

In order to avoid the pitfalls, it helps to know where they are, so let's begin by looking at some of the common RFP mistakes organizations make when looking for help with their Agile Architecture initiatives:

- **Confusing architecture with implementation.** In the unlikely event that your architects have already worked out your Agile Architecture plan, that's one thing, but if you need help with Agile Architecture, that means that you're not ready to specify any kind of implementation yet. Agile Architecture RFPs should say nothing about the specific technology you might expect your provider to recommend. As a result, you should steer clear of any vendor who says that you'll get Agile Architecture by buying any specific product.
- **Trying to do too much.** Your executive team read this book (or more likely, a summary of this book) and now they want an Agile Architecture? So you put together this hugely detailed RFP that delineates everything your provider would be expected to do to take you from your current sorry state to the world of Agile Architecture nirvana. Sorry, it just doesn't work that way. There are far too many unknowns as well as a plethora of cultural and political issues to overcome before you can delineate further tasks on your Agile Architecture road map.
- **Expecting providers to put Agile Architecture advice in their response.** You want to make sure your provider has sufficient Agile Architecture chops, but asking them to provide detailed advice in their proposal is unfair, because after all, the best practices they offer are core to the value they'll provide to you. Customer references are a better way of qualifying providers.
- **Expecting to be able to compare proposals via purely objective criteria.** Government organizations in particular often have the requirement that they must solicit some set minimum number of proposals, and then compare them using formal criteria to avoid any hint of favoritism or discrimination. Unfortunately, such formal criteria are woefully inadequate for evaluating proposals for Agile Architecture–related professional services, because there is so much variation from one organization to another among Agile Architecture approaches. As a result, such objective criteria are bound to focus on less important details (frequently technical capabilities), rather than the more important architectural skills and human interaction capabilities.

Now that you know of some of the biggest pitfalls to avoid, here are some pointers for putting together effective Agile Architecture RFPs:

- **Expect and encourage an iterative approach to Agile Architecture.** Taking an iterative approach to your Agile Architecture initiative that combines both top-down (business-driven) and bottom-up (technology-driven) activities to show business value along the way is an Agile Architecture best practice. As a result, it makes sense for many organizations to approach their RFPs iteratively as well. Put out an RFP for an Agile Architecture pilot project, and move on to the next step only after completing that pilot and evaluating the results. Where you start and in what order to tackle the various iterations will depend both on your organization as well as lessons you learn along the way.

- **Look for strong organizational change capabilities.** The technology part of Agile Architecture is the easy part. Much more difficult is dealing with the organizational and political changes your organization must go through to make progress with Agile Architecture. You might find that your RFP centers on change management, negotiation, and evangelism skills even more so than more traditional architecture skills like modeling, requirements gathering, and system design.

- **Allow for subjective evaluation techniques.** Though considering which provider takes your boss to the best restaurant won't do, it still makes sense to evaluate the proposals you receive by considering how good a fit the provider will be with your organization, both technically as well as organizationally. Successful Agile Architecture initiatives rely on change across the organization, so finding a provider who can act as an effective change agent is essential. The most technically astute provider may not have the capability to drive change in your organization, and will thus hit a brick wall, whereas the most effective provider may not have the deepest technical capability.

- **Don't focus on Agile Architecture at all.** This piece of advice is the most counterintuitive, yet possibly the most important. You have some set of problems that are prompting you to consider architectural change, or you wouldn't be writing an RFP in the first place. Instead of delineating some approach to solving the problems in the RFP, put your energy into describing the problems and let the provider respond with their own approach for solving them. Then, evaluate the responses in part by analyzing how well the approaches will help you implement Agile Architecture. You're not looking for specific activities here, but rather the overall approach and philosophy of the provider.

The bottom line with Agile Architecture RFPs is that the entire RFP process is not well suited to Agile Architecture initiatives. The core business motivator for Agile Architecture is business agility, and to be truly agile the business must be able to leverage changes in the business environment for competitive advantage. Traditional RFPs, however, fly in the face of this requirement for agility, as the RFP by its very nature casts requirements in concrete.

Even for organizations with sufficient in-house capabilities to tackle Agile Architecture on their own, the traditional requirements → design → develop → test → deploy methodology is entirely inappropriate for Agile Architecture, because of the need to build for ongoing requirements change. So, for an organization looking to bring in a third party, the requirements → RFP → design . . . approach makes no sense either. Instead, organizations should look for providers who can serve as partners to move Agile Architecture initiatives forward on both the organizational and technical fronts, with a continual focus on solving the business problems.

In fact, the most successful third-party relationships for both the organization and its providers follow this pattern. The best Agile Architecture consulting firms are the ones that focus more on solving business problems than delivering an architectural approach, and who work closely with their clients on a partnership basis that focuses more on overall business improvement than on specific, well-defined projects. Similarly, the most successful Agile Architecture initiatives that leverage third-party expertise are those that bring providers into many different aspects of the business. Such relationships, however, rarely come through RFPs. In fact, the best Agile Architecture consulting and advisory firms avoid responding to RFPs altogether, because the organizations that spit them out are frequently not ready for Agile Architecture in the first place, and thus don't make very good clients.

The Dangers of Checklist Architecture

The sad truth is your organization may not be ready for Agile Architecture—even though you personally are sold on the idea. We applaud you for being an architecture evangelist in your organization, to be sure—but there's no sense hitting your head against a wall. In fact, pushing architecture on an organization that's not ready for it can backfire, as excessive pressure can lead to initiatives that do not lead to business value—for example, the dreaded *checklist architecture* problem.

With checklist architecture, it appears that there are clear business requirements that the architecture will address—only there aren't. In fact, checklist architecture is just another way to achieve dramatic levels of business/

IT misalignment; and furthermore, this mistake can be a spectacular waste of money.

Checklist architecture occurs when there are a fixed set of goals for the architectural initiative, either final goals or interim milestones, where the goals only *indirectly* correlate to the business drivers for the initiative. Problems arise when the architecture team drives toward the goals without heeding the underlying business problems, especially as those business problems change over time.

Checklist architectures are endemic to government architecture initiatives. For example, DoDAF was developed primarily in response to the Clinger-Cohen Act, which mandated EA at the Federal level. DoDAF compliance, in turn, means creating a number of *views*, or architectural artifacts of various sorts. And although these views should help drive a successful architecture implementation that meets the business needs of the organization, far too often the views are the end result, rather than tools for achieving true business value. In fact, this limitation of the first version of DoDAF led to improvements in version 2 meant to address the checklist architecture problem.

We also ran into checklist architecture in the private sector at a client who had instituted a number of *Performance Objectives*, or POs. In this company, every team meets with their manager at the beginning of the year and hammers out POs for the year to come. These POs are intended to drive activity on the team in alignment with business needs, and then form a basis for rewarding the team members for achieving their goals for the year.

What happened, however, is by the end of the year, the team was driving toward the POs without any regard for whether they would end up addressing the business challenges. When we pointed out that the POs wouldn't solve the business problems, the response was that the business problems weren't important, the POs were. After all, they had to achieve the POs by the holiday break in order to get their bonuses!

The checklist architecture problem isn't even unique to architecture initiatives. After all, it's possible for this problem to torpedo any sort of effort that experiences a shift in business requirements. When the initiative involves *architecture*, however, the checklist problem explodes, because architecture is so hard to pin down. In fact, pinning down an architecture effort—that is, distilling broad requirements for architecture into specific action items—is a reasonable part of any architecture planning effort. But the more complicated the architecture is, the less it lends itself to specific action items—or more precisely, action items that remain stable over time.

In the case of Agile Architecture where a core business driver is business agility, a checklist architecture is virtually guaranteed to be counterproductive. One way of looking at this limitation is the realization that the checklist approach is essentially a traditional systems approach. Checklist architectures fix business requirements in stone, which will discourage or fully eliminate emergent properties like business agility.

Even though the traditional approach to a checklist architecture is inherently flawed, we don't mean to say that checklists themselves are bad. After all, it's important to have measurable milestones and goals that enable the organization to ensure the initiative is on track to meet business needs, and that also provide a means for measuring the effectiveness of individuals and teams that are participating in the overall effort. The secret to creating a checklist that doesn't lead to the dreaded checklist architecture problem is to approach the problem from an Agile perspective.

For example, one of the Agile principles in the Agile Manifesto is an increased focus on individuals and interactions as well as customer collaboration. These characteristics are missing from checklist architecture, because the technology team works toward the checklist instead of working toward solving the core business problems that originally drove the initiative. It is essential, therefore, for the architecture team to establish interaction with the business stakeholders as a core part of their checklist—not in the sense that "interacting with stakeholders" is itself a checklist item, but rather that there's a policy for establishing interactions with stakeholders that drive the checklist *and how it changes over time*, as part of the governance framework.

Agile Architects, remember, must always be thinking in terms of *change*. Whenever there's a requirement, artifact, or policy, it's not sufficient for the architect to ask what that requirement or artifact or policy *is*. The architect must also ask how it will *change over time*. Once architects focus more on how things change than on what they are, the next set of questions should focus on what sorts of changes are desirable and what sorts are undesirable, and how to achieve the desirable changes and avoid the undesirable ones. If this change-focused approach to architecture sounds a bit like herding cats, well, that's what it means to do Agile Architecture!

Establishing an approach to changing the milestone checklist *as a matter of policy* is a fundamental Complex Systems Engineering (CSE) technique. Our governance framework must favor the behavior we desire and discourage the behavior we seek to avoid. Over time, we'll end up adapting to changes in the environment. In other words, the architect focuses on change itself more so than the specific things that are changing. Establishing a governance framework that allows for changes in the checklist by favoring changes that keep the checklist in alignment with changing business needs is the true best practice approach for establishing goals and milestones for any Agile Architecture.

CONCLUSION

Computing is not about computers any more. It is about living.

—NICHOLAS NEGROPONTE

Assume for a moment that we're correct that the Agile Architecture Revolution is a revolution in the truest sense of the term. Now, imagine yourself 20 years hence, looking back on the part of the twenty-first century that has passed. What do you see?

The role technology plays in both our work and personal lives would be virtually unrecognizable to yourself today. After all, there's no reason to expect the rate of innovation to slack off—and furthermore, the transformative role that technology innovation has on our work organizations as well as our lives more broadly will only increase.

Remember, 20 years ago we had no Internet, mobile phones were few and far between (and only made calls!), personal computers were expensive, uncommon, slow, and difficult to use, and businesses mostly ran on complex, rigid, bespoke, stand-alone applications. Compare that world to the smart-phone-enabled, Service-oriented, social media–rich world we have today. Now extrapolate even more change 20 years into the future.

Crystal ball fogging up a bit? Fair enough. Predicting what's going to happen next week is hard enough, let alone two decades hence. That being said, we hope we've burst enough bubbles, challenged your preconceptions, and pointed out sufficient crises and disruptions, both now and imminent, to make the case that we're in the midst of a true revolution.

What characterizes revolutions most, of course, are its crises—and crises are the central lesson of the ZapThink 2020 vision. Take Cloud Computing, SOA, and mobile computing, mix with our five Supertrends—Complex Systems Engineering, Deep Interoperability, Location Independence, Democratization of Technology, and Global Cubicle—and we have a recipe for a true paradigm shift.

This paradigm shift, as with all such shifts, is part of a larger trend from old ways of thinking to entirely different approaches to building and consuming applications. Here are some aspects of this shift:

Old way of thinking	New way of thinking
Partition intolerant	Partition tolerant
Vertical scalability	Horizontal scalability
ACID	BASE

(Continued)

Process engines	RESTful BPM
State management with objects (threads, session beans, etc.)	State management with HATEOAS
Web Services-based SOA	REST-based SOA
Legacy enterprise apps poorly shoehorned into the Cloud	Next-generation enterprise apps built for the Cloud (enterprise SaaS)
Middleware centricity	Cloud centricity
Imperative programming	Declarative programming
The network is the computer	The Cloud is the computer
Build to fixed requirements	Build for change
Integration-centric architecture	Governance-centric architecture
Requirements, policies, methodologies	Meta-requirements, meta-policies, meta-methodologies
Dogmatic approaches	Iconoclastic approaches

In addition to these broad predictions for the next few decades, we have some more detailed predictions for the year 2020—the year the ZapThink 2020 vision comes to fruition:

- **We'll still be talking about Enterprise Architecture.** One of the biggest lessons of the past 10 years is that the business still doesn't understand or value Enterprise Architecture. CIOs are still, for the most part, business managers who treat IT as a cost center or as a resource they manage on a project-by-project and acquisition-by-acquisition basis. Long-term planning? Put Enterprise Architects in control of IT strategy? Forget it. In much the same way that the most knowledgeable machinists and assembly line experts would never get into management positions at the automakers, so too will we fail to see EA grab its rightful reins in the enterprise. We'll still be talking about how necessary, underimplemented, and misunderstood EA will be in 2020. You'll see the same speakers, trainers, and consultants, but with a bit more grey on top (if they don't already have it now).
- **More things in IT environments we don't control.** IT is in for long-term downward spending pressure. The technologies and methodologies that are emerging now—Cloud, mobile, Agile, iterative, Service-Oriented—are only pushing more aspects of IT outside the internal environment and into environments that businesses have little or no control over. Soon, your most private information will be spread onto hundreds of servers and databases around the world that you can't control and have no visibility over. You can't fight this battle. Private Clouds? Baloney. That's like trying to stop tectonic shift. The future of IT is *outside* the enterprise. Deal with it.
- **IT vendors will still be selling 10 years from now what they've built (or have) today.** There is nothing to indicate that the patterns of

vendor marketing and IT purchasing have changed in the past 10 years or will change all that much in the next 10 years. Vendors will still peddle their same warmed-over wares as new tech for the next decade. And even worse, end users will buy them. IT procurement is still a short-sighted, tactically project-focused, solving-yesterday's-problems affair. It would require a huge shift in purchasing and marketing behavior to change this, and we regret that we don't see that happening by 2020.

- **Everything will be Cloud, everything will be mobile.** Not only will we take the Cloud for granted, but we'll consider all devices to be extensions of the Cloud. Furthermore, the idea that any technology is bolted down to a particular location will seem quaint. All our technology will move around seamlessly, supporting work and home lifestyles that are inherently mobile.

- **Cyberspace will be our next battleground.** Guns, battleships, tanks, strike fighters—all the paraphernalia of twentieth-century-style warfare will become little more than accoutrements on the periphery of the true battlefield: cyberspace. We'll fight new kinds of enemies with new tactics and strategies, on location-independent battlefields that care nothing for national borders.

- *Plus ça change, plus c'est la même chose* **(the more things change, the more they stay the same).** Progress with technology will never affect human nature. Politics, bureaucracy, selfishness, greed, and incompetence will still be with us. But then again, so will creativity, insight, compassion, ambition, and whimsy. Give a caveman a cell phone, and he's still a caveman. Our tools are *always* a means to an end, never an end in themselves.

Some of the previous predictions may seem gloomy. Perhaps the current economic and political environments are putting a haze on the positive visions of our crystal ball. More likely, however, is the fact that the enterprise IT industry is in a long-term consolidation phase. IT is a relatively new innovation for the business, after all, having been part of the lexicon and budgets of enterprises for 60 years at the longest.

Just as the auto industry went through a rapid period of expansion and innovation from the beginning of the past century through the 1960s, to be followed by consolidation and slowing down of innovation, so, too, will we see the same happen with enterprise IT. In fact, it's already begun. Five vendors control over 70 percent of all enterprise IT software and hardware expenditures in the enterprise. Enterprise end users will necessarily need to follow their lead as they do less of their own IT development and innovation in house.

Now, this trend doesn't apply to IT as a whole—we see remarkable advancement and development in IT *outside* the enterprise. There is a digital divide between the IT environment inside the enterprise and the environment we experience when we're at home or using consumer-oriented Web sites, devices, and applications. As we move away from vertically scalable enterprise applications that require and promote central control to a Cloud of distributed resources that cross organizational boundaries, organizations will need to rethink—and in many cases, reinvent—their approach to governance, security, scalability, and change. Reducing or eliminating this digital divide will require difficult, often discontinuous change—in other words, a new way of looking at architecture. Welcome to the Agile Architecture Revolution.

LIST OF ABBREVIATIONS

ACID—Atomic, consistent, isolated, and durable
ADM—Architecture Development Method
ADSL—Asymmetric Digital Subscriber Line
API—Application Programming Interface
ASP—Active Server Page
B2B—Business-to-business
BASE—Basic availability, soft state, and eventual consistency
BPEL—Business Process Execution Language
BPM—Business Process Management
BPMN—Business Process Modeling and Notation
BPR—Business Process Reengineering
BYOD—Bring your own device
CAP—Consistency, Availability, Partition Tolerance
CD—Compact disc
CEO—Chief Executive Officer
CFO—Chief Financial Officer
CGO—Chief Governance Officer
CIO—Chief Information Officer
CMO—Chief Marketing Officer
COA—Cloud-Oriented Architecture
CORBA—Common Object Request Broker Architecture
COTS—Commercial off-the-shelf
CRM—Customer Relationship Management
CSE—Complex Systems Engineering
CSV—Comma-separated value
DCOM—Distributed Component Object Model
DDoS—Distributed denial of service
DMZ—Demilitarized Zone
DNS—Domain Name Service
DoD—Department of Defense
DoDAF—Department of Defense Architecture Framework
EA—Enterprise Architecture or Enterprise Architect
EACOE—Enterprise Architecture Center of Excellence
EAI—Enterprise Application Integration
EII—Enterprise Information Integration
ERP—Enterprise Resource Planning
ESB—Enterprise Service Bus

ETL—Extract, transform, and load
EULA—End-user license agreement
FTP—File Transfer Protocol
FUD—Fear, uncertainty, and doubt
GIGO—Garbage in, garbage out
GPS—Global Positioning System
GRC—Governance, risk, and compliance
H4x0r—Hacker
HATEOAS—Hypermedia as the engine of application state
HOA—Hypermedia-Oriented Architecture
HQ—Headquarters
HR—Human resources
HTML—Hypertext Markup Language
HTTP—Hypertext Transfer Protocol
IA—Information Assurance
IaaS—Infrastructure-as-a-Service
IANA—Internet Assigned Numbers Authority
IEEE—Institute of Electrical and Electronics Engineers
IMO—International Micro OraTib
IP—Internet Protocol
IPv4—Internet Protocol version 4
IPv6—Internet Protocol version 6
ISBN—International Standard Book Number
IT—Information Technology
JMS—Java Message Service
JSON—JavaScript Object Notation
JSP—Java Server Page
LOB—Line of business
LOIC—Low Orbit Ion Cannon
MDA—Model-Driven Architecture
MIME—Multipurpose Internet Mail Extension
MTV—Music Television
NIST—National Institute for Standards and Technology
OMG—Object Management Group
OOAD—Object-Oriented Analysis and Design
OS—Operating system
PaaS—Platform-as-a-Service
PO—Performance objective
POTS—Plain old telephone service
POX—Plain old XML
QA—Quality Assurance
QoS—Quality of Service

RAM—Random-access memory
REST—Representational State Transfer
RFP—Request for proposal
RMI—Remote Method Invocation
RMM—Richardson Maturity Model
ROA—Resource-Oriented Architecture
RPC—Remote Procedure Call
SaaS—Software-as-a-Service
SCM—Supply Chain Management
SD—Software development
SI—System Integrator
SIP—Session Initiation Protocol
SLA—Service-Level Agreement
SO—Service Orientation
SOA—Service-Oriented Architecture
SOAP—(Formerly) Simple Object Access Protocol
SPEAR—*Semper Paratus*: Enterprise Architecture Realization
SQL—Structured Query Language
SSA—Software Security Assurance
TCP/IP—Transmission Control Protocol/Internet Protocol
TOGAF—The Open Group Architecture Framework
TSE—Traditional Systems Engineering
UDDI—Universal Description, Discovery, and Integration
URI—Uniform Resource Identifier
URL—Uniform Resource Locator
URN—Uniform Resource Name
USCG—United States Coast Guard
VM—Virtual Machine
VPC—Virtual Private Cloud
VPN—Virtual Private Network
W3C—World Wide Web Consortium
WADL—Web Application Description Language
WOA—Web-Oriented Architecture
WSDL—Web Services Description Language
XML—eXtensible Markup Language
XSD—XML Schema Definition
Xtr3m H4x0r—Extreme hacker

ABOUT THE AUTHOR

Jason Bloomberg is President of ZapThink, a Dovel Technologies Company. He is a global thought leader in the areas of Cloud Computing, Enterprise Architecture, and Service-Oriented Architecture. He created the Licensed ZapThink Architect (LZA) SOA course and associated credential, and runs the LZA course as well as his Cloud Computing for Architects course around the world. He is a frequent conference speaker and prolific writer.

Mr. Bloomberg is one of the original managing partners of ZapThink LLC, the leading SOA advisory and analysis firm, which was acquired by Dovel Technologies in August 2011. His book, *Service Orient or Be Doomed! How Service Orientation Will Change Your Business* (John Wiley & Sons, 2006, coauthored with Ron Schmelzer), is recognized as the leading business book on Service Orientation.

Mr. Bloomberg has a diverse background in eBusiness technology management and industry analysis, including serving as a senior analyst in IDC's eBusiness Advisory group, as well as holding eBusiness management positions at USWeb/CKS (later marchFIRST) and WaveBend Solutions (now Hitachi Consulting). He also coauthored the books *XML and Web Services Unleashed* (SAMS Publishing, 2002) and *Web Page Scripting Techniques* (Hayden Books, 1996).

INDEX